SEVE

GOLF'S FLAWED GENIUS
ROBERT GREEN

'Do you want to know the great drama of my life? It's that I have put my genius into my life; all I've put into my works is my talent.'

Oscar Wilde

PORTICO

For Jane, Ben and Sam

First published in hardback in the United Kingdom in 2006

This paperback edition published by Portico in 2008

An imprint of Anova Books Company Ltd
10 Southcombe Street
London
W14 0RA

Photographs:
Front cover © Alamy
First plate section: 1 © Empics; 2 © Getty Images; 3 © Corbis; 4 © Getty Images; 5 © Getty Images; 6 © Rex; 7 © Getty Images; 8 © Getty Images
Second plate section: 1 © Getty Images; 2 © Getty Images; 3 © Getty Images; 4 © Getty Images; 5 author's private collection; 6 author's private collection; 7 author's private collection; 8 author's private collection; 9 author's private collection; 10 author's private collection; 11 © Getty Images

ISBN 9781905798247

A CIP catalogue record for this book is available from the British Library.

10 9 8 7 6 5 4 3 2 1

Typeset by SX Composing DTP, Rayleigh, Essex
Printed by WS Bookwell, Finland

This book can be ordered direct from the publisher.
Contact the marketing department, but try your bookshop first.

www.anovabooks.com

SEVE
GOLF'S FLAWED GENIUS

CONTENTS

ACKNOWLEDGEMENTS

I am indebted to many people for their help and co-operation with this book, some of whom – through their choosing – will remain anonymous.

Notably, my thanks to Sonia Land, for the 13 years of perseverance, Sandy Cadiz-Smith, Sergio Gomez, Richard Simmons, Jake Ulrich, Russell Carmedy and Tom Williams. At Anova Books, to Barbara Phelan, Malcolm Croft and Chris Stone. Also, I am especially grateful for the time afforded to me by Nick Faldo, David Leadbetter and Mac O'Grady. Oh, and Seve . . .

INTRODUCTION:

GETTING TO KNOW THE MAN

In *The Fight*, his book about the extraordinary Muhammad Ali/George Foreman 'Rumble in the Jungle' in Zaire in 1974, Norman Mailer wrote of Ali: 'What is genius but balance on the edge of the impossible.'

That's a fitting thought for this book, too. Part of the skill of Severiano Ballesteros has been to make the seemingly impossible seem routine. And there's more to the connection than that. Ali has been one of Seve's very few idols. A back injury incurred while boxing as a 14-year-old blighted Seve's career; not to the grotesque extent the sport so horribly assaulted Ali's wellbeing, but nevertheless to the long-term detriment of his own special gifts.

And Seve knows about fighting. He fought against class prejudice to gain acceptance at his golf club. He fought for and against the European Tour. He fought America's administrators off the course and its golfers in the Ryder Cup. He fought countless perceived adversaries, some real and some imaginary. He fought his own technical shortcomings to make himself one of the finest golfers ever, arguably the most charismatically entertaining in the history of the game. Oh yes, the fight is something Seve is hugely familiar with. It has been said before that his best position may be when he's beside himself. The fight has been his motivation and inspiration to greatness.

But then perhaps the title of this book should be *Floored Genius*. For a decade, Seve was surely rendered as low as a man of his talent, charisma and, yes, genius ever could be. It's like that old Irish maxim – you really don't want to start the journey from here. You would ideally do it from . . . well, maybe from 1984, the year of his victory in the Open at St Andrews and the circumstance of his most glorious pomp; or maybe 1988, his Open triumph at Lytham, the last of his five major championships; or it might be 1995, the year of his last tournament win and the year he played a remarkable role as Europe regained the Ryder Cup in his last appearance in the competition as a player; or then again it could be 1997, the year he captained the European Ryder Cup team – an entity which he did more than anyone else to bring about – to success in Spain. But we can't start the book from any of those places. We're in the here and now, as sports psychologists like to say, and we're stuck with that.

What we're stuck with is the fact that in July 2007, almost precisely ten years after he captained that victorious Ryder Cup team, Seve announced his retirement from competitive golf. In fact, pretty much from golf, period. At an emotionally charged press conference ahead of the Open Championship at Carnoustie, he explained his decision.

'For a few months, there was something confused inside of me. There was a fight, internal fight. [See, that word again.] My head say, 'I think you should retire' . . . but my heart was telling me it would be better to continue playing and compete. So it was difficult for quite a while. But finally I decided this year to go and try the Champions Tour [the senior circuit, for over-50 golfers, in America.] So I went there, the weather was nice but I only played one tournament and I came back. So that really made me think deeply and to really question . . . and I made probably most difficult decision of my career as a player. I decided to retire.'

He later added: 'I don't have the desire [anymore]. I'm not willing to give away things that I did before. You have to remember I gave away all my teenage years [to golf]. I worked really hard from morning to night and I put all my energy and effort into the game, focused 100%, and I thought that was enough.'

It was enough to have Tiger Woods, easily the best golfer in the world, maybe the greatest ever, to declare the next day: 'He was a genius.' You could google away merrily for years and not find Tiger paying a compliment like that to another golfer, very recently retired or not. He tosses tributes around as much as he does triple-bogeys. Woods also said: 'Seve has been probably the most creative player who's ever played the game. I've never seen anyone who had a better short game than him. I've been lucky enough to have had an opportunity to pick his brain on several occasions around the greens; watched him hit shot after shot and have him explain how he did it, why he did it. It was just phenomenal.'

That accolade will give you more than a sense of the talent we are talking about here. In the words of another contemporary giant of the modern game, Ernie Els: 'There's not enough great things I can say about Seve.' Nor could the press.

One of the reasons Seve enjoyed such spectacularly appreciative coverage in the British media was his inherent understanding of what was wanted of him, even in a foreign culture, although it should be added that he is also mostly good company, entertaining, infectiously mischievous and – not least – that he thrilled even the most bunker-hardened golf writers of a generation with his gloriously individual brand of seemingly reckless brilliance. But had any other player alleged that some of the business practices of the European Tour were 'nearly like a Mafia', an analogy particularly clumsy given that he was in Italy when he said it, he would have received far harsher coverage at the hands of the press than Seve got. Whether or not he had a point is something we'll look into later . . .

In a previous biography, published in 1982, *Seve: The Young Champion*, Dudley Doust wrote that Seve's mind is a 'private forest, a place impenetrable, indeed dangerous to others'. He is a complex character – charming and manipulative, gregarious and withdrawn, open and suspicious, generous and mean – depending on how the mood takes him. That is probably a necessary facet of being a flawed genius. It is part of the price you pay, a kind of Faustian pact, for being a champion – the selfishness, the remorselessness, the single-mindedness. Indeed, the phrase 'flawed genius' may be axiomatic. It has to be that way; there's no other sort.

In his much-acclaimed book *In Search of Tiger*, Tom Callahan quoted one Tiger Woods-watcher as saying of the world's best golfer, maybe the best ever: 'He doesn't want to change anything, because he feels it's all part of the perfect combination of what it takes to be who he is. If he got rid of his meanness, his pettiness, his cheapness, it would be like, "Well, maybe I'll lose something then."'

This is a world in which nothing must be given away. It's an attitude which indicates a craving to have a constant reminder of just how tough it was to get this far; it's been a fight, a fight against the odds. Another book, *Bernie's Game* by Terry Lovell, about the Formula 1 supremo Bernie Ecclestone, has the subject haggling for 20 minutes to knock 100 Swiss francs off the price of an expensive toy for one of his daughters. Ecclestone was with his colleague, Max Mosley, who pointed out to Bernie that his time was not worth so little as that. Ecclestone said he knew, 'but I've got to keep in practice'.

Seve, too, was relentlessly competitive. In 1990, I was working with him on the shooting of an instruction video, *The Short Game*, in Dubai. While waiting for the film crew to set up again, Seve insisted I try to hit the shot he was practising, something he called the 'parachute shot', a full swing to hit the ball just a few yards, in this case from a poor lie to a hole cut just the other side of a bunker. He explained the technique – open clubface, ball forward, an exaggeratedly wide stance, weight on the right side and so forth – and I had a go. The first one went into the sand. The next finished six inches from the hole. He hadn't hit one as close as that himself. 'See what I mean?' he said. 'It's not hard.' He took the sand-wedge back and had another effort. This one he holed.

That evening, we had dinner at the hotel. We got on to the matter of major championships. At this stage in their respective careers, Seve had won the five he would end up with, Nick Faldo had won two (of his eventual six). Seve said he thought Faldo had been lucky in one respect, and in two instances. Paul Azinger had bogeyed the last two holes at Muirfield to enable Faldo's round of 18 consecutive pars to be sufficient to win the 1987 Open, even though he had not started the final day in the lead; Scott Hoch had missed a tiny putt on the first hole of their sudden-death playoff at the 1989 Masters, which meant Faldo was able to go on and win at the next. 'That sort of thing never happened to me in any of my five majors,' Seve said.

We briefly argued back and forth over essentially the same issue – me saying that while I couldn't pretend to understand what it was like to be at the sharp end of a huge golf tournament, I thought Faldo's play under the gun on both occasions had demonstrated that he deserved to win; Seve insisting that he had enjoyed more than his fair share of good fortune. After a few minutes of this, Seve had clearly had enough. 'I thought you'd back down,' he said. Subject over. The truth is that Seve always expects people to back down. Why wouldn't he? They usually do.

Seve is a man who knows what he wants alright, as I was emphatically to find out a decade or so later, through a protracted, at times tortuous, process at the end of which we not only once failed to get his autobiography published, we managed the trick twice. One thing is for sure when you're involved with a project like that. You certainly get to know the person with whom you're dealing, frequently in ways you'd have preferred not to encounter.

My first Open Championship as a journalist was the one in which Seve made his distinctive name renowned throughout the sport. He was 19 at the 1976 Open at Royal Birkdale. He was the unknown who took an early lead in the championship. Everyone expected him to disappear from the leaderboards. He didn't. Mostly, he didn't for the next 15 to 20 years. At Birkdale he finished runner-up to Johnny Miller, then possibly the best golfer in the world. Over five different periods in the latter half of the 1980s, Seve was officially ranked the world's No. 1 golfer for a total of 61 weeks. Tiger Woods, Greg Norman and Nick Faldo are the only players who have put in more time at the top.

Of course, it wasn't just that Seve was a great golfer. It was the way he played, attacking the course like Brazil used to play football – 'score three if you like, because we're going to score four'. The way

Seve set about his task, bogeys were almost a certainty. So, too, was the fact that they would invariably be outnumbered by the birdies, and at least one of those per round would be extraordinary. A 'Seve par' became the recognised lingo for making four via the trees and the sand. Indeed, birdies were frequently made the same way.

In a rating of world No.1 golfers in the November 2004 issue of *Golf Digest*, Seve was only given five out of 10 when it came to the soundness of his swing and his ability to minimise mistakes. He got 10 out of 10 for both his putting and for his short game and talent for improvisation. The following underlines those points.

At the 1987 Masters, Seve came to the 72nd hole needing a par to tie the clubhouse leader, Larry Mize, and a birdie to beat him. His drive was perfect. The birdie was a serious possibility; after all, he had just birdied the 17th. With an 8-iron in his hands, Seve then shoved his shot into the right-hand greenside bunker. Now a bogey was on the cards. Or not. 'For anyone else a bunker shot on to the dangerous 18th green with a third Masters victory hanging in the balance would have been unsettling, to say the least,' wrote Sarah Ballard in *Sports Illustrated*. 'But Seve in sand is like Brer Rabbit in a brier patch: he's home. Long before he ever played a real golf course, Ballesteros was hitting sand shots on the beach of Pedrena, the village on the shore of the Bay of Santander in the north of Spain that is still his home. The bunker shot stopped six feet away, the putt rolled dead into the heart of the cup . . .'

Seve never did win that third Masters. Quite shockingly, and very dramatically, Mize beat him and Norman in the ensuing playoff. But a third Open Championship was to be his, in 1988.

So, as the room-service waiter legendarily asked George Best, encamped on his bed with champagne and a glamorous woman, where did it all go wrong? Without the application of too much dramatic licence, you could say it was perhaps on the eve of his first win as a professional – aged 17, the Spanish Under-25s Championship at Pedrena, the club where he learned to play the game. The weather was cold and damp but Seve was so determined to excel that week that he hit hundreds of balls in the miserable conditions, to the extent that he so aggravated his back injury that he considered withdrawing. Instead he played and won – but at a price. A long, lingering price. He insists that no one can ever comprehend the degree of pain his back has caused him throughout his career. 'I knew from way back that his back was shot,' Nick Faldo told me. 'I remember we were in Japan in the 1980s. He told me that his back was gone. For him, trying to get through the '90s was too much.'

As Seve told Faldo: 'The more I practise, the more I hurt. The less I practise, there goes my game.' Thirty years on from that golf tournament at Pedrena, Seve was involved in an unseemly incident, a scuffle that he instigated, at the same club with a European Tour rules official, José Maria Zamora. That takes us back to the 'Mafia' remark.

But notwithstanding that dispute, the break-up of his marriage, his back problems and his sometimes less than astute business decisions, his life and career have been filled with much happier events, too – the five major championships, his vital stimulation of the nascent European Tour, his epic Ryder Cup career. Despite some of the mistakes he has made, as well as because of all he has contributed to golf – especially in Britain and elsewhere in Europe – there is widespread affection for Seve. Even the personal devastation of his recent divorce from his wife, Carmen, the mother of their three children, has not ravaged the rich well of fondness for him. He is not the first famous man to fall into discredit due to a keen interest in women who are not his wife, and he won't be the last. But, as with much of what he has done, it could have been handled better.

I hope this book will help to bring an accurate portrayal, an unprecedented one, of a complicated character, an extraordinary man, who did more than anyone else to bring excitement, style and verve to the previously pedestrian world of European golf. For those too young to comprehend the impact he had, I can assure you that it was immense. So was he. He was indeed the Tiger of Iberia.

A SNAPSHOT OF SEVE

Early afternoon, late September 1987 – the Ryder Cup at Muirfield Village, Dublin, Ohio, the course that Jack Nicklaus built; the venue for the United States' attempt to regain the trophy they had lost at The Belfry in England two years previously, their first such setback in 28 years.

The chief architect of that reverse had been Seve Ballesteros – the man whose emergence as a force in world golf in 1976 at the age of 19 had been instrumental in causing continental European golfers to be invited to join forces with those from Great Britain & Ireland in 1979 after it had finally been conceded that GB&I alone were no match, and certainly no contest, for the United States.

On this warm autumnal day, Seve was playing the first hole in the first series of fourball matches in partnership with his compatriot and Ryder Cup rookie, the 21-year-old José Maria Olazábal. Over this and the ensuing three Ryder Cups, they would go on to prove themselves the greatest pairing in the history of the matches. In the recent past, that very morning's foursomes, they had demonstrated their worth by coming back from 2 down after six holes against Larry Nelson and Payne Stewart to win at the last. Europe and the USA were tied at 2–2 going into the afternoon fourballs. This time, the Spaniards were up against Curtis Strange and Tom Kite. On the first green occurred an incident that encapsulated Seve's skill, bravado, what he brought to the Ryder Cup and his oft-expressed antipathy towards Americans.

The identity of his opponents would have had something to do with it. He and Strange had not yet become the best of enemies (Seve had won four major championships to Strange's none at this point) but Strange was touted by the American press as presently the best player in the game, a piece of palpable nonsense largely based on the fact that he was on course to becoming the leading money-winner on the US PGA Tour for the second time in three seasons. With Kite, though, Seve did have history – one he has subsequently played down, as we shall see, no doubt partly out of respect for the fact that Kite was his opposite number as captain when Seve was effectively the Ryder Cup host, in the match at Valderrama in Spain in 1997. But you don't necessarily have to believe that.

In his book, *Summers With Seve*, published in 1991, Ian Wright, one of Seve's former caddies (not a rare species), wrote: 'So if anyone wants to see Seve wound up and motivated, all they have to do is mention Americans in general or Tom Kite in particular . . . whenever Tom Kite's name comes up, I watch the bristles rise.'

Nick de Paul had been Seve's caddie when he played against Kite in the singles at the 1985 Ryder Cup. Seve won three of the last five holes to force a half as Europe swept to a tumultuous and comprehensive victory that afternoon. De Paul told Norman Dabell for his book, *How We Won the Ryder Cup*: 'I should have realised I was going to be in for a hard time . . . when I saw the draw. Tom Kite had it in for Seve. There was bad blood somewhere . . .'

Most likely that emanated from the less-than-gracious reception Seve was widely accorded when he first played on the PGA Tour in 1978 – 'he's here to steal our money,' was how Seve characterised the widespread reaction to him – but by 1987 there was something specific. Kite had been paired with Seve during the final round of the 1986 Masters, when Seve had perpetrated the most regrettable shot of his career, hitting a straightforward 4-iron into the water on the 15th hole to cede the advantage in the tournament to Jack Nicklaus. It was a mistake from which he could not recover that day. To some extent – admittedly this is an exaggeration, albeit not a big one – it was a mistake from which he has never recovered. On the opening hole that afternoon, Kite had got involved in an altercation with Seve's caddie and brother, Vicente, which set the mood for the day and for their relationship – at least as it was in 1987.

Fast-forwarding nearly 18 months to the Ryder Cup, this incident still fresh in the mind of Seve at least, what we had on that first green at Muirfield Village was this. Seve had hit his approach shot short and left of the green, about 40 feet from the pin. Olazábal (sometimes referred to in this book by his nickname Chema, a diminutive of the Basque pronunciation of his name: JoCHE MAria) was on the green, about 20 feet above the hole. Kite, also on the green, had putted first and left his ball about three feet from the hole. Seve was next away but Seve – speaking in Spanish, reasonably enough – elected for Chema to go first with his difficult, slippery downhill putt, which he considered to be a harder shot than his chip. Olazábal left it short and went to mark his ball. Seve, again in Spanish, told him to putt out.

The Americans, not understanding what was being said, asked what the heck was going on. Indeed, Strange seemed so discombobulated that he actually said: 'Can you speak in Christian?' More reasonably, he felt Olazábal might be on the 'comeback line' of his putt if he went on to putt out. Seve, this time in English so the Americans could understand, said: 'Don't worry. This is an easy chip. I'm going to hole it.' He did. After telling Olazábal to pick up his marker now that his putt was no longer needed, Seve said, loudly enough: 'Don't worry. Curtis isn't going to hole his putt anyway.' He didn't. The Spaniards won their match by 2&1, Europe swept the day to lead 6–2, and ultimately they inflicted the first defeat on the Americans on home territory.

I think that incident says much about Seve and will be seen to typify what follows in this book: sublime skills and a willingness to embrace confrontation. It illustrates the colossal talent he had, an innate ability that has regularly provided vicarious thrills for millions of golf fans around the world. The anecdote may also indicate why there have been proportionately fewer of those in the United States than elsewhere.

In Tom Callahan's *In Search of Tiger*, Woods says of Seve: 'He's amazing around the greens. He showed me a few little things. There are some things you can learn only from another player.' As Arthur Conan Doyle, a quietly keen golfer himself, once said: 'Mediocrity knows nothing higher than itself, but talent instantly recognises genius.'

The outstanding Spanish player of the younger generation, Sergio Garcia, paid the compliment like this. 'You see him doing these little shots. Then you go home and try, and try, and keep trying and trying. But maybe only he can do them.' No player in the history of golf has had a better short game than Seve.

Garcia also said: 'With the heart, I don't know how anybody can be as good as Seve.' There has never been any doubting his *côrazon*. No questioning he had the *cojones*, too – except maybe that one lonely time in the middle of the 15th fairway at Augusta on that unlucky 13th day of April 1986, when in fact he lost his ball in the pond. That was four days after his 29th birthday, just over four weeks after the death of his father, and it seemed that the whole world – led by a vengeful PGA Tour and a rampant Nicklaus – were out to get him.

Seve's is a remarkable tale. This is how it began.

1. HOW IT ALL BEGAN

The Spanish have a word for it. *Destino*. Given that so much of his career, both highlights and low points, was enjoyed and endured at Augusta National, it is somehow fitting that the birthday of Seve Ballesteros should frequently fall during the week of the Masters Tournament. His 20th was on the Saturday of his first appearance there, in 1977, when two men who would figure large in his golfing life duelled for the title, Tom Watson eventually outgunning Jack Nicklaus. When Seve won there in 1980, the youngest-ever champion until Tiger Woods came along with his own awesome and compelling brand of precocity in 1997, the tournament began the day after he turned 23.

On 9 April 1957, two days after the Masters had been won by Doug Ford (not a vintage year), the baby Severiano was born in Pedrena, a homely fishing village on the southern shore of the Bay of Santander in Northern Spain, where the drama of the scenery is matched by the ferocious power of the seas in the Bay of Biscay. His parents were Baldomero Ballesteros Presmanes and Carmen Sota Ocejo. They named him after his paternal grandfather. His parents and three elder brothers – Baldomero (ten years older), Manuel (plus eight) and Vicente (plus five) – lived in a one-storey house directly above the barn in which they kept their cows.

It was a family of six that should have been seven. His parent's first child was named Manuel. Their second son was Baldomero. One summer's day when Manuel was two, a woman who helped look after the boys was riding with them in a donkey-drawn cart. The animal put its foot in a wasps' nest. Hundreds of them swarmed around the group, stinging incessantly. The woman managed to protect the smallest, Baldomero, but she could not take care of both children. Manuel died three days later, a loss sustained in circumstances too horrible to contemplate. The family's next child was thus christened Manuel, too.

During the Spanish Civil War, Ballesteros Snr had been on the side of the Franquistas. The Santander region was predominantly Republican, and when in June 1937 Baldomero was recruited against his will to fight Franco, he registered his disgust by shooting himself in the left hand. He was sentenced to 20 years in prison. While in hospital having treatment on his injury, he escaped and went to join Franco's forces. Franco himself would live until 1975, the year after the young Seve would turn pro.

As the baby of the family, Seve was somewhat spoiled by his parents. On the other hand, he got to do the most menial jobs around the farm because his brothers delegated most of those to him. When it came to mucking out the cows, there was seldom much doubt about whose name was on the rota. His pocket money was only five pesetas a week, a sum he would double by selling the crème caramels his mother made for him on to Vicente.

Seve's first display of sporting prowess was as a middle-distance runner, built up by undertaking something like a two-mile run four times a day to and from school – he went home for lunch – which he started when he was seven. He has kept the miniature trophy that he has for winning a 1500-metre race when he was 10.

After school, he would help his father around the farm, harvesting crops and feeding the cows. Not terribly exciting, but then there wasn't a lot going on in Pedrena, a village with rutted roads and few pavements, in those days. (It's not exactly Madrid today.) There was one place from which you could make a phone call, which meant the operator knew every secret in the village. There was one cinema. There was one taxi and a car, the latter owned by Seve's uncle,

Ramon Sota, Spain's most distinguished golfer of the day, who finished sixth at the 1965 Masters. An aptitude for golf was already in the family. There were three cafes, one of which, El Culebrero, boasted the village's first television. By day, Seve would do his best to enjoy the black-and-white thrillers or western adventures imported from Britain or America even though they had been dubbed into Mexican rather than Spanish, which made them hard to follow. By night, when he was no longer allowed inside, he would watch with his face scrunched up against the window pane. Watch meant just that. Since he was standing outside, he couldn't hear a thing.

Don't be entirely fooled by this slightly romantic image of a bygone era. This was post-Franco Spain. The mood in the village could be intimidating and the priests and soldiers were people not to be crossed. You didn't want them to catch you doing anything wrong, or hardly anything at all.

At home, meanwhile, the Ballesteros family had a radio but no television until Manuel, himself a professional golfer, won one in a tournament. As is traditional in those parts, the *montaneses* – people from the mountain regions of Cantabria – are close-knit, putting very much more emphasis on family than friends. Outsiders are inherently regarded with suspicion. That upbringing, while comfortable and cordial, doubtless shaped Seve's attitudes in later life, sometimes for the better and sometimes not. He had a couple of friends at school, but no one close.

At nights, Seve shared a bed with Vicente in a windowless room. Baldomero and Manuel were in another room, his parents in a third. The dining room and the kitchen were together and there was one bathroom. It wasn't luxury, but there were many people in more straightened circumstances than Seve and his family. And they most likely didn't have a consuming passion in the offing.

It has been written that Seve was born to play golf. His right arm is about an inch longer than his left, just perfect for taking a stance to hold a golf club. Whatever else may be said about his golf game, it's a part of his make up he took advantage of.

The first item he ever owned to do with golf was an old clubhead. Aged seven, he would find sticks that would make a shaft by ramming them into the hosel of the clubhead. He would have to hit stones and pebbles because his brothers wouldn't let him use their precious golf balls. They all played the game. Indeed, all three were professionals, although Manuel, who was Seve's chief inspiration, was the only other one of them to make any sort of impression as a player – he won the Timex Open in Biarritz in 1983, where he consigned Nick Faldo to being runner-up.

In this haphazard fashion, Seve would play his own games in the neighbouring fields and on the beach, where the firm sand with its true surface would prove to be a marvellously ideal environment on which to cultivate one of the greatest putting strokes in history.

When he was eight, Manuel gave him a 3-iron. In general, his golfing education was looking up. He had just begun caddying at the local club, although the rules stipulated that caddies were not allowed to play the course. Since the club pro was Uncle Ramon, Seve knew he ought to play by the rules. Since he was Seve, he didn't. Around dawn or dusk, he'd be out there with his 3-iron, now hitting balls rather than stones. 'Everything I learned as a boy was from copying Manuel,' he said. 'I watched his swing and tried to imitate the things he was doing.'

He was hooked – probably hooking as well, but quite definitely hooked. The 3-iron is not an easy club to master, particularly for your first one. But Seve had no choice. From that genesis, having learned to play all his shots with a club that was only suitable for a few, he developed a short game that has never been bettered. He would frequently skip school, understandably preferring to play golf rather than study books. His parents didn't realise that he was regularly leaving his club in drainage pipes on the course and swapping it for his school bag after lunch, when he was ostensibly on his way back to school. Dodging around the course like a culprit in his efforts to avoid coming across a legitimate members' outing, he would play a few holes in this necessarily surreptitious manner.

All the while, his parents thought things were going fine at school, or at least they did until he got expelled. One day when he was 12, Seve was mortified to discover that one of his school books had inadvertently been ripped, possibly by his father. One thing was for sure: Seve knew it wasn't his fault. But the school was strict; it wasn't only the priests and soldiers who had to be obeyed. His teacher made him hold out his hand and she hit it with a whip. The boy was hurt and angry when he got home for lunch, no less so when he found that his parents weren't in. There was a bottle of wine on the table. He had some, then he had a bit more. By the time he got back to school, he was drunk. He saw the teacher, went up to her and began to hit her. They threw him out.

This transgression proved a great career move. His parents were by now coming round to the idea that, as with his brothers, golf was a big deal for Seve. With school now being out-of-bounds, they enrolled him for private lessons in the evenings. This may have been less fun than hanging around outside cafes trying to watch television but it did mean the daytime was free for playing golf when and where he could, and for caddying at the club. Close to perfect, in fact.

The Real Club de Golf de Pedrena was founded by the King of Spain and was opened in 1928. Seve's family had connections with it since before its inception. His maternal grandfather had sold a plot of land to the club for its project. The family link was maintained with Ramon Sota's retention as the professional. And Seve assiduously went about his trespassing. He would wait until everyone had left and then practise for a couple of hours on the par-three 2nd hole, which is close to the road and out of view from the clubhouse, or else on the back nine, which is even more remote. This fox-like cunning was supplemented at home by using a can as a hole and practising his chipping with that as his target. And remember, all this was done with only a 3-iron, with which he had to hit the ball high and low, left and right, long and short, from short grass and from long grass.

His biggest frustration during these formative years was the gratuitously humiliating restrictions imposed on the club caddies. Not only were they not allowed to play on the course, Seve was once banned from caddying for a week for making a practice swing. It was no surprise that this atmosphere bred a taste for rebellion. 'If they had two dozen balls in their bag, we would take one dozen and hide them,' said Seve. 'We would also step on balls in the rough and collect them later.' Since most members had a lot of money and were bad at golf, this provided a splendid opportunity to sell such balls on, very possibly to the member who'd recently 'lost' them. Alternatively, Seve would retrieve these balls at a suitable moment and later practise with them on the beach, or sneak on to the course at dead of night and play by the light of the moon.

There was one member in particular whom Seve had reason to look upon kindly, one who permitted his young caddie to play with him and his friends at weekends, despite the complaints from the club, who tried to adamantly lay down the law that caddies could not play on the course – except for once a year, that is, in the caddies' championship.

There were three divisions in the Pedrena caddies' championship. The first time Seve played in the lowest, aged nine, with something approaching a full set of clubs, he finished fifth, shooting 51 for the nine holes with a 10 on his card. He was runner-up the next year, won the second division with a 79 over 18 holes when aged 11, and went into the top division when he was 12. He didn't win that year but when he was 13 he won the 36-hole event with 65–71. Also aged 13, and more of a sign of what was to come, he beat Manuel – eight years his senior and a tour professional – for the first time over 18 holes.

Attitudes towards him at the club now altered in the wake of this convincing display of young talent. Instead of being rebuffed, he was accepted. He was allowed to practise on the course. And how he did. He would hit hundreds of balls every day; the best part of four years spent doing little more than honing his game, refining that God-given ability. Almost the only life he knew was home and the golf course. Friendships were even less of a factor than they had been before. His route to adulthood through adolescence would mostly be a lonely one. But he didn't mind. This wasn't hard work. He was doing what he really wanted to do, doing what he loved. He was on the way to greatness – and he was sure of it.

Seve won the caddies' championship twice more before getting the chance to take his caddying skills to the other side of Spain. He had earlier caddied for Manuel in a tournament, but in late October 1972, Seve was among the caddies recruited from Royal Pedrena to travel to southeast Spain to caddie in the inaugural La Manga International Pro-Am.

La Manga was an ambitious new project – today it is arguably the foremost sports complex in Europe – and consequently it had no caddies of its own. For Seve, the long bus journey was worthwhile if only because it meant he encountered Gary Player, the first famous golfer he had met. *Manos de Plata*, they called him, 'Silver Hands', on account of his deft touch, notably from sand bunkers. Six years later, the two would play together in the final round at Augusta as the legendarily tenacious South African rallied from seven shots back to win the Masters. Also at La Manga that week, on the victorious team in the pro-am, no less, was a businessman by the name of Mark McCormack, the founder of the International Management Group (IMG), the world's leading sports entrepreneur. His path would cross Seve's many times in the future, although not in the way he fervently would wish – as Seve's manager.

It wasn't long before Seve's reputation began to go before him. Dudley Doust, who passed away earlier this year, recalled Spanish professionals, not only Manuel, telling the British press in the summer of 1973 that there was an extraordinary talent in their midst. 'One day he will be better than all of us. You watch. You will see.' But within a few months of those accolades, Seve's formative plans for being a professional golfer had hit a snag largely of his own making.

It was a custom on New Year's Eve that the young folk of the village would set out for the evening with the intention of making mischief. It was unfortunate for Seve that the plans for 31 December 1973 involved Pedrena Golf Club. At that time, the club were trying to improve the drainage on the course and they had the necessary large tubes on site, awaiting work to begin after the holiday. The same sort of pipes that had provided sanctuary for his beloved first golf club were about to be his undoing. One of his friends had a bright idea. 'Let's push those tubes down this hill.' So they did, about 20 of them, and by the end of the evening they were scattered all over the 6th fairway. Seve insisted he didn't actually push any of the tubes – he was merely loitering with intent, you might say – but when it got out who the group of youths had been, Seve was the only one who had any relationship with the golf club. Inevitably, he was the one who had to pay the price. The imposition of a month-long ban from the club's property only affected him. As if that was not bad enough, he had been intending to turn professional in the January. Now he couldn't.

At this point, he got just what he didn't need – a helpful offer from a nephew, of a job working in a boatyard. His mother, disillusioned by the treatment of her boy by the golf club, thought this a good idea, since he was clearly going nowhere in his chosen sport. Fortunately, his father's view prevailed. 'He said I must start playing golf for a living, because I was good,' Seve recalled. He would sit out the ban, turn pro, and see what happened. Come the beginning of February, he returned to the club to caddie and to practise, and then took the exams he required in order to turn professional, which he did on 22 March, 1974.

It is instructive to note that Seve did this without having had any amateur career to speak of. A few caddies' championships at Pedrena apart, he'd had no competitive experience. In America, that would have been unheard of – his counterpart (not that Seve has ever had a genuine equivalent) would surely have gone to university and played college golf. In Britain, players who would become Seve's peers, such as Nick Faldo, had auspicious amateur records. A little over 10 years later, another Spanish player, José Maria Olazábal, would complete the unprecedented feat of winning the British Boys', Youths' and Amateur Championships before turning professional.

Yet for Seve, there had been nothing other than those caddies' events, learning from Manuel and his own dedication, talent and self-belief. He had sacrificed the routine pleasures of the mid to late teens in order to devote everything to golf. Depending on how the mood takes him, he can get almost maudlin about this – 'No one can understand how much I gave to my golf in those days and how much I lost regarding other things in life' – and he will suggest that if he could turn the clock back, he may have pursued his career at a slightly more leisurely pace. Of course, he can't have the time again and in any case it is hard to believe that this rationalisation with hindsight has not been coloured by the back problems he has suffered from even before he got out of his teens.

Aged 14, he was in the boxing ring with a friend from the village. As Seve took a blow, the other boy trod on his foot. When Seve fell back, he landed hard on his spine. He was in pain for a few weeks, and while the pain did ease with time, on other occasions it would feel stiff and awkward. It is likely, although not certain, that was the genesis of the injury that has plagued him ever since. Carrying heavy bags and sundry other stuff around the farm wouldn't have helped either, and neither would the incessant working on his golf swing. Time went by and, as referred to in the introduction, his severe practice regimen ahead of his first professional victory, in the 1974 Spanish Under-25's Championship at Pedrena, may have been the straw that . . . er, broke the camel's back.

His first tournament as a professional had been the Spanish National Professional Championship, at Sant Cugat in Barcelona at the end of March 1974. He was accompanied on this – what would otherwise have been his first trip alone outside the Santander region – by his big brother, Baldomero. He finished 20th in the tournament, which was won by Manuel Pinero. Afterwards, he cried in the locker-room. Crazy as it sounds, he had expected to win. 'He was sobbing with his head on his knees,' said Pinero, who would later be a Ryder Cup teammate of Seve's.

There followed a tournament at La Coruna, in Northern Spain, and then continental Open tournaments in Portugal, Spain and France. Seve missed the cut in them all except Portugal, his first tournament outside Spain, where, on his 17th birthday, he shot 89 in pre-qualifying and didn't make the field at all.

His return to La Manga for the Spanish Open wasn't so hot either. At dinner the night before the first round, another Spanish player owned up to having taken a 10 in a tournament at Royal Birkdale. 'Impossible!' declared Seve. 'Nobody can score double figures on one hole.' The next day he took an 11 at the par-five 9th and shot 83. A 78 the next day meant he had at last managed to break 80 in a tour event and, amazingly, only left him a shot shy of making his first cut. With his prize-money earnings not threatening to hit three figures in pounds, and expenses well into the hundreds, it was a rather chastened 17-year-old who headed home for practice, practice and more practice.

Seve's next tournament was that Spanish Under-25s Championship at Pedrena; the one where, knowing every blade of grass, he had recorded his first win as a professional and collected a cheque worth £500. But in the aftermath of victory, he felt neither great elation or coruscating pain. He felt satisfied. He had never won a tournament before, but since – so his logic ran – he had turned professional in order to win golf tournaments, what he had just achieved was absolutely normal. As Pinero had also said in Barcelona: 'He always expects to win.'

He didn't win the Santander Open, the tournament following the under 25s, but he did finish second. He also addressed the matter of money – i.e. his lack of it. Via an introduction from his brother Manuel, Seve met Dr Cesar Campuzano, a local man who had a radiology practice in Madrid. He agreed to underwrite Seve's expenses in return for 50 per cent of his winnings, and it was this finance that funded Seve's trip, with Manuel alongside, to South Africa at the end of the year. (His parents, evidently bullish about his prospects themselves, sold a cow to help their sons on their way.) Dr Campuzano's munificence was not to be stretched. From this point on, Seve started to win prize-money, his earnings outstripping his costs, so he effectively became self-sufficient.

Through Uncle Ramon, meanwhile, Seve had been introduced to another wealthy local man, Emilio Botin, an eminent banker. In fact, Seve's father used to look after the Botin's house when they were away from Santander and he would also caddie for Snr Botin occasionally. The Botin family used to spend a lot of time in Pedrena, especially in the summer, and Seve started giving golf lessons to the Botin children once his elder brother, Vicente, who originally undertook that function, had to leave in order to do his military service. Seve would do this both at the club and in a room at their house that was fitted out with a net. Among the children was the fifth of the six, Carmen, who took her first lessons under Seve's supervision. She would later become his wife. Carmen's father also offered to sponsor Seve, but the deal with Dr Campuzano was not only in place, the terms were more favourable to Seve.

In October 1974, Seve had put in a tremendous performance at the Italian Open. The autumnal weather was almost stereotypically Venetian, with fog and mist playing around the Lido course. The first round had to be reduced to nine holes, but once the tournament had been completed after 63 holes, the fifth man home was, in the words of the *Mark McCormack Golf Annual* for that year, '17-year-old Spaniard Severiano Ballesteros, brother of Manuel and nephew of Ramon Sota'. The winner was Britain's Peter Oosterhuis, on the way to being the leading money-winner in Europe for the fourth year running. Johnny Miller, the 1973 US Open champion, was runner-up. What really impressed the 17-year-old prodigy-in-waiting was that he wasn't impressed at all. He had seen some of the best golfers in the world at first-hand and had seen nothing to fear. He felt what he had always known. He could beat anyone and everyone. There was no reason on earth why he could not be the best golfer on it.

The following week was the El Paraiso Open, on the Costa del Sol, where Roddy Carr, who would later become Seve's manager for a period, first came across Seve. Carr's father, Joe, was one of the great figures of amateur golf and the younger Carr was a former Walker Cup player himself, but by 1974, he was a struggling tour pro, paired with Seve. 'I'll never forget it,' he said. 'It was the second round and I had to make the cut to make my card [exempting him from having to pre-qualify for tournaments]. That's the most intensive negative pressure you could ever experience. I was drawn with this kid from Spain. We get on the first hole and he hits a 5-iron into 20 feet and slams the club down on the ground. I thought it was a fairly decent shot. He misses the putt and kicks the bag off the green. This went on the whole way round. I'm thinking, "Jesus Christ, does he expect to hole every shot?" And it was getting to me. I was getting annoyed. He was passionate. If he didn't hit a 2-iron into 10 feet, he was pissed off. If he didn't hole every putt, he was pissed off. And he had a temper in those days. I battled my way through and made the cut but I went in and said to his brother, Manuel: "I'm not actually going to report him, though I should, but someone ought to explain to him that he is not going to hole every shot and that he has to cool it or he'll be impossible to play with."'

How Manuel dealt with that is not known. By the end of the tournament, he was probably feeling pissed off himself. He had just lost a playoff to Oosterhuis. Seve had tied for 17th, five shots ahead of Carr. The impetuous behaviour Carr had witnessed that week was just one manifestation of Seve's intense, at times irrational, search for perfection in those early years. When he didn't attain it, which inevitably was often, he would sometimes deprive himself of dinner in the evening, a punishment for what he saw as his own stupidity.

For Seve, 1975 was a satisfying season. It wasn't great because he didn't win, which he thought he should, but he had top-10 finishes in the Spanish, Portuguese, Swiss and Madrid Opens and he was third, behind his hero Gary Player, at the Trophée Lancôme in Paris. His visits to the links of Britain (a links is a course built on sand-based land originally reclaimed from the sea; the type of course on which the Open Championship is always played), where he would enjoy three of the highest points of his career, were dismal affairs, however.

Seve hated Royal St George's, the links on the Kent coast and the venue for the PGA Championship in May. As far as he was concerned, it was as alien as playing golf on the moon. At St George's, you can't readily see the course from the clubhouse. Seve asked Manuel where it was. His brother pointed at the rugged linksland, amid which Seve could begin to recognise something resembling golf holes now that he looked carefully. 'It's there,' said

Manuel. Seve explained this inhospitable experience to Dudley Doust by saying it was 'so cold, so much wind, so much different from any other course I had known'. He was handed three golf balls by the tour representative from Dunlop, who promised him three more if he made the cut. He looked out morosely at the five-foot rough and thought 'These will last me about six holes.' He shot 78–84. In the Open at Carnoustie in July, it was 79–80. Almost needless to say, he missed the cut there, too.

Come season's end, Seve was in America. This was partly at the behest of the man who had become his first manager, an American called Ed Barner, who looked after the business affairs of Johnny Miller, Billy Casper (a three-times major champion) and Roberto de Vicenzo, the Argentinian who had won the Open in 1967 and would later become a mentor of sorts for Seve, notably prior to his win in the 1979 Open at Royal Lytham. It was de Vicenzo who had alerted Barner to Seve's potential and it was Barner who encouraged Seve to try to earn his playing privileges on the US PGA Tour in the 108-hole qualifying school.

After five rounds, Seve was well placed to become the youngest-ever golfer to hold a PGA Tour card. After five and half rounds, he seemed a shoo-in. He had reached the turn in 33 and as long as he remained standing, he looked certain to qualify. The problem, however, wasn't physical. It was in his head. Thoughts of what this would mean – endless weeks of travelling, mostly alone, in a big country with a different language from the one he knew, away from his family and his village – swamped his brain. 'I was scared. I wasn't ready. I didn't want to be there.'

So he did something that is a necessarily rare thing for a great athlete to do, albeit Seve was not yet worthy of being called great. He gave up. Seve could hardly believe what he was doing but he did it anyway. He came home in 40 and was happy to have missed out on his card. Like greeting an unfamiliar friend, he embraced failure.

Later in November, he paid his first visit to Japan, to play the Dunlop Phoenix tournament, and in December he and Angel Gallardo represented Spain in the World Cup in Bangkok. Two 17th places were the outcome as he closed out his promising season, a year in which he had consolidated on 1974 and had established himself as something more than a footnote to those who followed professional golf. In 1976, he would hit the big time.

2. THE GLORY YEARS:

HIGHLIGHTS & HEARTACHES

Although the most distinguishing thing about his first appearance in the Open Championship had been his ineptitude, Seve was back for the championship at Royal Birkdale in 1976 because he had finished top of the 1975 Continental Order of Merit. Nothing was going to shock him as much the second time around – indeed, he had tied for 23rd in the PGA Championship at his hated Royal St George's just two months previously (he'd win that title there in 1983) – and he knew that he should be able to play links golf.

'I knew how to hit the ball low and how to hit bump-and-run shots,' he said, 'but they were really only practice shots for me. I had hardly played on courses where you needed to use them.' Well, now he was going to play one again. The fact that earlier in the season he had had top-ten finishes in Portugal, Spain and France helped his confidence, too.

His preparation for the Open was far from orthodox. The week beforehand, he was bailing hay with his father on the farm in Pedrena, a job that had to be done by hand since they didn't have the necessary machinery. When he got to Southport, near Blackpool on the Lancashire coast, his first task was to try to steer the non-exempt Manuel through qualifying at Hillside, right next-door to Birkdale, by being his caddie. In this he failed, and Manuel did not return the favour. Seve had been hoping that his bagman for the Open would be Dave Musgrove, who had caddied him to eighth place in the French Open at Le Touquet, also a links course, in early May. Musgrove would be walking with Seve down the final fairway at Lytham in three years' time but on this occasion he was committed to, coincidentally, Roberto de Vicenzo. However, Musgrove had a solution. He had a chum called Dick Draper, a local policeman. He'd never caddied before but he was on holiday for the week and he was up for it, so why not?

The weather that week was of the sort which must have had the Southport Tourist Board thinking that all its summers had come at once. In fact, it was so hot that it felt like they had. And it was so dry that the course actually caught fire. In these torrid conditions, Seve realised that he would have to hit every approach so that it would land about 20 yards short of the green and then run on. In the first round, he applied this strategy so successfully that, with a three-under-par 69, he was tied for the lead. In the clubhouse, Manuel graciously accepted congratulations from players who were surprised to see the name Ballesteros on the scoreboards since they thought he'd not made it through qualifying. He had to explain the case of mistaken identity before accompanying Seve to the press centre to act as his translator.

'All good fun,' the press thought, as we sat in the enervating heat of the tent in which the interviews were conducted, but we were pretty sure the Ballesteros brothers wouldn't be back in front of us that week. One delightfully idiosyncratic aspect of the translation rigmarole was that someone would ask a question in English, Manuel would explain at length to Seve in Spanish, who would then reply to Manuel at equal length, also in Spanish. Manuel's explanation to the press in English would then be along the lines of 'He feels confident.'

Press scepticism that the above entertainment would be a one-off was incorrect. After another 69 from Seve on the Thursday (the Open was then held from Wednesday to Saturday; it didn't switch to a Sunday finish until 1980), the Brothers Ballesteros were in the tent again. Seve was leading the Open by two shots from the golden wonder boy of American golf, Johnny Miller. That flailing swing and wondrous putting touch were proving an irresistible combination.

The brothers were staying in a small private house in Southport. They went out for dinner, later walking around the streets and enjoying the glorious July evenings. There was a disco-pub they were particularly fond of, although Seve was more interested in the music than the drink. This first sensation of fame was a welcome one. Seve felt warm and wanted. Photographers snapped him constantly and he was on both the front and back pages of the national press. He was the story of the week – an unknown, good-looking, non-English speaking Spanish teenager leading the biggest golf tournament in the world.

The fuss didn't abate after the third round. Seve recovered from a rocky opening – he bogeyed the first three holes – to shoot a 73. Miller shot the same. Seve still led by two shots, but now there was only one more round in which he could fall over. And after this third day, after what he had seen at that tournament in Venice in late 1974, Seve could think of no reason why Miller should get the better of him. Manuel, on the other hand, could hardly believe what was happening. 'He was obviously thinking, "My God, my brother could win the Open,"' said Seve. Not only was Manuel incredulous, Seve felt, 'he was almost embarrassed, because he knew how important the Open was. I hardly understood that, partly because I hardly spoke English'.

There was a media maelstrom surrounding Seve, the pleasant aspects of which he was relishing, but he didn't comprehend that much of what was going on was speculation about how he was on the verge of becoming the youngest Open champion of the 20th century (in the event, he'd have to wait three years for that), the first continental European winner since Arnaud Massy in 1907 (ditto) and the biggest surprise winner since . . . well, maybe ever.

His inability to understand anything but the most rudimentary English insulated Seve, and so it was within this serene cocoon that he stood on the first tee of the final round of the Open, playing in the final group, again paired with Miller. 'It was probably the most relaxed I've ever felt while being in contention,' he said. 'I felt no pressure, no obligation.'

On the first hole, a long par-four, Seve was in trouble off the tee and faced a 20-foot putt for his par. He holed it. Miller missed from four feet for his four. Seve was three ahead. 'Oh my God', thought Miller. 'That's going to give him confidence.' Seve looked at Miller and read what the other man was thinking – 'He may play unbelievable and win the tournament.' The scarcely credible was beginning to look likely.

That was as good as it got. Within a hole, the lead was down to one. Seve bogeyed the 2nd, Miller birdied it. Matters were soon spiralling out of control, along with his swing, as Seve visited hitherto uncharted areas of Birkdale on almost every hole. He took a double-bogey at the 6th, a triple-bogey at the 11th. When Miller chipped in at the 13th for an eagle three, it was over. In a gracious acknowledgement of defeat, Seve shook Miller's hand. He then looked at a leaderboard and was alarmed to see how many players had overtaken him. A birdie at the 14th and an eagle at the 17th sorted that out, but he needed a birdie four at the last to tie for second.

On the 17th tee, Miller had spoken to Seve – in Spanish. As a native of California, it was no surprise that Miller had at least some fluency with the language, but he hadn't spoken a single word of it to Seve over their previous 34 holes together. 'I was a little bit shocked,' admitted Seve. 'He said, "It's important for you to finish well because Mr Nicklaus is already in the clubhouse [on three under par]." So I eagled that hole and birdied the last, with a nice chip-and-run between the bunkers.'

That 'nice chip-and-run' from some 15 yards short and left of the green was to prove a harbinger. Over the next 20 years, we would witness and thrill to such strokes of genius. Rather than settle for a regulation pitch shot over the bunkers which would require him to make a medium length putt for his four, Seve took on the only shot that could get him close to the pin, knowing that if he failed to execute it properly he was running the risk of taking six. His chip was perfect, threaded through the tiny gap between the bunkers, leaving him a four-foot putt in order to tie for second. In those days, Seve missing a four-foot putt was like England footballers scoring in a penalty shoot-out. It hardly ever happened. Nor did it on this occasion. It seemed fitting even at the time that Miller, the champion, had already putted out. The final act of this Open was Seve's.

At his press conference later, Miller said: 'It was Seve's driver that killed him. [A refrain that would be heard down the years, with sonorous regularity.] I really think that if he could have contained himself and used a 1-iron, he might have won.' He added: 'I think the best thing for Seve today was that he finished second. His day will come.'

Seve had no clue what Miller was talking about. 'I thought that was ridiculous. It is always better to win than come second. But in retrospect I could see what he meant. A lot of things happen, and happen very quickly, when you do something like that, and it is not usual for someone so young to win a major championship. In a way, even three years later, I was not fully prepared for what happened.'

In the shorter term, three tournaments later, after third places in Sweden and Switzerland, he won for the first time on the European Tour – the Dutch Open, by eight shots from Howard Clark. He had always known that this day would come. In the wake of Birkdale, so had everyone else.

Top-ten finishes were now the norm: third in Germany, fifth in Ireland, eighth in England. Against an eight-man field at the Donald Swaelens Memorial Trophy in Belgium, Seve had Gary Player as runner-up. In another elite event, the eight-man Trophée Lancôme at St Nom-la-Breteche near Paris, it was Arnold Palmer. In what he insists was all innocence, Seve's remark in the final round – 'Mr Palmer, you are driving the ball very, very straight today' – was a straightforward compliment. Palmer's retort – 'Not as straight as you're putting' – reflected the fact that at the time Palmer was on his way to relinquishing a four-shot lead over the last nine holes. Seve came home in 31 to beat him by a stroke. 'I had heard he was tough but I didn't know he was *that* tough,' said Arnold. He knew now.

Seve finished the season at the top of the European Order of

Merit, the youngest player ever to do so, but his year wasn't over. It concluded with a first-ever victory for Spain in the World Cup of Golf in Palm Springs, California. Manuel Pinero and Seve won by beating the United States team of Jerry Pate and Dave Stockton, the reigning US Open and PGA champions, respectively. The glory was soured by a second-round dispute during which Pate suggested that Pinero's caddie had cleaned his player's ball in breach of the rules, but in the calm light of day back home in Pedrena, Seve could regard 1976 as almost unequivocally a success story. The cloud on the horizon was the looming presence of military service with the Spanish Air Force.

Although the authorities co-operated to the extent that a good part of his service was spent giving golf lessons to military dignitaries, his obligations severely curtailed his time and opportunities in which to practise. In April 1977, *Golf Digest* in the United States, the world's best-selling golf magazine, put Seve on its front cover with the headline 'Can this teen-ager win the Masters?' This was more extraordinary than it might seem. *Golf Digest* will routinely have an instruction story on at least 10 of its 12 covers each year, so to devote one to a young foreigner about whom so little was known, especially in the United States, was a tribute to the admiration and excitement his exploits of the previous season had inspired.

Of course, having played so little golf, Seve had no chance of winning the Masters. He shot 291 to tie for 33rd, 15 shots behind the winner, Tom Watson. (For the record, only three men have won at the Masters at their first attempt – Horton Smith in the first one, in 1934; Gene Sarazen in the second, in 1935; and Fuzzy Zoeller in 1979. Tiger Woods won on his pro debut in 1997 but he had played in it as an amateur.)

Seve's military service went by largely without incident, other than one reprimand for playing on the European Tour without formal permission, and once it had been completed he set out to take up where he'd left off. After winning the French Open, he beat Nick Faldo, then an emerging player, in a playoff for the Uniroyal Tournament at Moor Park, north of London. Later, he won the Swiss Open, won twice in Japan, once in New Zealand and he helped Spain to retain the World Cup with Antonio Garrido as his partner on this occasion. That victory in the Philippines made it seven wins in six different countries. You won't be surprised to learn that with results like those, he again finished top of the European Order of Merit.

He repeated the trick in 1978, this time winning seven tournaments in as many different countries: Kenya, the United States (at the Greater Greensboro Open, of which more later), England, Germany, Sweden, Switzerland and Japan. Taking into account his last four tournaments of 1977 (including the World Cup), his victories in Kenya and America made it six wins from six starts. As every month went by, so grew his reputation. And not only for winning. There was his driving, too.

In 1977, Seve had won eight long-drive competitions, with such renowned behemoths as Jim Dent and Evan 'Big Cat' Williams up against him. In those days, Seve was always long and he could be straight – drives in those events had to land within a specified dispersion range in order to count. But in the latter years of his career, even when he was winning, he became short and crooked – in the words of David Leadbetter, probably the world's No. 1 golf instructor, 'a bad combination'.

Seve's most famous single shot of 1978 was a drive, a blow that hit and held the 10th green at The Belfry. The hole, which would come to be regarded as an essential ingredient of four subsequent Ryder Cup matches, measured 310 yards and in his Hennessy Cup match (between the Continent of Europe and Great Britain & Ireland) in September against Faldo, Seve took it on. The carry was something like 280 yards and there was general astonishment – excepting the fact that it was becoming increasingly hard for anyone to be amazed by what Seve could do on the golf course – when Seve's ball settled down 10 feet from the cup. The fact that these days, with the enormous advances in equipment technology, a drive of around 300 yards occasions yawns rather than gasps should not detract from what he did. Having said that, the most unlikely aspect of the whole thing was that he missed the eagle putt.

Seve was Europe's main man, there was no doubt about that.

However, by the end of June 1979, he had been assailed by the odd doubt about himself. He hadn't won since the Japanese Open the previous November and in May '79 he had been given a horrible reminder of mortality. A friend of his, the 29-year-old Spanish golfer, Salvador Balbuena, died of a heart attack at the French Open. Seve gave his prize-money (he tied for third) to Balbuena's widow.

Over the first weekend of July, Seve at last got off the mark for the year, winning the Lada English Classic at The Belfry by six shots from Neil Coles. Three weeks later, he was at Royal Lytham & St Annes, on the Lancashire coast, for his fifth tilt at the oldest title in golf.

Roberto de Vicenzo helped plan the route to victory; a lengthy route. The Argentinian observed that if you hit it far enough at Lytham, the rough was thin and sparse and in any case there would then be less distance to go to the green. The thick stuff was back towards the tee. Seve could simply hit over it all. He need not be so worried about accuracy. This was perhaps just as well. In reviewing the 1979 Open, Colin Maclaine, the chairman of the championship committee of the Royal & Ancient Golf Club of St Andrews (R&A), which organises the event, said: 'That the winner, Severiano Ballesteros, chose not to use it [the course] but preferred his own, which mainly consisted of hay fields, car parks, grandstands, dropping zones and even ladies' clothing, was his affair.' I'm afraid I can't shed any light on the particular incident of the ladies' clothing, but the car park was quite a story.

Seve began with a 73, two over par, ordinary stuff, but there was nothing ordinary about his 65 the next day. He birdied four of the last five holes, mightily impressive stuff in any circumstances, but especially so in a major championship and even more so given the ferocity of Lytham's notoriously rigorous finish. Curiously, the one hole he didn't birdie was the easiest of the lot, the short par-four 16th (he would make amends in spades for this oversight in the final round), and two of the four were exceptional – a chip-in on the 15th and a three at the last after playing what was effectively a 150-yard pitch-and-run under the wind with a 5-iron from an awkward lie.

Hale Irwin, the recently crowned US Open champion who led the field (and Seve) by two shots at the halfway point, was told that Seve had played the last five holes in 16 shots. Genuinely incredulous, he said: 'He must have left some out.'

Seve played with Irwin in the third round. In some respects, it was 1976 revisited. Then he and Miller played raggedly on the Friday. This day, he and Irwin did. Both shot 75, but the pack was not so much chasing as chastened. Irwin ended the day with Seve still the closest man to him. After two holes on Saturday, the last occasion on which the first day of the weekend would be the last one of the Open, Irwin had lost his lead. Seve had a birdie two at the 1st, Irwin took a double-bogey six at the 2nd.

Irwin never regained his advantage, but as Seve inadvertently sought out previously unknown parts of Lytham with his driver, both Rodger Davis of Australia and Isao Aoki of Japan held the lead at some stage. Seve had to wait until the final six holes to produce the killer blows.

The first came at the 13th, a 342-yard par-four. Seve attempted to drive the green. He was within a yard of pulling it off, the yard by which his ball failed to clear the last bunker. His drive had carried an estimated 298 yards – this with old equipment, remember. From the hazard, he conjured up a marvellous bunker shot that reached the edge of the green. The birdie putt from 30 feet was greeted with a two-armed salute. That thrust was then parried by the course. He bogeyed the 14th. But a deft chip saved his par on the 15th and he led the field by two shots. Now it was car-park time.

Seve's drive on the 16th was right of Franco. Fortunately, it wasn't too wayward to miss a temporary car park that had been set up for the final day. He'd have a clear line into the green, at least he would once a bit of automotive reshuffling had occurred.

While he later took a lot of flak for that errant drive, not least from an ungracious Irwin who mumbled that Seve had been lucky – 'I can't understand how anyone can drive that badly and still win an Open Championship' – and that he wouldn't win another major, Seve was only implementing the strategy that he and de Vicenzo had agreed upon: to hit it as near to the green as possible. (You could even say he was ahead of the game – doing that is essentially the strategy today of the likes of Tiger Woods and Vijay Singh: just bomb it.) Seve was also mature enough to realise he would get a free drop from the cars in that trampled-down rough. And for all the subsequent jokes about how the only driving that Seve could do in a straight line had to involve cars, he had taken left – where the danger was – out of the equation; the fact that he only had 90 yards to go to the flag showed that he couldn't have been that awry. His sand-wedge second shot was into the wind. It finished 20 feet from the stick and the putt was never anywhere but the centre of the hole. Walking to the 17th tee, he was home and hosed.

At the 17th, he saved par from a greenside trap, for the 14th time in 15 efforts during the week, and he could play the last with the luxury of a three-shot lead. Walking through the crowds that traditionally flood the final fairway at the Open, Irwin waved a white hanky in surrender. Whether it was mock or not was debatable.

Seve took two putts from some 70 feet and received the tumultuous acclaim reserved for the Open champion. Not since England's Tony Jacklin stood on the same green 10 years previously had there been a more popular winner. He finished the championship on one under par to win by three strokes from Jack Nicklaus and Ben Crenshaw. Irwin had stumbled home with a 78. If some wanted to carp that he was the car-park champion, Seve didn't care. He'd got the claret jug, not a ticket or a wheel clamp. He was aged 22 years, 3 months and 12 days. He and his three brothers, who engaged in a lachrymose embrace even before he'd completed the formalities of signing his scorecard, indulged in a little champagne. It was the happiest day of his career, but not the most surprising. As far as Seve was concerned, he was just accomplishing what he had always known he would.

The Open Championship – or the British Open, as it is often incorrectly if understandably called outside Britain, especially in America – is the oldest of golf's four major championships, hence the reason there was no need to specify in which country it's played. It was founded in 1860 and is held each July over a links course in Scotland or England; once, in 1951, it was held in Northern Ireland. The other three of golf's four majors are held in the United States. In other words, golf does not have the cosmopolitan breadth of tennis, where the four Grand Slams are held in Australia, France, England (Wimbledon) and the United States.

Golf's American threesome are the Masters Tournament, held each April at the Augusta National Golf Club in Augusta, Georgia; the US Open Championship, held in June; and the US Professional Golfers' Association Championship (USPGA), held in August. The latter two events, like the Open, do not have a permanent venue.

Seve first played the Masters in 1977. From the outset, he loved Augusta National. It's not easy to reconcile with the reality once you have seen both, but for Seve the course was reminiscent of Pedrena. He felt at home. He was pleased on the Friday evening of that debut that he had made the halfway cut, of players who would play the final 36 holes, despite taking seven on the 18th, and he was later thrilled to learn he had been invited back for 1978 even though he had not finished among the top 24 who were guaranteed a return trip.

In 1978, he made the cut again, after playing the second round in the company of Jack Nicklaus, who at this point had won 14 of the record-setting 18 major championships he would win. On the first hole, Seve chipped in from over the back of the green, from a situation that had six written all over it, for a birdie three. 'Seve, that was one of the best shots I ever saw,' said Nicklaus. Although Seve didn't necessarily believe this, and his limited English was indeed very limited back then, it was quite some compliment. Throughout the day, Seve enjoyed playing with and talking to Nicklaus.

He had no great expectations on the Sunday, and final, morning. He was seven shots behind the leader, Hubert Green, which was too far away to win. Or not. Seve's playing partner on Sunday was his idol from the past, Gary Player, who was also seven behind. That hot afternoon, Seve had to grind it out for a 74. Player was on fire, shooting a 64 to win by a stroke. The difference between the men was closer than that. After eight holes, they were both two under par for the day. Legend – and cliché – has it that the Masters doesn't begin in earnest until the back nine on Sunday. Gary played it in 30 while Seve's game was falling apart. He learned one fundamental lesson that day: never give up. On the 13th hole, Player said to him: 'Seve, I will tell you something. These people don't think I can win. You watch. I'll show them.'

Seve was getting closer to donning the champion's green jacket himself: 18th in 1978, 12th in 1979. Then in 1980, he turned the Masters into a procession for the best part of three and a half rounds. His swing was shorter and flatter than it had been at Lytham, in part to ease the strain on his back, and mentally he was sharp and prepared. Through a girlfriend, a television presenter from Barcelona, he was introduced to a psychiatrist who advocated a positive mind-set theory called 'sufrologia'. Seve had taken this up in late 1979 – i.e. after he had won the Open – and going into the Masters, he was pleased with the effects it was having on his attitude and his concentration. 'What the doctor says to me is private but it helps me to relax and convinces me that I am good,' he said. (It would prove generally symptomatic of Seve's reluctance to stick with just one swing instructor in later life that this 'mental training' regimen didn't find favour for too long.)

In Seve's mind, he had won this Masters before he got there. In the minds of everyone else, he'd certainly got it won come Saturday evening. After rounds of 66–69-68, he led the field by seven shots. He started the final round, playing with the Australian pro, Jack Newton, birdie-par-birdie-par-birdie. It was a rout. By the time he reached the 10th tee, he led by 10 shots. So this was one Masters that ended before the back nine on Sunday, although Seve did his best (or worst?) to make it interesting. However much the sufrologia sessions had helped up to this point, there is no doubt that his concentration was shot. Like everyone else, he knew he'd got it won. The lack of a target to aim for very likely hurt him that afternoon. For example, Seve, not the most assiduous reader of golf history, in part because it was usually written in English, was not aware that if he could play the back nine in two under par, having gone out in three under, he could set a new record-low total for the tournament, the same mark of 270 that Tiger Woods would set in 1997.

The first mistake came on the 10th green, where he sloppily three-putted from 25 feet for a bogey five. At the 12th, a notoriously beautiful but devilish par-three, measuring just 155 yards, Seve selected a 6-iron for his tee shot. He then did what you are never supposed to do unless you're chasing the leader on Sunday. He went for the flag instead of the safe part of the green. His ball went into the blue-dyed waters of Rae's Creek. Having to drop a shot under penalty and playing his third from the drop zone, he pitched on to the green and two-putted for a five. Newton, who had birdied the 11th, now birdied the 12th as well. Seve's apparently invincible 10-shot lead of some 20 minutes previously was down to five.

Water, water, everywhere . . . it was now beginning to seem that way for Seve. Not that there were any albatrosses in sight. Far from it. On the par-five 13th, he was in the wet stuff again. Instead of the once-in-a-lifetime bonus of an albatross two, he suffered the ignominy of a bogey six. He had hit his second shot too easily, having chosen his 3-iron for the shot after hitting a good drive. Maybe a hard 4-iron would have been the better option. In most circumstances under pressure, the harder, full shot is more successful than the one with something left off it. Seve was to suffer from this mistake once more at Augusta in 1986, with a more devastating impact.

On this afternoon, he still had the lead, but it was now down to three. Newton had just notched up his third consecutive birdie. There was now every chance that Seve could suffer the most calamitous collapse in major-championship history. 'What you are doing is stupid,' he told himself. 'Now you must try very hard or you lose the tournament.'

On the 14th, he suffered another unsettling experience. A near-frenzied spectator yelled out: 'Come on, Jack.' Temporarily shocked, Seve remembered what Gary Player had said to him two years before – 'These people don't think I can win. You watch. I'll show them.' He got his par, a fine, steady one, with two putts from 25 feet.

Confidence seeping back into his psyche, he hit a drive and a 4-iron to the heart of the 15th green. Suddenly stabilised, he was now comparatively unfazed to notice that in the group ahead, Gibby Gilbert had birdied the 16th to move to within two shots. Seve's two-putt birdie on the 15th restored his three-shot advantage and his temperamental equilibrium. The last three holes were negotiated with three tranquil pars.

He won by four shots from Gilbert and Newton; along with Gary Player, he had become the only non-American victor at Augusta. The Masters tradition back then, thankfully since abandoned, was for the club chairman, then Hord Hardin, to ask a few questions of the new champion for the edification of the television audience. 'Tell me, Seve, something people are always asking me . . . er, um, uh, just how tall are you?' was the gist of what he managed.

Back home in Spain, the news of Seve's triumph was carried on television, but not until the next day. At Augusta National, as if piqued by the identity of their new champion, the club resolved to rip up its Bermuda-grass greens. From now on, the greens would be of bent grass, firmer and faster. Let the putting seriously begin.

As the defending champion, Seve missed the halfway cut in 1981, but the following April he finished one shot out of the playoff in which Craig Stadler beat Dan Pohl. Seve finished strongly, with birdies on three of the closing four holes, but this valiant effort was rendered redundant by earlier mistakes that Sunday. Still, he did have 1983.

That was a glorious Masters for Seve if not for the spectators: the weather was so miserable that Friday's scheduled play was washed out, forcing the tournament to a Monday conclusion. Seve kept calm amid the storms and went into the final round paired with Tom Watson, the great American golfer of the day – as Johnny Miller had been in 1976 – who was widely and rightly regarded as the best golfer in the world. (The World Golf Rankings were not formally intro-duced until April 1986.) Watson had won the Masters twice, in 1977 and 1981, the Open Championship four times and the US Open once.

Indeed, he was the reigning Open and US Open champion. In the coming summer, he would win the Open for a fifth time. It would be the last of his eight major championships. But as is nearly always the case, no one could tell that the curtain was about to fall on the best days of a career. And this wasn't one of Watson's best days.

Entering the final round, Seve was on 211, five under par, a shot clear of Watson and one behind the men in the last group, Stadler and Raymond Floyd, who, like Seve, had also won the Masters once apiece.

Having won the Masters before the back nine in 1980, and then threatened to fritter it away, Seve effectively won this one by the 5th tee. He opened with a 7-iron to eight feet and made the putt for a birdie three. At the par-five 2nd, he hit a fantastic 4-wood second shot. From 255 yards off a downhill lie, he carried the right-hand bunker and stopped the ball 15 feet short of the flag. 'That's a shot I don't even have,' said Tom Kite later. Had Seve missed the eagle putt, it would have been an awful anti-climax, so he didn't. At the 4th, his 2-iron tee shot finished nearly in the hole. Four under for four holes on the day, nine under for the tournament, three shots ahead of Floyd and Stadler and four clear of Watson. He later birdied the 9th and could afford two dropped shots coming home (a mini 1980, if you like). He won by four.

There was one interesting incident on the way in. Time was running out for Watson as they reached the par-five 15th. Both players were forced to lay up short of the pond with their second shots, leaving their third shots roughly equidistant, but it was just Watson to play first. 'It's easy to hit the shot heavy into the water, and easy to spin it back in if you catch it too cleanly,' thought Seve. Watson thought so, too, and he motioned for Seve to play first. Seve stood his ground. Watson motioned again. Again Seve declined the offer. He wasn't going to give Watson one chink of hope by chunking his ball into the water.

Seve's four-shot margin might have been less. His second shot to the final hole went through the green. In hugely uncharacteristic fashion, he fluffed his first chip shot. The second went in for his par.

Not for the last time, Seve was irked by Watson. In the subsequent press conference, Watson suggested Seve had been lucky that his second chip went in because it was going quickly; who knew what might have happened if it hadn't hit the hole – it might have gone off the front of the green. When this was put to him, Seve was scathingly dismissive. 'Sure, and I suppose then I take 10 putts and don't even finish in the top 10.'

But nothing could ruin this victory for Seve. In one respect, it was his finest hour. This was the first time his father had ventured outside Spain to watch him play. After the tournament, they had time to kill in New York before flying home. They drove around Manhattan in a rented limo-with-chauffeur, drinking whisky from the bar in the back as they took in Central Park, Harlem and elsewhere. In short, generally relaxing. Such behaviour is not typical of Seve – chilling out isn't his normal style. But then his father always commanded a very special place in his affections. The 1983 Masters also provided a golfing footnote. It meant that Seve had won his first three major championships on different days – Saturday, Sunday and Monday.

As became his own little tradition at a place that thrives on the stuff, Seve missed the cut in 1984. The defending champion had to kick his heels in Augusta for two days waiting, as is the custom, to help his successor into the club's green jacket (Ben Crenshaw, in this case) at the victory ceremony.

In 1985, it seemed that Crenshaw might be about to return the favour. Down the stretch on Sunday, Germany's Bernhard Langer was taking advantage of Curtis Strange's sudden if unwanted attraction to the apparently magnetic allure of the course's water hazards by seizing the lead, but with Seve as his playing partner, no one was sure Langer would hold up.

Most notably, Langer had played with Seve in the final round of the 1984 Open at St Andrews and had seemed at times to be overawed as his Ryder Cup colleague claimed the title for the second time, a story which comes later. During the closing stages of the tournament, it appeared that Langer's chief function, even though he finished joint runner-up with Tom Watson, was to sign Seve's card. Then, at the World Matchplay Championship at Wentworth in the autumn, Langer had said what others had sometimes said *sotto voce*. 'Seve is very intimidating – always on the course and sometimes off it. I learned my lesson at the Open and I will handle him differently now.' He added: 'He never likes it if you criticise him in any way. If you only say he's good, he thinks you're putting him down.'

With those sentiments doubtless in the minds of both combatants, it seemed that Seve might be too tough mentally for Langer, only three months younger but light years away in terms of experience. But Seve's chips and putts for birdies somehow stayed out of the hole (although he had holed a bunker shot at the 2nd) and when Langer rolled in a 12-footer for a birdie on the 17th, he had two shots in hand over Strange and three on Seve. Walking to the 18th tee, Seve patted him on the back and said: 'Well done. This is your week. It's all yours.' Maybe his surprise at this gesture was why Langer bogeyed the hole, but it was still good enough to win his first major championship.

For Seve, disappointed as he was, there would be other chances to win the Masters. Three big chances.

By early 1986, Seve's father was very ill with lung cancer. He'd had an operation to remove one lung in a Houston hospital and had come home shortly before his son was due to go to America to prepare for the Masters. Seve made him a promise: 'I will come back and take you to the Masters. I am going to win the Masters for you this year.' Seve's golfing preparations for the Masters were also not what you'd call ideal unless your name was Irony. He was mired in a bitter spat with the PGA Tour over his playing rights there, the broad details of which we shall return to later. The upshot was that having lost his membership for refusing to play in the required 15 tournaments per season, the only events he could play in the States were the three major championships over there, at New Orleans in defence of the USF&G title he had won in 1985, and on mini-tours.

In late February, he played on one of the latter, a 54-hole event called the Florida Cup Classic on the Tournament Players' Association Tour, where he finished tied for 22nd in front of a total of about 220 people. He earned $1,375. He never got to the next tournament. He received a phone call from Baldomero, urging him to return home to their father. He died within the week.

Within two weeks, still deep in mourning, Seve returned to America for his one-shot at a PGA Tour event. He missed the cut in New Orleans. He therefore headed for Augusta on the basis of nine competitive rounds all year – three in Florida, two in New Orleans and four in the Spanish PGA Championship. No doubt it was emotions inspired and fired by the death of his father that caused him to say, out of character: 'This tournament is mine.' It was simple repugnance for the PGA Tour commissioner, Deane Beman, whose height was never his long suit, that led to Seve saying: 'Beman is a little man trying to be a big man.'

Despite the sad circumstances and lack of preparation that presaged his arrival at Augusta, Seve was still Seve and therefore among the favourites. Sure enough, at halfway the bookmakers weren't wrong. On five under par, 139, he led the field by a shot. A level-par 72 on Saturday did no damage, leaving him a shot off the lead which was held by the glamorous and gregarious Australian, Greg Norman. Alongside Seve on 211 were Nick Price, who had just broken the course record with a 63, Bernhard Langer and Donnie Hammond. Tom Kite, Seve's partner for the final round, was in a group on 212 that included Watson. Comparatively unnoticed among this gathering of the contemporary great and good was the greatest of them all – the Golden Bear, Jack Nicklaus, the most formidable golfer in history, lurking on 214.

Seve and Kite teed off at 1.48 p.m., the same time as Seve had started in 1980. A good omen? As it transpired, about as encouraging as being paired with Damien Thorn. The two men had been singles opponents when Europe had won the Ryder Cup the previous September, when Seve claimed a moral victory by winning three of the last five holes to force a half. There was rancour in the air. On the first green, Kite complained when Vicente, Seve's brother and caddie,

made a movement, well off the green, while Kite was about to hole a
one-foot putt for his par. 'What is wrong with this guy?' they said to
each other. By the 8th, Seve had picked up a shot on the day, while
Kite had dropped one. They were both well short of the green in two
on this uphill par-five. I was standing with (now Sir) Michael
Bonallack, then secretary of the R&A, at the back of the green. We
first saw Kite hole a nearly full wedge shot for an eagle three. The
crowd went crazy. Across on the 9th fairway, Seve saw Watson give
Kite an enthusiastic gesture of encouragement. Seve had the ideal
answer. His pitch-and-run from 40 yards went into the hole for an
eagle of his own. Cue more pandemonium. 'I just don't believe it,'
laughed Bonallack, happily outraged by what the man had just done.

At eight under par, Seve led the field by a shot. A wayward drive
on the 9th almost ineluctably led to a bogey, but three pars followed
and Seve arrived at the 13th tee still tied for the lead. The 13th is the
final element in the three-hole act that is Augusta's 'Amen Corner':
the par-four 11th, the par-three 12th and the par-five 13th. Seve's
prayers seemed to be answered. His drive was perfect, drawing round
the corner of the trees and settling in the middle of the fairway. He
nailed a 6-iron, his ball finishing six feet from the cup. He holed the
putt. At nine under par, he led Kite by two. He led Nicklaus by four.

As this was being played out, Seve's second eagle in six holes, I
was in the stand behind the 13th green with Herbert Warren Wind,
the doyen of American golf writers. 'That should do it,' he said to me,
matter-of-factly. (In his subsequent review in *The New Yorker*, Wind
would write: 'Ballesteros is a puzzlement – a highly emotional man
whose attitudes are inconsistent.')

With the benefit of hindsight, Seve and his brother took a lot of
stick for what happened after Seve hit that 6-iron. Vicente went over
and shook hands with him – 'That was a fantastic shot' – in an action
somewhat reminiscent of what Seve had done when Johnny Miller
had holed his eagle chip on the 13th hole in the final round of the
1976 Open. Critics said that showed a lack of concentration on Seve's
part; a touch of hubris that was about to be rewarded with nemesis.
He insisted that they were just congratulating each other on having

chosen the correct club, albeit he did later concede this much. 'I thought that when I eagled the 13th, I was the champion. Eight times in 10 I would have been. I don't want to take anything away from Jack Nicklaus, he played fantastic golf, but I think for me not to win was almost a miracle in all the circumstances. It was *destino*.' Whether that amounts to a tacit admission of culpability is a moot point, but when Vicente shook his hand, he still had the putt to make, which he did.

Seve's tee shot on the 14th, with a 3-wood, was also perfect. Then it wasn't. It hit a TV cameraman who was walking where he shouldn't and ended up perhaps 40 yards short of where it would have finished. An easy pitch and a possible birdie became a fight for a par. His drive on the par-five 15th was another belter, long and straight. Might this lead to his third eagle of the round? It was then that his troubles really began.

He and Kite had to wait forever to hit their second shots. Alright, that's metaphorical, but five minutes is a very long time to hang around when you are on the verge of winning your third Masters, of sticking it to Deane Beman and the PGA Tour and their stupid rules, when there's a father who's no longer with you but for whose memory and in whose honour you so badly want to win this thing; and you are having to do all this playing with a guy you don't particularly like, when you've hardly played any competitive golf all year, when you have the world's greatest-ever golfer now hot on your tail with 99 per cent of the crowd roaring him on; oh, and you're between clubs with, very unluckily, a far-from-ideal lie in the fairway.

The delay was all Nicklaus's fault. After Seve's eagle on the 13th, Jack had retaliated with one of his own on the 15th to go to seven under par. On the 16th, his tee shot had come within something like an inch of going in for a hole-in-one. The formality of that birdie meant his walk from the 16th tee to green was as tumultuous an ovation that a golf course has ever heard. There were thousands of people crammed around that hole, on a nearby hillside and around the 15th green. 'The noise was deafening,' said Nicklaus. 'I couldn't hear anything. I mean nothing.' The fact that the noise was enveloping the 15th green meant that Watson and Tommy Nakajima, who had birdie putts on the hole, waited until Nicklaus had got his two on the 16th before they putted out. Which in turn meant Seve had to wait . . . and wait . . . and wait.

He's a professional golfer, he had won four major championships and countless tournaments around the world, but while he never admitted it to me, it's hard not to think that in all that spare, unwanted, time he had on his hands, some of those aforementioned thoughts didn't mess with his thinking. Especially, perhaps, thoughts of the father he had recently lost; of that promise he had made; of how he had won with his father there in 1983 and now would win this in his absence. 'I was going to win for me and my father,' he told Peter Kessler of *Golf* magazine in 2003. Then there was that lie. 'He had an awkward lie up on a knob,' Kite told *Sports Illustrated*. 'It was a tough situation: the lie, the circumstances, what Nicklaus was doing, the noise. It was so noisy you couldn't even hear each other.'

By now, of course, Nicklaus was eight under par, only a shot behind Seve. Of what happened next, Nicklaus was later to say that Seve's swing was that of a man who hadn't played enough golf under the gun. Seve and Vicente talked over what to hit. Seve's initial thought was the 5-iron. But then, as he had on the 13th hole in the final round in 1980, he decided to club up. 'Let's play the 4-iron,' he said, 'a nice, soft, easy 4-iron.' The logic wasn't completely skewed; the most important thing with the second shot on the 15th at Augusta is to clear the pond with your shot – assuming you're not going to lay up, and from where Seve had driven his ball, lay up wasn't in his vocabulary. It seldom was anyway. Whatever, whether distracted by myriad feelings and thoughts, discomfited by his lie or uncertain about the club selection, he hit the shot heavy. Horribly heavy. Nice and easy does it was again a very bad idea. His ball wasn't even close to making it over the water. 'It was, no question, the worst swing made by a genuinely world-class player during the 1980s,' wrote John Huggan in *Golf's Greatest Eighteen*. 'It took a long time before I was confident with my 4-iron again,' admitted Seve.

Spectators at the Masters are, slightly quaintly, described as 'patrons'. Good manners, as instructed by the tournament's founder, Bobby Jones, are impressed upon them. What happened here slightly broke with that convention. If one can have such a thing as a huge muffled roar followed by a collective hush and then a communal moment of quiet contemplation . . . well, this was it. Nicklaus admitted to hearing 'a funny sound' as he stood on the 17th tee, the mixture of shock and cheers that greeted the drowning of Seve's golf ball. The fans weren't rooting that way because they hated Seve. They just wanted to see 46-year-old Jack Nicklaus – a golfer who had won only two tournaments since 1980, who had been described that very week in *The Atlanta Constitution* as 'done, through, washed-up and finished' – win a record sixth Masters, and his 18th major championship. It was simply Seve's misfortune that he was in the way.

Later Seve would deny the error was down to the pressure. 'It's just that I hit too easy a swing with a 4-iron. I should have hit a hard 5.' But there was far more to it than that, as he admitted to me the next day at Atlanta Airport. 'A lot of things happened yesterday,' he said, almost gnomically, 'both on the 15th and before the 15th.' The whole subject is one to which he still finds denial the best response, but that sentence sums it up. There was stuff on the 15th and there was all that stuff beforehand, and not only Kite getting grumpy with Vicente on the first green.

Meanwhile, back at the golf course the previous afternoon, Seve's ball might have been in the water on the 15th but *he* wasn't all washed up. If he could get up and down in two shots, after taking his penalty drop, he would save his par and still lead at nine under par. Now he got seriously unlucky, twice. His pitch was good but his par putt from 10 feet somehow stayed out. Now tied for the lead, on the 16th his tee shot was all over the flagstick. Miraculously, if your name was Nicklaus, it somehow landed over the bunker and then stopped just short of the green. Normally, one would have expected the ball to release towards the hole and be stiff for a two, but we weren't talking about anything normal here. Instead, Seve had to stand in the bunker to hit his putt. As he prepared to do that, a TV cameraman in a gantry at the back of the green did a thumbs-up and mouthed to the crowd below: 'Jack's just birdied 17.' He had, too. Seve's birdie putt missed by inches and now he trailed by one.

Seve three-putted the 17th and it was left to Norman and Kite to fail to make the putts on the last green – Norman for a par, Kite for a birdie – that would have forced a playoff. As if God would have let them.

After his three-putt on 17, Seve said 'Thank you' to the crowd for their now sympathetic applause. Walking up the 18th, he blew kisses to the gallery. To the world, he looked the epitome of the gracious loser. Inside, he was in bits. He could not believe he had lost. In a way he hadn't lost. He had been beaten by *destino*. 'The problem was the wait,' was how he attempted to rationalise his blunder. 'I don't want to take anything away from Jack but it was destiny. I was destined not to win and he was destined to finish his career with a great victory.'

Nicklaus's victory was fantastic, an epic denouement to an epic career. If Seve had won then, in a different way, the story would have been every bit as dramatic. And if Seve could replay one shot from the millions he has hit in his life, that 4-iron would be it. 'I think that if I had hit the green instead of the water, I would have won maybe six Masters.' We'll never know that. Nor will he. 'It burns me inside,' he said. And it always will.

In Thomas Hardy's novel, *Tess of the D'Urbervilles*, the President of the Immortals ended his sport with the eponymous heroine only when she was hanged. And the Muse of the Masters wasn't yet done with Seve Ballesteros.

The following year, he led the tournament not after 68 holes but after the full 72. But two things were between him and a third green jacket: Greg Norman and Larry Mize, the former the flamboyant Australian who was reigning Open champion, the latter a journeyman American tour pro who happened to be a native of Augusta. They had tied on 285, three under par, after a tough week on a hard-baked golf course. As they headed for the first playoff hole, the 10th, it would be fair to say that the third man – Larry Mize, not

Harry Lime – was generally regarded as the bit-part actor in what would surely be a sudden-death shoot-out between perhaps the best two golfers in the world. 'He looked like a mâitre d' who was going to show them to their table,' wrote Dan Jenkins in *Golf Digest*.

All three hit good drives. Seve's second shot called for a 5-iron. His ball carried perhaps three feet too far, one extra yard that meant that instead of funnelling down towards the hole on the left-hand side of the green, it stayed up on the back edge. With Norman 15 feet away, Mize only 10, it looked like Seve might need to make his putt in order to stay in the playoff. But the putt was dangerously quick, the more so if you played it too aggressively. Above all, he wanted to get it close. Even then, he knocked it three feet past. Norman and Mize both missed their chances; Seve needed his putt to stay alive. He didn't make it.

The light was tricky, with the early evening shade making it hard to see the line. That may have explained why Seve seemed to get himself misaligned. His ball went past on the left. He was out. Utterly disconsolate, in tears, he trudged back up the steep hill of the 10th fairway towards the clubhouse, leaving Mize and Norman to get on with it. Before the playoff, he had had time to reflect on the enormity of what this could mean – a chance at redemption just one year on. Now it was not to be. This time, our brief conversation at Atlanta Airport the next day saw him displaying a defiant sense of perspective.

'Hi,' I said cheerily. 'How are you?' Then: 'Sorry, stupid question.'

'Not stupid at all,' he replied. 'I'm fine. I have my health. Nobody died.'

But he felt like death. 'Even more than the blow to my confidence after '86, I lost faith in my putting when I missed that short one,' he said later. 'I started missing a lot of short putts after that, especially the crucial ones.'

Mize won the Masters at the next hole, chipping in for a wholly improbable birdie three from well wide of the 11th green. Since the previous major championship, the 1986 USPGA, had seen Norman denied victory by Bob Tway holing a bunker shot on the final hole of regulation play, the general belief was that Norman had just suffered two successive thrusts from fate that beggared belief. This was not an opinion that Seve entirely shared.

The week after, at the Suze Open in Cannes, the only tournament Seve would win in 1987, he explained his theory that Greg had left the door open for this to happen. 'Norman thought Mize was bound to make a bogey, so he played his second shot too safe. [He left it 50 feet from the hole.] Mize then knew that Norman could three-putt from there, so he thought that if he bogeyed the hole he might still be alive. That meant he could be more relaxed when he played the chip shot. If Norman had played more aggressively and finished closer to the hole, Mize would probably not have holed his chip.' Similar circumstances had occurred with the Tway shot (Tway's holed sand shot was for a birdie after Norman, holding a one-shot lead, had missed the green with only a wedge in his hands) and Norman was subsequently displeased to hear of Seve's analysis, telling *Sports Illustrated* 'Seve is so detrimental to his name right now' by voicing those views.

That was not the end of Seve's near-misses at Augusta. The fates held that back until 1989. Now Seve was the reigning Open champion, having won for a third time at Royal Lytham & St Annes in 1988; back to feeling upbeat. Mentally at least, he could not have wished to have felt more self-assured. He had suffered the odd setback, such as four-putting the 15th green (when he had committed the same sin on the 16th green in 1988, he had explained his error by saying: 'I miss, I miss, I miss, I make'), but at the halfway stage he was only two shots off the pace set by Nick Faldo and Lee Trevino.

Bad weather delayed the conclusion of the third round until Sunday morning. In the gloom of Saturday afternoon, Seve had bogeyed the last three holes he played but he was fast out of the blocks on Sunday, making birdies at the 14th, 15th and 17th to be in at level par, three shots behind the leader, Ben Crenshaw. He was two ahead of Faldo, who had stumbled home in 77 on the resumption of play. Starting the final round, Seve kept his momentum going magnificently. He birdied the first, holed a bunker shot at the 2nd, canned a 40-foot putt on the 4th and a 30-footer at the 5th. A birdie at the 9th took him out in a five-under-par 31 and in the lead. Par home would have got him into another playoff. He missed that target by two.

The weather had by now turned nasty again. On the 10th, Seve pull-hooked his tee shot into the trees. No problem, he thought, I'll get a free drop. Not so fast. His playing partner was Ken Green, a sometime dyspeptic American tour pro. 'Next thing I know, I see him preparing to drop [without penalty],' Green told *Golf Digest*. 'I had to hoof it all the way back to see what the hell was going on. That's when the official said: "At Augusta we have this local rule – if it's crowd damage, we give the player a drop." Seve's particular interpretation of crowd damage was people just walking and the grass being matted down.' Green disputed the ruling and sought an alternative opinion. He got one, the one he thought was right, from Michael Bonallack, no less. Seve had no choice but to pitch out and he bogeyed the hole.

Three solid pars followed before he missed a birdie putt from six feet on the 14th and then from eight feet at the 15th, this time distracted by a huge roar for a Norman birdie up ahead. He was running out of time. His 6-iron tee shot at the 16th, as in 1986, looked down the throat of the flag. This time it didn't make it over the bunker. It caught dry land and toppled sadly into the water hazard. He double-bogeyed the hole. His birdie three at the last was an empty flourish; a what-might-have-been goodbye wave to what was his last genuine shot of victory in the Masters. On the back of two huge birdie putts at the 16th and 17th, and Scott Hoch's missed tiddler on the first extra hole of their playoff, Nick Faldo won his first Masters and his second major.

As mentioned before, Seve was the second non-American, and the first European, to win the Masters. In his wake there followed Bernhard Langer (1985 and 1993), Sandy Lyle (1988), Nick Faldo (1989, 1990 and 1996), Ian Woosnam (1991) and José Maria Olazábal (1994 and 1999). Put another way, no European had won the Masters before Seve did, but they won 11 in 20 years after his first success. They have won none since 1999.

Seve didn't play in the Masters between 2003 and 2006. In 2007, to general surprise – even if these were the days he was talking about soon fulfilling a serious schedule on the US senior tour – he turned up to play the course that he sometimes seemed to own. By now, it being longer and tighter, he hardly knew his way around. He shot 86-80 to finish dead last after two rounds, although there was some consolation. In an interview with Jock Howard for *Golf World* last summer, Seve intimated he had taken home his champion's green jacket, which is supposed to remain on the Augusta premises. 'They can come back here and collect it if they want,' he said. My bet is that they'll leave him alone.

As we shall see later, and not only in the Ryder Cup, Seve was effectively alone when it came to being in the forefront of instilling a generation of European golfers with the belief that they could beat anyone. He was especially thrilled with the first victory of his compatriot, Olazábal. Before the final round, Seve left in his locker a note that read (in Spanish, of course): 'Be patient. You know exactly how to play this course. Allow the others to become nervous. You are the best player in the world.' He wasn't, of course, even if he was the best that week. But when Seve said it, you could believe.

3. MORE MAJORS AND A
PLACE IN HISTORY

After Seve's triumph in the 1979 Open at Lytham, Tom Watson won three of the next four, in 1980, '82 and '83. The missing one was at Royal St George's at Sandwich in Kent, the place Seve had quickly come to loathe on his first encounter with links golf in 1975.

Going into the 1981 Open, Seve had, two weeks before, won the Scandinavian Enterprise Open. His form and confidence were high. During the final practice round, he had ripped a 1-iron through the roaring wind to the heart of the 15th green. He turned to his caddie and pronounced: 'Now we are ready.'

But the weather wasn't ready to co-operate. Aside from the fact that it is always played on a links, the aspect that sets the Open Championship apart from the other three majors is the impact that the weather routinely has on events. The tee-off time you draw can be vital, especially at those Open venues – i.e. all of them except for Birkdale and Muirfield, where the courses are laid out in two loops of nine, each of which returns to the clubhouse – where the course is basically configured in an outward and an inward nine. Be really unfortunate and you can draw the worst of the weather both days for the first two rounds. Such was essentially Seve's fate at Sandwich. You can't win a golf tournament on the first day but you can go quite a way towards losing it. Seve shot 75–72 to trail the leader, Bill

Rogers, by nine shots at the halfway mark. Demoralised, he finished the week 17 strokes adrift, in a tie for 39th. He was not much of a factor the next two years either, but then his drought ended.

The 1984 Open was played over the Old Course at St Andrews, universally regarded as the oldest golf course in the world. This may or may not be strictly accurate but no one seriously disputes that St Andrews is the spiritual cradle of the game, the 'Home of Golf', the most famous piece of golfing ground in the world. This particular corner of the east coast of Scotland, the 'Kingdom of Fife', is home to the university of St Andrews. But as distinguished as the university is, it is for golf that the town is renowned. The essence of the game envelops its buildings and streets as surely as the sea mists that regularly perpetrate themselves upon the inhabitants. In the countless bookshops and pubs, there is no getting away from the game. The very location of the course is an incessant reminder of what the place is all about. The 18th hole is part of the town itself.

The golf course looks utterly unprepossessing. No one would dare build it today. It may be the course that established 18 holes as the norm for a round of golf (this in the 1760s, when the layout was reduced from 22 holes) but nowhere else would you find a top-ranked course with just two par-threes and two par-fives. When the great American golfer of the day, Sam Snead, later a hero of sorts to Seve, came to St Andrews for the 1946 Open, he recorded that he thought it was 'an old abandoned sort of place . . . so raggedy and beat up I was surprised to see what looked like fairway among the weeds. Down home we wouldn't plant cow beets on land like that.' And he won the championship!

But Bobby Jones, the greatest amateur golfer who ever lived, the one and only winner of the original Grand Slam – the Open and Amateur Championships of Britain and America – in 1930, later said: 'I could take out of my life everything except my experiences at St Andrews and I'd still have a rich, full life.' Jones, who founded the Augusta National Golf Club and the Masters Tournament, was made a Freeman of the Burgh of St Andrews in 1958. He died in 1971. The next year, the 10th hole, previously nameless, was christened 'Bobby Jones'. Only one other hole, the 18th, called 'Tom Morris' in tribute to the four-time Open champion and legendary 19th-century son of the town, is named after a person.

Jack Nicklaus, the greatest golfer of his generation and winner of the Open over the Old Course in 1970 and 1978, was driven by Jones's edict that to be considered a great, a golfer must win at St Andrews. 'There isn't a place I would rather win a championship than on the Old Course at St Andrews,' he said.

So it was to St Andrews that Tom Watson arrived in 1984 seeking to win his third consecutive Open. That feat had been achieved by Peter Thomson as recently as 1956, but if Watson were to win, he would join Harry Vardon, the British giant of the game at the turn of the century, as the only six-times winner of the claret jug. And he wanted the title for another reason. He had won it at each of the other four Open venues in Scotland – Carnoustie (1975), Turnberry (1977), Muirfield (1980) and Troon (1982). This would complete the set, and at the place where everyone wants to be champion at least once.

Seve had designs on the crown as well. He hadn't won thus far in 1984 but after working on his game with the assistance of two friends, Vicente Fernandez and Jaime Gonzalez, both Argentinian tour pros, he felt comfortable and in control. His first three rounds were 69–68–70. At nine under par, he was tied with Bernhard Langer, his final-round playing partner. In front of them, leading the championship on 11 under par, were the novice Australian, Ian Baker-Finch – and Watson. The latter had fired a 66 on Saturday and was perfectly placed to realise a lifelong ambition or two. But as Seve left the interview room that Saturday, he said to the assembled press: 'I'll see you all in here tomorrow evening.' He didn't mean as a loser.

Throughout the next afternoon, he looked at the leaderboards. Birdies at the long 5th and the short 8th gave him the lead, this for the first time in the Open since he had won at Lytham five years before. Seve bogeyed the 11th before a birdie at the 14th got him into a tie for the lead with Watson, who had birdied the 13th. Nothing was happening for Langer, Baker-Finch was on his way to a 79, and no one else was remotely threatening. It was between the two of them.

The breeze strengthened as Seve arrived on the 15th tee. He reached into his bag and took out his navy blue sweater, chosen to go with his white shirt and navy trousers. He put it on. He was now clad exactly as he had been at Lytham. (This nautical sartorial combination was one he mostly reserved for the Open, but for Seve blue has been the colour ever since he wore a shirt of that hue when he clinched his debut tour victory in Holland. He also wore blue, in different shades, for his two Masters victories. For the record, the royal blue shirt he wore to lose the 1986 Masters was a Nike model. Clearly, as Tiger Woods has repeatedly demonstrated on major-championship Sundays, they work better in red.)

Seve parred the 15th and 16th without drama or anxiety but as he got to the 17th tee, he had reason to be fearful. The 'Road Hole', as it is called, is generally reckoned to be the toughest par-four in the world. Measuring 461 yards, it calls for a blind drive over the corner of the Old Course Hotel (more romantically, there used to be railway sheds there before the line that used to run alongside the course was ripped up) to a narrow, sinuous fairway. Into the hotel grounds on the right is out-of-bounds, which is where Seve had gone when leading the championship in the second round in 1978. That year, he played the hole 5-6-6-5 for the four rounds, six over par. He finished the Open seven shots behind Nicklaus. The safe line off the tee, to the left, invariably means that you get tangled up in thick rough and the green is then much harder to hit and hold. The green is shallow and raised on a shelf. In front of it is a bunker so hideous that Hitler wouldn't have been seen dead in it – 'eating its way into the very vitals' of the green, wrote Bernard Darwin. Behind is a road, from where the ball has to be played up to a ledge on which the green sits.

Seve had suffered only five bogeys in the championship to this point, three of them here, two of those with one-putts. He badly wanted a par this time around. Again he drove left. The rough was thick and matted down but Seve's lie was not too bad. He could get a 6-iron on the ball. The question was whether that could get him the

200 yards to the green. It did – the shot of a champion. Two putts from 50 feet secured the par. It felt like a birdie.

On the last, as straightforward a par-four as the 17th is fiendish, Seve hit a good drive and a wedge to 12 feet below the hole. The putt was on line all the way but seemed as if it would stop on the lip. As if making one final determined effort, the ball toppled into the cup for a birdie three.

'I knew the putt was very close,' he said. 'You never think whether the ball is going to go in or stay out. You just watch it. I could see it was close and then – it goes in. It was the happiest single shot of my life.' His celebrations were extravagant, like a matador enjoying the best kill of his life. That image of his moment of exultation is iconic and Seve has adopted it for his corporate logo and even had it tattooed on his arm. It meant that much. 'I nearly killed my caddie,' said Seve of the embrace he gave Nick de Paul. 'I was so excited.' What added to his pleasure was the fact that his mother, who had never attended the Open before, was with him. Apart from anything else, Seve's parents could certainly pick which majors to make their first.

There was more pleasure, of course, in the identity of the man he beat. Watson could have caught Seve with a 4-3 finish of his own, but after an ideal drive down the 17th (in fact, it started out so close to the out-of-bounds that Watson initially thought he might have to hit another tee shot), he went with a 2-iron for his second shot. It was a bad misjudgement; way too much club. His ball finished on the road and he took a bogey five, just before an unknowing Ballesteros was sinking *that* putt on the 18th. By the time Seve had signed his card, he knew Watson needed to hole his second shot at the last to force a playoff. That forlorn hope didn't happen.

The frostiness between the two men was apparent in the aftermath. Seve was mildly offended by Watson's half-hearted handshake and curt congratulations. He told Gary Player: 'Look how that guy congratulated me!' But Watson's disappointment was understandable. He knew he'd never have a better chance to win an Open over the Old Course. What he didn't know was that he'd never win another major. For Seve, there was still a last hurrah.

Seve's best round in the Open was probably the closing 65 that propelled him to victory in 1988, the first time the Open had returned to Royal Lytham since 1979. It was a scintillating performance in which he only missed three greens and three fairways in a marvellous display of controlled, powerful golf. Seve dominated this championship from the outset. He had begun the week as 8–1 co-favourite with Sandy Lyle, the Scottish golfer who in 1985 had become the first Briton to win the Open for 16 years and who was the reigning Masters champion. The bookmakers liked the fact that Seve didn't have a brother on his bag (Vicente had taken the rap in many quarters for Seve's muddled thinking during the closing stages of the 1986 Masters). Instead, about to become the third different caddie to win an Open with Seve, Ian Wright was the man.

As Nick Faldo had done the previous year, on his way to victory in the Open at Muirfield, Seve opened his title bid with three consecutive birdies and added two more at the 6th and 7th, both par-fives. Five under par through seven holes; what was that about not being able to win a tournament on the first day? And this was a cold day, with the temperatures below 50 degrees and the wind at over 40 miles per hour.

Out in 30, Seve found the back nine altogether more unpalatable, as is usual at Lytham. He came home in 37, making two breathtaking bogey fives, at the 14th and 18th. For the former, he had to take a penalty drop from an unplayable lie after his second shot, from where he hit a blind 7-iron to within 15 feet and made the putt. At the last, his drive was deep into the bushes but another one-putt got him out of jail. His four-under-par 67 not only gave him the lead, it was, according to Jack Nicklaus, 'one of the great rounds ever in the British Open'.

But a 71 on Friday left Seve trailing Nick Price by a shot, and he was two behind after the third round, which was played on Sunday after Saturday's play was washed out. As at Augusta in 1983, matters would conclude on a Monday. And very aware of what had happened to him at Augusta in 1986, Seve said: 'So far I am beating the pressure but, as you know, the pressure is very difficult to beat.'

Unusually for the last round of a major championship, they went out in threeballs. Ballesteros, Price and Faldo were the last group out. It was no shock to see that Seve was again dressed in navy and white: his Open lucky colours. He birdied the first hole and was still a shot behind Price playing the 7th. Price hit a wonderful 2-iron second shot to within four feet of the pin. From the fairway you can't see the bottom of the flag on this hole, but the roars of the crowd told Seve that Price was close. He only had a 5-iron in, which he hit to six feet. He holed his putt for an eagle; so did Price. Faldo three-putted and was on his way out of contention.

Seve caught Price with a 20-foot birdie on the 8th. After pars at the 9th, both made birdies at the 10th, Nicky from four feet and Seve from 20. Against a par of 5-4-3-4, Seve had just had four straight threes. On the par-five 11th, another birdie gained him the lead at last, an advantage he promptly squandered after a poor tee shot at the 12th.

Price, who had frittered the Open away in 1982 and had yet to win a major championship, was far from finished. His second shot to the 13th almost went in for an eagle two. Seve knew he could not afford to let Price get ahead again. He matched the birdie by holing from 18 feet. As if joined at the hip, they both bogeyed the 14th and parred the 15th.

To the 16th, where Seve, the 'car-park' champion, had so dramatically sealed the title nine years previously. This time it was a 1-iron into the fairway (there's maturity and experience for you) and a 9-iron, from 135 yards, that finished three inches from the hole. That birdie gave him the lead again, and for good. Later, Seve couldn't resist saying: 'It's a pity that I didn't find any cars on the 16th today. Perhaps next time the R&A should park them on the fairway.'

There was one more anxious moment to overcome, as his drive on the last flirted with the right-hand traps. It finished in wispy rough from where – in his keenness not to go into one of the deep bunkers that protect the last green (he was only in four sand traps all week, as opposed to 15 in 1979) – he hit a 6-iron just over the left-hand side of the green. This was deliberate. Before going out to play, he had looked out over the 18th green and observed that if he required a four to win, the safe play was to go left. How his gorgeous 9-iron chip shot from there didn't go in for a three remains one of golf's enduring mysteries.

Ian Wright began to celebrate. Seve told him to cut it out. 'Just a minute,' he said. 'Nick still has to putt. I've seen things happen before.' Such as what Tway and Mize did to Norman. If Price could hole his 30-foot putt for a birdie, there would be a playoff. Determined that his valiant effort to win would not come up short, Price sent his putt long and missed the one back. The two-shot margin the record books show Seve to have won this one by does tend to disguise how thrillingly close it was.

There was no doubt how much this victory meant to Seve. Since he'd stood in the 15th fairway at Augusta with the 1986 Masters in his control, he had lost his confidence, two Masters and chances at the US Open and USPGA in 1987, as we shall see shortly. He had made Little Bo Peep seem careful. And it wasn't only that. Other European golfers were climbing furiously aboard the bandwagon that he had hitherto been driving alone. Lyle had won both the Open and the Masters, Langer had won the Masters and Faldo had won the Open. The European Ryder Cup successes in 1985 and 1987 had been in large part down to him but an individual triumph was well overdue.

'I didn't believe I would never win another major,' he said afterwards, 'but I was a little bit worried. I was starting to wonder, you know, that my time was, you know? . . .' He claimed this victory was his catharsis. 'Now that shot [the 4-iron into the water at Augusta] will be way back in my mind. Instead, from now on, I will remember how I played today.'

Vicente, too, got his share of praise. He may not have been Seve's caddie but Seve credited him with a putting tip he'd passed on at Westchester in upstate New York the previous month, to put his hands closer together on the grip. 'My game at Lytham was much as before,' he said. 'The putting was the difference; my best since I won at St Andrews in 1984.' For the time being at least, the demons exercised by that playoff miss at Augusta in 1987 had been exorcised.

The Sun newspaper summed up how the nation felt. 'What a marvellous performance by the new Open Champion Ballesteros. If a Brit couldn't win it we're glad it was him. Great golfing Sevvy.' (*The Sun* doesn't take the chance that its readers might not know how to pronounce 'Seve'.) There was one additional facet to Seve's enjoyment of the week. Although his girlfriend, Carmen, had been at the 1984 Open, this was the first one she had attended as his fiancée, now aged 23.

(There was one unusual footnote. Bernhard Langer finished with a round of 80, coming home in 46, including five putts from five feet at the 17th. He hadn't so much got the dreaded, supposedly incurable, yips, it was as if his photo should have accompanied the word in the dictionary. Yet even though there were to be no more major victories for Seve, Langer would recover sufficiently to win the Masters – the game's most testing examination of putting – in 1993 and be playing well enough to make the victorious European Ryder Cup team in 2002. Funny game, golf.)

Three years after Lytham II, the Open returned to Royal Birkdale, the venue where Seve had first courted the attention of the wider sporting world. The R&A paired him with Johnny Miller for the first two days. After the first of those, thanks to an eagle-birdie finish, Seve's 66 left him alone atop the leaderboard. With a round to play, he was very much in the thick of things, two shots behind Baker-Finch (now a much stronger competitor than he had been at St Andrews in 1984) and the American, Mark O'Meara. On Saturday evening, reflecting on the fact that he was the only man within four shots of the lead who'd ever won a major, Seve said: 'I feel so confident. The crowds are with me. They give me an extra club in my bag. You must be brave and play solid golf to win an Open. I have done it. They [the other players on the leaderboard] haven't. It is my destiny.' He added: 'I don't think any player is afraid of me. The thing is, they are afraid of the trophy more than me. The trophy means so much.' That comment led to one tabloid headline of 'They're Scared Of Me' on Sunday morning.

In the event, it wasn't his *destino* and they weren't scared of him or the trophy. At least Baker-Finch wasn't. Seve shot 71, which wasn't bad but was never going to be enough to make up the deficit. This was especially the case once Baker-Finch had gone to the turn in 29. He went on to win by two. Seve's hopes were shot when he bogeyed the 1st and then missed a short putt for a par at the 3rd. In the media centre, Dudley Doust observed that as that putt went by, 'his shoulders didn't slump, they lifted'.

Maybe so. Maybe Seve's confidence was really such that he didn't fancy the pressure and tension of being in contention through-out a long afternoon when he didn't rate his chances of being able to finish the job. Perhaps, considering his career in totality, he'd gone to the well too often; the strain of putting himself under pressure – at least in an environment as formidable as contending for a major championship – had become too much to bear. In only one more Open would he be any sort of factor. At Royal St George's in 1993, the Open won by Greg Norman with a wonderful 64 on Sunday, Seve had a two-under-par 68 to begin with and was two shots off the pace, but thereafter he was never able to mount a challenge.

He hasn't made the cut in the Open since 1995; only entered it once since 2001. His withdrawal in 2002 occurred shortly after his disqualification at the Irish Open, where he signed for a 10 on the final hole rather than the 12 he had taken, in the process turning an 89 into an 87. That incident was not so much the beginning of the end as the end of his belief. He did play at Hoylake in 2006, with his eldest son as his caddie. 'I think that's the main reason he has come back', said José María Olazábal. 'To take his son on the golf course and let him see how the game is played'. By now, though, Seve wasn't capable of showing anyone how to play the game. He shot 74-77, not too awful but nowhere near making the cut. 'I was nervous', Seve admitted. 'I felt down because deep inside I felt I didn't have the game to play the Open. But I also really felt the people behind me, and my son as well. I played with the heart, as always.'

He is eligible to play in the Open until he's 60, but he retired well short of that mark.

He hasn't entered the US Open or the USPGA Championship since 1995, either. The story of his assaults on those two titles is a different one, and very much shorter.

Seve freely admits his biggest regret in golf is that he never won the US Open. But it's no surprise. He never felt comfortable on golf courses where the emphasis is on saving par rather than making birdies. 'The US Open is all about negatives,' he once told me. The way the course is routinely set up by the United States Golf Association (USGA), the driver is taken out of a player's hands (although for Seve this could be no bad thing) and the thick rough around the green tends to assure that all golfers are reduced to the same level – i.e. all they can do is try to hack it out – rather than the more skilful exponents of the short game, such as You Know Who, being rewarded for their superior technique, ability or imagination.

Seve's relationship with the US Open got off to quite an encouraging start. At Cherry Hills in 1978, only a final round 77 denied him a top-10 finish. A Sunday repeat of the 69 he had on Friday would have seen him, not Andy North, home as champion. The next year, at Inverness, he missed the cut. Then things got worse.

On the flight from Madrid to New York in June 1980, Dudley Doust reported, Seve had a premonition. 'I remember saying to myself: "Seve, you should not be going to the US Open. Something bad is going to happen."' Not going was not seriously an option – he was the Open and Masters champion, after all – but then disqualification should not have been an option either.

After a first-round 75 at Baltusrol, five over par, Seve was in evident danger of missing the cut. His tee-off time on Friday morning was 9.45 a.m. He thought it was 10.45 a.m., which was why he didn't leave his hotel until 9.25. As he reached the course, thinking he had about an hour in which to practise and prepare for his round, he was told he was late on the tee. His scrambling was to no avail. His playing partners, Mark O'Meara and Hale Irwin (yep, him again) had already reached the first green. Under the Rules of Golf, Seve had to be disqualified.

His fury was almost tangible. He railed against his manager, Joe Collet, who was looking after him, Ed Barner having flown overseas on other business. Baldomero, the brother charged with caddie duties that week, copped his share of the blame as well. But inside, Seve knew that one person and one person alone was at fault.

He had been unlucky that the car journey to the course had taken longer than usual. If normal service had applied, he would have made the tee-off time, even if his lack of pre-round practice might have made it harder to make the cut. Indeed, he would have had to shoot 71 to do that, so the likelihood was that the incident was a temporary humiliation rather than a career-hurting error, but he was or certainly should have been aware enough not to allow this to happen. He had nearly missed his tee-time at the 1978 Greater Greensboro Open, a scare which he survived with sufficient élan that he made that his first tournament victory in the United States. So at Baltusrol, he had been forewarned. Whatever, by the time Jack Nicklaus had holed out to win his fourth US Open on the Sunday afternoon, Seve had long been back in Pedrena.

Seve did have a chance to win the US Open at Oakmont, just outside Pittsburgh, in 1983. An opening 69, two under par, gave him a share of the lead. After two rounds, he was on 143, two shots off the lead and five shots ahead of the man who would win, Larry Nelson.

At times, conspiracy theories have no trouble flourishing in the fertile Ballesteros brain. This was such an occasion. Seve had gone with his 1-iron, rather than his wayward driver, for most tee shots that week. On the last day, he noticed the tee markers were well back and that the rough had been trimmed. To his way of thinking, this could only mean one thing: the USGA didn't want this Spaniard 1-ironing his way to the championship. 'I think someone realised Severiano might be the champion,' he told *The Independent*, 'so they moved the tees back as far as they could.' The way the course was now set up, not using a driver was a penal act of masochism. A closing 74 left him tied for fourth, six strokes adrift. He had also been unsettled by the sight of his playing partner, Tom Watson, dressed in blue – his colour! Seve thought it might have been a tactic to get into his head.

Two years on, at Oakland Hills, it was a tie for fifth. With a round to play, Seve was on level par, which would ordinarily represent good shape after 54 holes of the US Open. But he trailed the leader, T. C. Chen from Taiwan, by seven shots. This huge advantage largely evaporated on the par-four 5th, where Chen double-hit a chip shot on the way to running up an eight. Apart from spawning an inevitable rash of cheap jokes ('Just like everything from Taiwan; great for three days and then it falls apart'), this opened the door to the other contenders. Seve's play on the back nine was more aggressive and when he made a rare two at the formidable par-three 17th, he was in with a chance if only he could birdie the last as well. He couldn't. His total was 281 and, for the second time in his career, Andy North could enjoy the luxury of a bogey five at the last to win the US Open.

Another two years later, 1987, and the championship was at the Olympic Club in San Francisco. Seve finished third, his highest-ever position in the US Open, five shots behind the champion, Scott Simpson. Two months later, it was the USPGA Championship at Palm Beach, where Seve had an outstanding opportunity to win despite messing up towards the end of his third round.

After 15 holes, he led the championship, but he finished 6-2-6, including two visits to the ubiquitous water. Two shots in arrears, he'd climbed back into a tie for the lead after just two holes on Sunday. The 3rd hole was a 533-yard par-five which he had birdied every other day. This time, he and Vicente seemed to be in a state of war during its entire length. A poor drive left Seve merely able to pitch out to the fairway. His third shot finished short of the green, his fourth in a bunker, his fifth over the green and into water – again. He had to one-putt from 10 feet to make eight. He finished five shots out of the playoff in which Larry Nelson beat Lanny Wadkins.

There was also the 1990 US Open at Medinah, Chicago. Halfway through the second round, Seve had been heading for the exit. Then, executing a shot that only he could have imagined, let alone hit, he punched a 6-iron from under a cluster of trees off the

10th fairway. Travelling 130 yards, the ball never got above waist high. It finished a foot from the flag. That birdie inspired him to a 32 coming in and, after a level-par 71 on Saturday, he was heading to the first tee of the final round on 213, three under par, four shots behind the co-leaders, Mike Donald and Billy Ray Brown, and level with the man who would win, his old mate, Hale Irwin. His hopes lasted for two holes. The 2nd at Medinah is a par-three over water and, yes, the *agua* did for him again. He snap-hooked his tee shot with a 6-iron and with that he gave up. 'I just put myself down,' he confessed. 'I was there to win and I hit it in the water. If things are going badly, it becomes a kind of routine.' The last 16 holes passed in a blur as he shot 76.

Despite that, in 1994 Seve got a special invitation into the US Open. He had been complaining in the press that he wouldn't be able to play at Oakmont, where he had performed creditably in 1983, because he had not been given a special exemption into the championship. 'It's wrong,' he said. 'I think I am part of its history.' Maybe, albeit not in a leading role.

It had previously been announced that Arnold Palmer, for his valedictory appearance in the championship in what was practically his hometown, Johnny Miller and Larry Nelson (the previous two US Open champions at the venue) had been extended invitations, and Seve was perhaps fortunate to get his way since some of his remarks had rather come across as peevish criticism of the invitation for the legendary Palmer, who had no chance of making the cut. He may also have been fortunate that José Maria Olazábal had won the Masters that spring, which qualified him for the US Open. The suggestion was that Olazábal would have been given an invitation if necessary, which would probably have scuppered Seve's hopes.

In any case, in late May the USGA added Seve to the list. They also added Ben Crenshaw, the widespread view on this being that it diminished the impression that they had been browbeaten into submission by the Spaniard. In the event, Seve finished in a respectable tie for 18th. He missed the cut in 1995 and never returned.

*

Where will history place Seve in the pantheon of the game's greats? It is largely by a golfer's performances in the major championships that this judgement is made. Rather harshly, in my view, Herbert Warren Wind opined: 'I think we may have overrated Seve. He wasn't a great player, finally.'

Is that correct? Seve won five major championships. As of March 2008, the following are the golfers who have won more:

Jack Nicklaus: 18
Tiger Woods: 13
Bobby Jones: 13 (as an amateur)
Walter Hagen: 11
Ben Hogan: 9
Gary Player: 9
Tom Watson: 8
Arnold Palmer: 7
Gene Sarazen: 7
Sam Snead: 7
Harry Vardon: 7
Nick Faldo: 6
Lee Trevino: 6

You could comprehensively dot that table with asterisks (for example, Hagen only had three majors to go for, since he was pretty much finished as a competitor by the time the Masters was inaugurated in 1934), but for sure Tiger Woods is the only one of those who might add to his tally. At spring 2008, there was no other contemporary competitive golfer who has won more than three – Ernie Els, Vijay Singh and Phil Mickelson – so Seve's pedigree doesn't look too shabby.

If you include his regular tournament victories (in total career wins, for example, he has 87 to Faldo's 39), his record looks even more impressive. If you take into account the flamboyant way he played and the joy he brought (which you can't), or his almost single-handed resurrection of the Ryder Cup (which you might be minded to put into the mix), and that along with Player he is the only golfer in that table who doesn't have a major championship played in his home country, then one might not unreasonably feel that he is one of the 10 best golfers who ever lived. I'd say that's pretty great.

Faldo, himself a decent judge on this topic, said (admittedly on Seve's DVD, *The Definitive Story of a Golfing Genius*): 'He's definitely in the top half-dozen all-time golfers, I'd have thought.'

In a foreword to the Dudley Doust biography of Seve, Lee Trevino wrote: 'By the time he finishes, in about 20 years, he may not be equal to Jack Nicklaus . . . but he'll be more than equal to the all the rest of us – myself, Watson, Byron Nelson and even Ben Hogan.' (Nelson won five.) That, clearly, was rather over-egging things, but then 20 years was far too much to expect. For most of the greats, 10 years is the maximum period they have at the top, between their first and last major championships. That applied to Jones, Hogan, Palmer, Watson and Faldo as well as to Seve. There are exceptions, but then Nicklaus (24 years) and Player (19) are extraordinary exceptions. In the case of Tiger Woods, we shall have to see, although I think we know the answer.

In 2005, Trevino updated his thoughts for *Golf Digest*. 'Seve at his best was the best golfer I ever saw. Jack [Nicklaus] was the greatest chess player ever. He made a plan. Tiger makes a plan. Seve never made a plan, he just made things happen. He had something we didn't have.'

Essentially, that something enabled Seve to survive at the top for the general maximum of 10 years, from 1979 to 1988. It was a decade cut through for him with tales of Kipling's 'two impostors', Triumph and Disaster. No one can claim that he managed to treat them both just the same, but for golf in Europe he was stupendous, thrilling, brilliant. What a period it was. It was the best of times and he gave them to us.

4. CONNERY, ELVIS OR PALMER?

At the moment Seve was so memorably celebrating his winning birdie on the 18th green of the Old Course at St Andrews, Spanish television's main sports programme was mourning the death of a thoroughbred brood mare called Kriti. The Seve show was only seen later, as part of a highlights package.

'Twas always thus, back then. Not so when José Maria Olazábal won his two Masters, in 1994 and 1999, when Spain had cottoned on to the achievements of its foremost golfers, but when Seve was collecting his majors, Spain was, for the most part, not looking on. He was a prophet without honour, if not short of profits. The later, he would say belated, recognition of his achievements – a celebration dinner in Madrid in 2000 to mark his 25th anniversary as a professional golfer; a subsequent accolade as Spain's sportsman of the 20th century – have not erased the frustration and sense of injustice engendered by those earlier snubs.

When he had chased Miller home in the 1976 Open, the story didn't make the press in Spain. When he won the Open in 1979, it was not that big a deal, and certainly not as big a deal as the return to the bullring of El Cordobes. When he won the Masters in 1980, the only sports story on the Spanish radio news was of a native swimming record. When he won at Augusta in 1983, that took second-place to a tape-delayed football match – though admittedly it did involve Real Madrid. (Ironic, in a way – Seve, a fan of Racing

Santander first and Barcelona second, hates Real Madrid; still more curious when you consider his father's devotion to Franco, in whose memory Real Madrid are such a potent symbol to many.) Even as late as 1997, when Seve captained the victorious European Ryder Cup team at Valderrama, he received messages of support from Tony Blair and other, less eminent, politicians, 'but not one message from any Spanish authority. I am really surprised once more'.

But that was there. Elsewhere in Europe, and especially in Britain, he was lionised. 'I think I am more like an artist,' he said. 'The way I played was exciting for the public and exciting for myself.' With his charismatic presence, he made golf seem almost sexy. He certainly made the European Tour what it is.

In 2003, Colin Montgomerie told Will Buckley of the *Observer* : 'He is the most charismatic figure the European Tour has ever had. He has an aura around him that few people in the world have. The only other person I have met with the same effect on people was Sean Connery. The thing about Seve is he can walk into a room and you know he's there even though you can't see him. Suddenly there is a buzz and you just know someone special is present.'

He became an example to the major winners from Europe who would follow him, notably Bernhard Langer, Sandy Lyle, Nick Faldo and Ian Woosnam, all born in the 11 months after Seve. They were, inevitably, the 'Famous 5'. And Seve has never been shy of taking the credit that is his due. 'I led all of them – winning the Masters, winning the Open, winning the Ryder Cup, winning in America. If anybody asks me what my biggest achievement is, I always say that I am very proud that I was the first to do all those things. I feel that I really helped to develop the game in Europe. Sport is not just how much you win, it's how you win. It's the way you win that connects with the people.'

He told me in 1988: 'I don't think there was anybody more excited than me when Sandy Lyle holed his putt to win the Masters. I was watching on television, jumping up and down. I was tremendously happy for him, and for Nick Faldo at Muirfield last year. Seeing Sandy and Nick win, and watching Bernhard with the

Masters [in 1985], I gave a little credit to myself. I think I was the one who proved we had the ability to win major championships. I think I helped give confidence to the European players.'

His influence extended beyond his own continent. Zimbabwe's Nick Price, who won three majors after narrowly losing out to Seve at Lytham in 1988, told *Golf Digest* in 2005: 'A lot of us who would win majors – me, Greg, Faldo, Sandy, Langer – were the same age, but Seve was our benchmark. He won four majors before any of us won any and he had immense charisma. The way people were riveted to him, he reminded me of Elvis.' First Connery, now Presley. Later there would be José Maria Olazábal, Paul Lawrie and Padraig Harrington, but, to date, that's it as for further European major winners. Since then, there have been no more majors for Europe, for all of Colin Montgomerie's eight Orders of Merit and the talents and intermittent excellence of players like Sergio Garcia and Paul Casey, Darren Clarke and Lee Westwood, Thomas Bjorn and Luke Donald.

According to Mac O'Grady, the PGA Tour player, Seve's quondam golf teacher and a fellow off-the-wall genius (he can play golf almost as well left-handed as he can right), Seve will, in his more vainglorious moments, claim to have earned 19 major champion-ships – his five, Faldo's six, two apiece for Langer, Lyle and Olazábal, and one each for Woosnam and Lawrie (that was before Harrington won the 2007 Open). That, of course, would give him one more than Nicklaus. Faldo has won one more major than Seve, but he has never been surprised at the Spaniard's greater popularity with the crowds, even in his own country of England. 'It was because he was the one hitting those magical shots. He was smiling and pumping his fist more and that sort of thing. And, dare I say it, he's probably marginally better looking than me [this said with a chuckle]. He endeared himself to the public because he made the effort to speak English. He had that while I was the head-down, blinkers-on grinder, so only the hardened golf fan appreciated what I was up to.'

In his autobiography, *Life Swings*, Faldo wrote: 'Seve and I would never become intimate friends; our rivalry was too intense for us to form any sort of attachment, but my admiration for him – especially the way he almost single-handedly made us believe the Ryder Cup was within our grasp – is unbounded. Our relationship was born out of respect rather than affection and I wish there had been a bit more affection.'

There always was that distance. In June 1988, a week before Faldo would lose the US Open in a playoff with Curtis Strange, a month before Seve would win the Open, I had lunch with them both at the Westchester Classic – that is, I was chatting with Seve when Nick came up and asked if it was OK if he joined us. (I think the other tables were taken.) Around that time, I used to have dinner with Faldo a couple of times a year or so on tour; he didn't like hanging around with other golfers too much. As Trevino said: 'How can you have dinner with a guy one night when you're going to try to kill him the next day?' But I doubt Faldo would have sat for lunch with Seve alone. In a way, they had me in common: a third party to defuse any potential tension. They didn't need to feel obliged to discuss stuff they'd prefer not to go into; no awkward silences to fill. It wasn't that they disliked each other but it was respect rather than anything stronger that tied them together. Coincidentally, a fortnight before that lunch they had done something together for *Golf World* magazine. Faldo was the reigning Open champion, Seve the previous winner of the Open at Lytham, and we were pleasantly surprised that Faldo agreed to pose with Seve and *his* trophy for the cover story of the July issue. That Seve went on to win at Lytham again just made us feel a bit smug for a while.

Once Seve won his first tournament, the Dutch Open in 1976, he hardly stopped. He won in Spain, France, England, Scotland, Ireland, Switzerland, Germany, Sweden and Monte Carlo. He won in Japan, New Zealand, Kenya, Australia, South Africa and Dubai. He won in the United States. The world was his Rolex Oyster.

Seve officially won 55 times in Europe (including the Tour's 'satellite states', such as Dubai) and he notched up a further 14 European Tour-recognised international victories. And then there were the Sun City titles and a few more besides. Eighty-seven in all.

That he was regarded as the 'European Arnold Palmer' – rather than the 007 or Elvis of European golf – was inevitable. It has long been acknowledged that the foundations of the PGA Tour in America were built upon three bricks in the 1950s: the coverage of golf on television, the entrance into the White House of a golf-mad president, Dwight Eisenhower, and the thrilling on-course exploits of Arnold Palmer. Palmer was a huge heterosexual figure, mesmerically drawing the attention of both men and women to the appeal of the game, largely because of the extravagant and unpredictable way he played – a tenacious presence, fearless big-hitting, gob-smacking recovery shots and a silky touch around the greens. Remind you of anyone? Like Seve would do later, Palmer always seemed to be engaged in a *mano e mano* battle with the golf course; a titanic struggle from which – like the good guy in a Western – there was only going to be one winner. Things obviously didn't always work out like that; it just seemed that way. And as Seve would do later, Palmer's allure drew in sponsors and spectators as if he were a magnet.

In truth, Gary Player is at least an equally good analogy to draw with Seve since, perforce, the South African had to travel the world to establish his reputation. Seve had to do likewise from Spain. In the foreword to Dudley Doust's *Seve: The Young Champion*, Lee Trevino also wrote: 'It won't be long before [Seve] is the greatest international player of all time . . . even more successful than Gary Player.' Not counting Senior Tour events (for which golfers have to be 50 in order to be eligible), Player has won 77 official victories, according to PGA Tour records. Seve has 10 more.

By contrast, Palmer could ratchet up the wins from the comfort of his own home in America; albeit it was Palmer whose support of the Open Championship reinvigorated its stature in the 1960s, when it was in the doldrums due to an almost complete lack of interest by the leading American players since World War II. Sam Snead only played once more after his win in 1946. Ben Hogan came, saw and conquered in 1953 and never returned. When Palmer came second, first and first in his first three appearances (inevitably, it was downhill

from there), that was the inspiration for the likes of Nicklaus and
Trevino to take up the torch that had been carried so successfully
before the War by those such as Bobby Jones and Walter Hagen.

Even in 1969, however, Jack Nicklaus was able to write without
fear of contradiction that 'the most important golf tournament in the
world [is] the US Open simply because it is the national
championship of the world's leading golf nation'. While there isn't
unanimity on the subject, that is not so today. The USPGA
Championship would be fourth of the four in the minds of at least 95
per cent of pro golfers. When they are conducted, polls in golf
magazines tend to show that either the Open Championship or the
Masters are the two titles most golfers want to win – certainly for non-
American golfers, and for some Americans as well. The US Open is
no longer atop the pinnacle on which Nicklaus placed it.

When Seve followed his Open win of 1979 with the Masters in
1980, they were back-to-back major triumphs. He hadn't played in
the USPGA, though that was down to dumb thinking on the part of
he and Ed Barner rather than a highly individualistic, and futile,
effort to cause a redesignation of the majors.

Despite his intermittent attempts to redraw his personal history
and suggest that if he had his time again he would base himself in the
States, the fact is that Seve played more in Europe than in America
because he was not only at home, he felt at home. Several tournament
promoters had been great supporters from the beginning of his career,
and given the fact that he was making a lot of money in Europe, and
had proved that he could win majors in America without basing
himself over there, why would he want to leave?

There was a downside to being so popular in Europe, however.
I remember having lunch with him at the Italian Open in Milan in
1990. 'The pressure on me is huge, every single week,' he said. 'I have
to make the cut at least, because the sponsor is relying on me so much
– for the publicity before the tournament and to be on television at the
weekend.' That tournament was a case in point. He had opened up
with a three-over-par 75. He was four over for the tournament after
11 holes of his second round. 'Airport courtesy car for Snr

Ballesteros!' But no. He had three birdies and an eagle coming in, shot 66–69 on the weekend and finished in fifth.

Seve was by then approaching the beginning of his decline, but his point was wholly valid and generally he delivered, certainly in the 1980s. When he finished 50th in the Open in 1987, it was his worst position in a European Tour event since a missed cut in Barcelona in 1982. Furthermore, that aberration at Muirfield apart, he had been in the top-10 in his previous 36 starts in Europe, of which he had won 13. His golf was not only remarkable for its range of quality but for its utter consistency as well. There were a few tales along the way.

In 1981, Seve won the first of his five World Matchplay Championships at Wentworth, beating Ben Crenshaw with a birdie four to win on the last green. It was during that tournament that he began his 'formal' relationship with Carmen. On 31 December 1981, he was at Sun City, South Africa, for the first round of the first-ever Million Dollar Challenge. Only five players had been invited – Player, who was effectively the host, Nicklaus, Trevino, Miller and Seve. He lost the tournament after a playoff with Miller which went nine holes and into 1982. He would win at Sun City in both 1983 and 1984.

In 1983, he not only won the Masters in the States, he took the Westchester Classic as well. In the autumn, he beat Palmer in the first round of the World Matchplay, holing an 8-iron chip-and-run shot that he absolutely had to make in order to take the match into sudden-death. 'I can't complain,' said Palmer. 'For years I used to do the same to people.' And that was Seve's game, too. 'I am very unpredictable and people like to see that,' he told me in 1985. 'I can go double-bogey to eagle; make three birdies in a row and then three bogeys. People don't like to see somebody shoot par-par-par. It's very boring and that's why I think they like to watch me.' As Nick Faldo was to say a decade on, if he had hit it in the woods as often as Seve did, 'I'd have thought there goes my game. Gone. Finished.'

Other than total commitment, you never knew what sort of game you were going to get from Seve. That was fine while he still possessed the mental resilience, allied to that fabulous touch, to cope with the setbacks perpetrated by his errors, but the delicate technical edge on which he played the game – walking the tightrope between brilliance and catastrophe – had to tip one way at some point.

Even in his prime, Seve's game was a bit like love and hate. They are opposites in one sense and yet so close together in another. He could be great and he could be awful, both on the same hole, never mind during the same round. In many respects, the opposite of both love and hate is indifference. If Seve wasn't going to find salvation in reliability by the mid-1990s, then it would inevitably be incompetence that did for him.

Seve's swing problems are something we'll look at more fully later. In the mid-1980s, though, he was topping the Order of Merit for the fourth time. In the immediate aftermath of his failure to win the 1986 Masters, his initial form in Europe indicated how much his confidence had been damaged. When he had the third-round lead in those days, he would usually win. But that year, although he won six times on the European Tour, he should have won a lot more. 'I didn't feel so invincible,' he explained. 'I was pessimistic. I believed that if something could go wrong, it would go wrong. I thought there was the devil in me. I said, "Where has the confidence gone? Where has the optimism gone?" It hadn't left me. It was inside me, but I couldn't bring it out.'

His first win came at the Dunhill British Masters at Woburn in June. But between Augusta and Woburn, he had squandered a two-shot lead on the last day at the Cannes Open and lost by four to John Bland; lost a last-round shoot-out to Howard Clark at the Madrid Open; done the same thing with David Feherty at the Italian Open; and failed to take his chances at the Spanish Open, where Clark had again been the beneficiary. Around this time, his concentration was so fragile that he would have his caddie attend the flag on putts as short as five feet in an effort to blank out the image of all the photographers on the other side of the pin, waiting to take his picture for the zillionth time.

After winning at Woburn, he won four of the next five in Europe

– the Irish, Monte Carlo, French and Dutch Opens. The missing one was the Open at Turnberry, on the west coast of Scotland, where a last-round 64 enabled him to tie for sixth, eight shots behind Greg Norman. His win in the Dutch Open was the 10th anniversary of his first victory on the European Tour. Fittingly, he again won by eight shots. He also set a new mark. 'I think it's a great record,' he said, 'to be the first man in the history of the game to win £1 million in Europe and $1 million in America.' His season's stroke average of 68.95 made him the first man on either side of the Atlantic to break 69 since Byron Nelson in 1945.

There was only one win in 1987, in the Suze Open at Cannes, the week after his playoff loss at the Masters. The week also witnessed the sort of brush with authority that has marked his relationship with the European Tour. Seve's caddie was Vicente. Seve had overlooked the fact that the previous December the Tour had introduced a rule prohibiting the use of professional golfers as caddies. Seve refused to hire anyone else but his brother and so paid a paltry £50 fine for continuing to employ Vicente, which he did all the way up to collecting a £25,000 cheque for this time winning a sudden-death playoff, against Ian Woosnam. 'It is a stupid rule,' he declared of the regulation. It was changed within a week.

In 1988, Seve headed the Order of Merit for the fifth time, taking seven wins in as many different countries – the Majorca Open de Baleares (Spain), the Westchester Classic (USA), the Open Championship (Britain), the Scandinavian Enterprise Open (Sweden), the German Open, the Trophée Lancôme (France) and the Taiheiyo Masters (Japan). At year's end, he was officially the No. 1 golfer in the world.

The show rolled on. There were three more wins in 1989, but only one in 1990, in Majorca in March. In July, he had his first-ever tournament hole-in-one, at the Monte Carlo Open. A month later, there was a more substantial reason to celebrate. Some 12 hours after he had blown a clear opportunity to win the English Open at The Belfry (that wasn't the reason), his first son was born. He was given the name Baldomero, in memory of Seve's father.

That joyous occasion was in contrast to how he felt about his golf. In 1990, he had missed six cuts and only been in the top 10 on 10 occasions. In 1988, in contrast, he had won seven times in 24 starts and had eight other top-10 finishes. People were wondering if the question was 'Whither Seve?' or 'Has Seve Withered?' His compatriot, Manuel Pinero, put it like this. 'He may be mentally tired. It's hard to stay at the top for more than 10 years and Seve has already been there for 15. And it's normal to become more interested in your family and other activities than playing in another golf tournament.'

Seve himself conceded 'I don't have the fire I used to [but] it happens to everyone. Maybe it's a bit surprising that it didn't happen to me sooner, with all the years of travelling, expectation and pressure. The problem is that I don't have the same degree of concentration that I used to have on the course. I have trouble keeping it up for 18 holes. I get distracted very quickly and very easily; my mind wanders off on to other things – like a movie I've seen or what we're doing for dinner – and that never used to happen before. So my concentration goes, so I make some bogeys, and then I lose my confidence. Then I start to hit more bad shots, and then I can never get my confidence or concentration back. The longer the round goes on, the worse things seem to get.' For example, at the USPGA Championship that year, he was an OK one over par until he took three putts from 10 feet at the 13th. 'Then I was gone.' He dropped three more strokes on the way in and shot 83 the next day. But there was some defiance when he said: 'I am only 33, I will keep working hard and I am very positive that I will have seven or maybe 10 years ahead as good as those in the past. I am very much aware that the golf I am playing on the course is not that of Seve Ballesteros.' The old 'self-as-third-person' ploy.

A renaissance of sorts didn't seem a preposterous idea in 1991, when Seve headed the Order of Merit for the sixth and final time, although he only won two official tournaments in Europe, the Volvo PGA Championship and the Dunhill British Masters. He did, though, win the World Matchplay Championship, now sponsored by

Toyota cars rather than Suntory whisky, for the fifth time. That was also a finale. In early May, he had won the Chunichi Crowns in Japan, his first title for 14 months, helped – although Seve was never keen to admit it – by some advice from David Leadbetter. 'His swing had got too loose,' said Leadbetter. 'He needed to make less of a hip-turn in order to create more resistance in his swing.'

From Japan, he returned home and lost a three-shot lead to Eduardo Romero on the last day of the Spanish Open, eventually losing the tournament at the seventh extra hole of a playoff. In the PGA at Wentworth at the end of the month, he was 17 under par with five holes to play and had a two-shot lead. He birdied the 15th but bogeyed the 16th. Up ahead, Colin Montgomerie had birdied the last two holes (both par-fives, so not an especially great achievement) and they were now tied.

Seve went with an iron off the 17th tee, to play safe. He hit it behind a tree. The spectators poured down the fairway with him. Monty may be British but everyone bar his relatives in this part of England was rooting for the Spaniard. There was a delay before Seve could hit his third shot, after chipping out, the crowds pressing so close in to him. The stewards seemed to have gone home. He backed off his shot. 'I know you are nervous,' he told his fans. 'I am nervous, too.' He played like he was nervous, making six. Now he wanted, badly wanted, a birdie four at the last to get into a playoff. Ultimately, he had to sink a seven-foot putt to do it or else suffer further speculative stories about how he was getting past it.

'When you are trying to read a putt, you have no room in your mind to think about what people will say if you miss,' he said. 'But afterwards, I thought about it. I know the sky would have fallen in on me. That was an extremely brave putt to make. People would have said it was terrible, that I am not like I was. But I have heard all that before.'

The ball went in. On the first playoff hole, the long par-four first on Wentworth's West Course, his 5-iron second shot finished less than a yard from the flag. The tap-in birdie three was a winner.

It is an interesting footnote that Montgomerie would later go on to win the Order of Merit for seven consecutive seasons between 1993–99, his total breaking Seve's record by one. When Seve shakily got the better of him in that playoff, the then 27-year-old Scot was looking for his second tournament victory. Monty headed the Order of Merit for an eighth time in 2005, but he still awaits, with diminishing hope, his first major championship at the time of writing. (He has lost the US Open and the USPGA in playoffs and in 2006 blew a great chance to win the US Open.) And Monty has never been the best golfer in the world. Having Tiger Woods around latterly hasn't helped that ambition, but when Seve won the Order of Merit in 1986 he was the best golfer in the world, as he was at times in 1988.

After a rise, the fall is inevitable. The Roman Empire discovered that. Seve's powers were on the wane, and it was not easy for him – nor would it be for anybody – to cope with the recognition of his own inexorable decline. In his autobiography, *Serious*, John McEnroe wrote: 'Arthur Ashe once said that there was as much difference between number 10 in the world and number five as there is between number 100 and number 10. Going from number five to number four, he said, is like going from 10 to five. And from three on up is inconceivable. I agree with him. The very top, like the summit of Everest, is weird territory, impossible to comprehend unless you've actually been there.' This was about tennis, of course, but it's equally applicable to golf.

Not that Seve was quite in the shade just yet. When he won the Dubai Desert Classic in February 1992, it was his 50th victory on the European Tour and it made him, temporarily, the leading money-winner in the history of the game. Money-winning records do not mean much in the great scheme of things – they completely fail to represent the achievements of the likes of Ben Hogan and Sam Snead, let alone Jack Nicklaus – but Seve's had mostly been earned in Europe, where the purses are much smaller than in the United States. It was yet another remarkable milestone.

A month later, he won the Turespana Open de Baleares in Majorca after a six-hole playoff against Jesper Parnevik. Two wins from four starts for the season. How good was that? In Dubai, he had said: 'I've won every year on tour since 1976 and maybe I can go on doing that until the year 2000. I'll be only 42 then, so why not?' Oops. After Majorca, he had only one other top-10 finish in 20 tournaments. The rest of the carnage included seven missed cuts, a closing 81 at the Masters and an 82 at the season-ending Johnnie Walker World Championship in Jamaica, which meant he finished dead last, 32 shots behind the winner.

In 1993, he failed to win on the European Tour for the first time in 17 years, slipping down to 42nd place on the Order of Merit, his worst position since 1974. But one bit of Seve magic deserves to be recorded here.

Standing on the final tee of the European Masters at Crans-sur-Sierre in Switzerland, he was 16 under par. After appearing to be out of contention for most of the afternoon, an eagle at the 14th and consecutive birdies at the 16th and 17th had emphatically brought him back into it, but a birdie three here was essential if he was to stand any chance of winning. His drive seemed to have put paid to that. Not only was it so far off line to the right that he almost needed a compass to track it down, when he did get there he found it lying under such thick trees and bushes that there seemed no way out. Indeed, he had hit a provisional ball off the tee because it had seemed likely that he'd never find his ball, or if he did it might be out-of-bounds in an adjoining swimming pool. Once he had found it, a chip back to the fairway looked like the only option. His ball lay about five feet away from a 10-foot high wall and there was no gap between the trees through which he could hope to thread a shot while keeping it below branch level.

But Seve is nothing if not resourceful. In 1995, I worked on a golf instruction book with him, one that dealt with the aspect of the game of which Seve was the unquestioned master. It was called *Trouble-Shooting*. In it, Seve talked of the 'window of opportunity'. He explained: 'When I am in the trees, as long as I can swing the club, I always find a way somehow. Most players look for the fairway. I always look for the target. That's where I want to go.' This was such a case.

'I would not have risked that shot if the situation had arisen earlier in the round,' he said. 'It would have been too much of a gamble to risk the shot while there were still several holes to play in which to make up lost ground. But on the last hole, it was the only hope I had of winning.'

Looking up, he figured out there was a gap he could get the ball through. It was a hugely risky shot, since hitting the wall was a possibility and the shot would have to be perfect if it was to complete its journey through the foliage. He took out his wedge, got the blade wide open, and smashed the shot towards the green. It ended up about 20 yards short of the pin. With a finale that a work of fiction would hardly dare describe, he then holed the chip shot. After that, fiction would probably not dare deny him victory, but that's what happened. Barry Lane came in at 18 under par to beat him by one.

By May 1994, it had been nearly two years since Seve had won a tournament. The Benson & Hedges International that year was at St Mellion in Cornwall. At the beginning of the week, one of the Bond brothers, who owned the course, went up to him and said: 'Good to see you here again, Seve. I hope you make the cut.' Clearly they didn't have much hope that he would rediscover any form. They were wrong. Seve led through the first two rounds but trailed Gary Orr by a stroke going into Sunday. A measure of his popularity could be gleaned from the remarks of two other players in contention. Orr said: 'If I wasn't playing, I'd be wanting Seve to win.' Sam Torrance added: 'If I can't win, I'd love Seve to win. He's done so much for the game. He's a marvellous man.'

Seve did win. He parred the first 15 holes on Sunday and then birdied the 16th and 17th to move clear. A par four at the last brought him home three shots ahead of the runner-up, Nick Faldo – 26 months to the day since his victory in Majorca, a sequence of 50 tournaments in which he had missed 17 cuts and only had four top-10 finishes. The victory lifted him from 164th to the top of the Order of Merit. At the end of the month, he finished sixth at the Volvo PGA Championship, a birdie four on the final hole meaning he had

During the 1976 Open at Birkdale, the championship at which the wider world became aware of Seve, the 19-year-old farmer's son spent a great deal of time in the hay but still managed to finish second.

Hail the champion. Seve salutes the crowd and they salute him as he strides the final few yards of the 1979 Open at Lytham, his first major championship safely in his hands.

The Master. His triumph at Augusta in 1983 was the second time Seve had won the Masters Tournament. Somehow, despite regularly threatening to, he contrived never to win it again.

Before the fall...Seve drives in the final round of the 1986 Masters, a tournament he would spectacularly lose to Jack Nicklaus in one of the most dramatic major championships ever played.

Heartbreak again. As this three-foot putt goes past the hole in the Masters playoff of 1987, Seve's hopes of the title go with it.

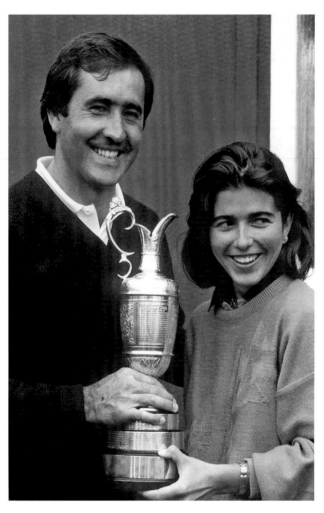

Sweet redemption. Seve with the Open trophy after his third victory in the championship, his fifth and final major, in 1988. With him is Carmen, then his fiancée, later his wife, now his ex-wife.

Stroke of genius. A miraculous recovery shot on the final hole of the 1993 European Masters, which led to a birdie when anybody else would have been happy with a bogey, was emblematic of the extraordinary talent Seve brought to the game.

Decline and fall. In his first tournament for two years, at the 2005 Madrid Open, Seve's golf was in such disarray that rounds of 77-73, to miss the cut, were widely regarded as being a decent effort.

reached a cumulative 1,000 under par for his 261 tournaments on European Tour.

At the beginning of October, he notched up a dramatic playoff victory at the German Masters in Berlin, beating two distinguished opponents: José Maria Olazábal and Ernie Els, respectively the reigning Masters and US Open champions. On the first extra hole, he hit a 3-wood off the tee and followed that with a 6-iron to within two feet of the stick. That was that. He had played the last 36 holes with only one bogey.

At the World Matchplay Championship a fortnight later, up against David Frost in the first round, he was round in 63 in the morning and four up. He won by 8&7, finishing with three birdies, making it 13 in the day. The next day, he again came face-to-face with Els, but this time he came off worse, losing by 2&1. Again he had 13 birdies, including twos at seven of the eight par-threes. He could hardly complain. He had only got into the field because IMG had felt compelled to invite him when John Daly withdrew and the press caused such a fuss about him being omitted in the first place. Admittedly, he had played like a drain for most of the past two seasons, but then he was Seve, he was in form, and he'd won the tournament five times.

The month, and the season, ended with the Volvo Masters at Valderrama. After rounds of 69-67–68, Seve had a two-shot lead over Montgomerie and Langer, who had fired a nine-under-par 62 on Friday, a new course record. Langer caught Seve with a birdie four at the 17th on Sunday and then hit a good drive down the last. Seve didn't. His ball finished at the base of a cork tree. He felt he should have been able to obtain relief because it had come to rest in a hole left by a burrowing animal. The referee, John Paramor, disagreed. Seve bogeyed the hole and Langer won by a stroke.

In 1995, Seve won for the last time – three times in all, as he likes to kid: the Tournoi Perrier de Paris at St Cloud in Paris in April, a team event in which he had Olazábal as his partner; the Peugeot Spanish Open at Club de Campo in Madrid in May (his last individual title); and the Ryder Cup at Oak Hill in September, where he was a member of the victorious European team.

At the Spanish Open, he began the last round a shot off the pace and opened up with three bogeys. But he birdied the 4th, no one else was doing anything good, and with four holes to play he was tied for the lead. At the 15th, he hit his approach to five feet and made that for a birdie. At the last, he pitched to four feet for another. It was his first win in his national Open for 10 years, his third in all. His last.

That season he finished 33rd on the Order of Merit. From then on, it was downhill – 69th, 136th, 108th, 143rd, 190th, 204th, 247th, 279th. His last top-10 finish was in Dubai in 1998. In 2004, he didn't play at all. The previous numerical regression hides such tales as the time he withdrew from the Moroccan Open after he was 13 over par for 12 holes, and the time he disqualified himself at the Irish Open after he lost count, signing for a 10 on a hole where he had taken 12.

In October 2005, 10 years on from that last win, he was back in the capital, this time for the 2005 Madrid Open at the same venue, his first tournament since the Madrid Open in 2003. He assured everyone that his back was strong enough to compete and he seemed convinced that he could at least make the cut. No one else was, though there were plenty of people in attendance. There had been 120 applications for media credentials, compared to the usual 50, and those expecting a car-crash kind of story looked likely to get their way when Seve's wild golf saw him begin bogey, double-bogey.

Back in Britain, on Radio 5 Live, the 10 a.m. sports bulletin carried the news. 'Seve Ballesteros was three over par after four holes, having been in trees twice on the 2nd for a double-bogey after a bogey at the first.' Such detail about such a failure speaks volumes for the attention Seve attracted, even then.

He reached the turn in 41, six over par, including a birdie at his eighth hole (the 17th, since he had started at the 10th) but he played the back nine in level par, with two birdies and two bogeys and a patented Seve-style par when he had to play one 5-wood from off his knees from beneath the trees. The six-over 77 was better than had seemed likely, if hardly in line with his pre-tournament boast of 'I'm looking at a top-10 finish, but why not a win?', a sentence that se

stupidly arrogant and presumptuous to many people. But that 77, in which he hit six fairways and six greens in regulation, was also eight shots worse than his nephew, Raul.

'Everything was fine until I walked on to the first tee,' he said, which is always a bad place for things to go wrong; it leaves so much scope for more problems. 'I started to feel a bit tight. I was a bit tense at three over par after two holes, which made it difficult for the rest of the day.' The next day he shot a respectable 73 but, obviously, he missed the cut.

In April 2006, Seve played in the pro-am that preceded the Spanish Open, a tournament his company promoted, but not in the main event itself. In June, he horribly missed the cut at the French Open, before – as we have seen – also having the weekend off at the Open. His days of tournament golf were almost over.

Having looked at Seve in the context of the game's greatest players in the last chapter, how has he fared over time compared to the other members of the Famous 5 that he so gloriously led and inspired?

* Sandy Lyle was the Masters champion in 1988, also the year of Seve's last major championship. His collapse has been more of a soggy soufflé than Seve's. He won only three tournaments after that season, one in 1991 and two in 1992.

* Bernhard Langer's last win in a major was the 1993 Masters. Since 1995, the year's of Seve's last victory, Langer has won nine tournaments, the last of them being a tie with Colin Montgomerie at the 2002 Volvo Masters (darkness meant their playoff could not be concluded) and was playing strongly on the PGA Tour in 2007. He was the 2004 Ryder Cup captain.

* Ian Woosnam won the Masters in 1991. Since 1995, he has won seven tournaments, the last of them being the (now Cisco) World Matchplay Championship in 2001. He was the 2006 Ryder Cup captain.

* Nick Faldo won the last of his six majors by unforgettably overhauling Greg Norman at the 1996 Masters. Since then, he has

won one tournament, the Nissan Open in Los Angeles in March 1997. He will be the 2008 Ryder Cup captain.

Throughout his career, Seve preferred to play in Europe even though he is adamant that he would have earned more money had he been based in the States, both from having a greater endorsement value and by regularly playing for higher prize-money, this even though he was paid huge appearance fees for playing in Europe (a contentious issue, discussed later). But whatever his motives, Seve's contribution to the development of the European Tour has been truly colossal, more than that of any other individual.

In 2003, Lee Westwood, winner of over 25 tournaments worldwide, said of Seve: 'He made European golf more exciting. He was the man the crowds came to see. He hit it all over the shop but the excitement was in watching how he got it up and down. The money we're playing for nowadays can be put down to the interest Seve attracted.' Not all contemporary tour players are as prepared to acknowledge that, and given some of his run-ins with the Tour, that's perhaps no wonder, but Thomas Bjorn, the Danish golfer who probably should have won the Open in 2003 and who came tantalisingly close to winning the 2005 USPGA Championship, put it well. 'The European Tour is what it is because of one man, and that's Seve. There are a lot of young players out there with no understanding of that, and they lack a lot of respect.' Seve thinks the same, and probably feels he couldn't have put it any better himself.

As for those successive Ryder Cup captaincies for Langer, Woosnam and Faldo (alas, poor Lyle), as with all aspects of their respective careers, Seve was ahead of the game when it came to that job. He led the European team in 1997, when the match was held in Spain, the first time it had been held outside Britain when contested on the European side of the Atlantic. But then when it comes to the Ryder Cup, Seve has been there, done that, got the polo shirts to prove it. Without him, who knows where it would be.

5. KING OF THE RYDER CUP

The Ryder Cup today is perhaps the most eagerly awaited competition in world golf. In the late 1970s, until Seve emerged as a force in the game, it was an occasion in need of an event. Simply, without him, it would not be what it is today. It was Seve who proved to other European golfers that the Americans were not invincible, even on their own soil and in their most cherished championships, and he was also the spark that ignited the Ryder Cup.

The Ryder Cup began in 1927, the first match being held at Worcester Country Club in Massachusetts. The United States won by 9½ points to 2½. (These days, there are 28 points at stake.) Great Britain & Ireland won the next match, at Moortown, Leeds in 1929. So it went. The US won at home in 1931 and 1935, GB&I won at Southport in 1933. But the Americans won at Southport in 1937, the last match before the war, and as indicators go, it was pretty accurate. The United States was in the ascendancy. Post-war, with Britain struggling with matters such as rationing, the plucky Brits were even more serious underdogs. The US won at Portland, Oregon, in 1947, by 11–1, and they kept on winning.

GB&I *nearly* won at Wentworth in 1953, did so at Lindrick in 1957, and they got a tie at Royal Birkdale in 1969, the ending of that match immortalised by Jack Nicklaus conceding Tony Jacklin, the reigning Open champion, a three-foot putt for a half on the last. Had Jacklin failed to hole out, the hosts would have lost again. 'I don't think you'd have missed that putt,' Nicklaus told him, 'but under these circumstances I would never give you the opportunity.'

A good example of how relaxed the Americans were about the fact that they would routinely win in those days was that not only did they not bother with wild-card picks – they only followed their opponents in that respect once they started losing – but that due to the arcane eligibility regulations laid down by the PGA of America, Nicklaus had not qualified for the match before 1969, even though by the time of the 1967 match he'd won three Masters, two US Opens, an Open and a USPGA.

That outstanding gesture of sportsmanship at Birkdale elevated Nicklaus to a special level in the game (yet another one), particularly in respect of the Ryder Cup. After the Americans had won again in 1971, 1973, 1975 and 1977, the latter at Royal Lytham, Nicklaus spoke to Lord Derby, president of the British PGA. He told him: 'The American players love to get on the Ryder Cup team because there is no greater honour in sport than representing one's country. But the matches just aren't competitive enough.' Had steps to reinforce the hapless losers been taken, say, a decade previously, as had been mooted, then it's likely that players from the old Commonwealth – Australia, New Zealand, South Africa, Canada – would have been invited as reinforcements. As it was, with the British and Continental tours having formally consolidated to form what by 1979 would be called the PGA European Golf Tour, it was to mainland Europe that Britain would look to revive a contest that was in danger of dying due to lack of interest. Oh, and it had been noticed there was a dashing young Spaniard with a nifty golf game who would be an ideal recruit.

Before the continental players were introduced in 1979, the overall victory record read United States 18, Great Britain 3, one tied. The Americans won the next three after 1977, but beginning with Europe's first win, in 1985, and excluding the 2008 match, the score reads Europe 7, United States 3, one tied. Seve played in three of those victories (and the tie) and captained one of the others. Things didn't begin too well, though.

*

For the 1979 match at The Greenbrier, West Virginia, two continental players made the team, two Spaniards: Antonio Garrido and Seve. As far as the latter was concerned, one thing was for sure – the Europeans were going to get beaten. 'The situation and atmosphere were very clear before we played. We were going to be second.' This was not the mindset the new Open champion liked to take into a tournament.

At one of the interminable functions that preceded the match, one of the visitors' official party referred in a speech to being proud of the Great Britain & Ireland team. Seve turned to Garrido and said: 'What the hell are we doing here?' Two British members of the team, Mark James and Ken Brown, seemed to hold a similar view, displaying scant respect for the captain, John Jacobs – one of the gentlemen of British golf, the first head (in 1971) of what would become the European Tour, and one of the most respected golf teachers ever – by being late to arrive at the airport before the team left and late for meetings once they got there.

Seve was used to being a winner. But not this week. Larry Nelson beat him four times. The one match Seve won was in partnership with Garrido, against Hubert Green and Fuzzy Zoeller, at foursomes. 'There was a bit of an incident on the 16th green, where we won the match,' he recalled. 'Antonio conceded a putt to Hubert and he threw the ball back to him with his putter. I guess Hubert was upset because he was losing. Whatever, he started to say something and Antonio got upset and it was a very difficult situation. I had to stand in between them. They both got very cross and I nearly had to act as a referee. At that moment, I could see that the Ryder Cup was important, even though we didn't play for money. We played for pride. That's when I started finding out how tough it was.'

One of the aspects of matchplay golf that Seve loves is that it's *mano e mano*: head-to-head competition. In the latter part of his career, such as in the Seve Trophy, as we shall see, he revelled in the fact that he didn't have to keep score on a card. Make a triple-bogey and it wasn't three dropped shots, it was just one lost hole. In matchplay, you only have to beat the man in front of you. At The

Greenbrier, however, not only did Seve not manage to do this very
well, the two teams were playing in front of almost no one. The sell-
out days had yet to arrive. What a contrast to what the Ryder Cup
would become.

There have been several epic Ryder Cup matches since the
continental Europeans joined the party. The 1981 renewal was not
one of them, especially for Seve. Other than the fact that the
Americans won by 18½ points to 9½ at Walton Heath (the match had
been scheduled for The Belfry, just outside Birmingham, until it was
clear the new course would not be ready in time), this was a Ryder
Cup indelibly associated with Seve. And he wasn't even there.

Due to his increasingly rancorous row with the European Tour
over the thorny and lucrative matter of appearance money, an issue
described in detail later, Seve had only played in Europe three times
before the team was going to be announced. But he wasn't worried
about retaining his place on it. As far as he was concerned, he would
get one of the two wild-card invitations available that would complete
the 12-man team. He had already received a call from the captain,
who remained Jacobs. 'John Jacobs called me in America and said,
"Seve, you join the European Tour and we will pick you for the
Ryder Cup", so I joined the Tour and he didn't select me. I will never
understand that.' Seve also recalled Jacobs saying: 'If you don't
qualify automatically, I cannot promise you 100 per cent you will be
in but I promise you will have my vote.'

As far as Seve was concerned, Jacobs' rider about his Ryder Cup
spot was inconsequential. Jacobs was the captain. The other two
members of the selection panel – Bernhard Langer and Neil Coles –
would not defy him. After all, Seve knew how things worked. As the
past winner of the Order of Merit, he had been on the panel with
Jacobs and Coles in 1979.

When I wrote a feature about Seve, published in *Golf World* in
May 1985, which outlined the first of the above exchanges, Jacobs –
a gentle man as well as a gentleman – was angry enough to ring to
dispute what I had written. I told him I was only quoting what Seve

had said. I even had the tapes to prove it. Subsequently, Jacobs arranged a meeting with Seve and Ken Schofield, his successor as head of the European Tour, to talk the subject over. Jacobs told Seve the discussion about whether he should get one of the wild cards had gone along the following lines. 'I asked Neil and Neil said "No" and I asked Bernhard and Bernhard said "No". So I was in the position that I didn't have any other way to go. So we all went for "No."' However, muddying the waters, Langer had told Seve at the 1983 Ryder Cup: 'I want to make sure that you understand I wasn't the one who voted against you.'

What really happened? Seve had assumed all along that Coles, the Tour chairman and a strong ally of Schofield, would be against him because of the appearance-money dispute. As for the apparently conflicting accounts of Jacobs and Langer, the likelihood is indeed that Jacobs, understanding that the majority of the players were not for Seve, decided not to push it. There was no formal vote. Jacobs was telling the truth, and so was Langer – he'd not had to vote against Seve.

Whatever, before this had the chance to happen, Seve rejoined the European Tour on 11 August, 12 days before the announcement of the European team for the match at Walton Heath, although he would not be playing any tournaments in Europe until the following month. Politically, his non-appearance in the last counting tournament, the Benson & Hedges International at Fulford, may not have been a smart move, although he refused to see it like that, not least because even if he had won he could not have qualified for the side automatically. 'We are talking about revenge here, against the team and against European golf,' he protested. 'That's not the way to do it. If I were the captain, I would pick the best players as wild cards even if I didn't like them personally, because that is the best way for the team and for European golf.'

But it wasn't only Schofield and the suits who didn't want him on the team. Langer's antipathy reflected a widespread sentiment among the players that Seve should have done more to support the Tour. Two prominent Spanish players, Manuel Pinero and José

Maria Canizares, felt that way, too. When he found out that they had been against his inclusion, he was sad rather than angry. 'That was a pity. I was very disappointed at that because I always felt that I helped them and they were good friends. I don't know if it was jealousy or whatever, but that was the one time they could help me and the one time they could hurt me, and they chose the second option.' It is likely that Pinero's opinion had been formed by his immense disapproval of Seve's decision not to represent Spain in the 1978 World Cup, an event he had played in the two previous years, because he would only get £1,000 for playing. 'If you refuse to play for your country,' Pinero had said, 'I'm not happy with you.'

Amid all this, it is often overlooked that Seve wasn't the only big-name player in need of one of the two wild cards. There was also Tony Jacklin, twice a major champion, and Peter Oosterhuis, four times a winner of the Order of Merit, who had just won his first tournament on the PGA Tour. Indeed, Oosterhuis was playing the PGA Tour full-time. The essential difference between him and Seve was that he hadn't resigned from the European Tour and he wasn't seeking full-on confrontation over appearance money. In the event, Oosterhuis got picked. Jacklin didn't. Despite whatever had gone on at The Greenbrier, Mark James got the other invitation. 'In 1979, Mark James was fined for bad behaviour during the Ryder Cup,' said Seve. 'It was a joke that they went for Mark James instead of me in 1981. It was a shock.'

Shorn of their best player, the Europeans went into the match against the best-ever American team. Jack Nicklaus, Tom Watson and Lee Trevino are three of the greatest golfers ever. Raymond Floyd, Hale Irwin and Johnny Miller were multiple major champions. Larry Nelson and Ben Crenshaw would go on to be. In all, 11 of the 12 had or would win majors, the exception being Bruce Lietzke. There was a touch of almost sardonic humour in the fact that the winner at Fulford had been Tom Weiskopf, the American who won the 1973 Open Championship but who wasn't among the American dozen bound for Walton Heath. The United States could afford to omit its major champions. Europe could not. Europe would surely have lost with Seve, albeit perhaps less decisively. But so far as he was concerned, after one poor match and one match of being treated poorly, the Ryder Cup could get lost, too.

For the 1983 match at the PGA National Golf Club in Palm Beach Gardens in 1983, Tony Jacklin took over from Jacobs. It would be the first of four successive captaincies for him. Indeed, he was so good at the job that he turned it into a second career. Much has been made of how Jacklin turned things around by insisting on first-class treatment for his players, such as flying there on Concorde and them being provided with the best cashmeres (for Florida!), but at least as important was that he had the total respect of his players because he'd been there and done it. He'd won two majors. Seve apart, he was whom the members of his team aspired to be like. But first Jacklin had to get Seve back onside, and back on the side.

He approached him over breakfast at a tournament one morning, and urged Seve to review his new-found but deep-held dislike of the Ryder Cup. After all, Jacklin pointed out, he felt he'd been shafted by being overlooked in 1981 as well. Jacklin had a job on his hands. Seve was reluctant to change his mind – when is he not? He went home to talk things over with his brothers. 'Baldomero said, "You have no choice. The British people love you. The team needs you".' So I agreed.' Over a decade later, Baldomero would be influential in convincing Seve to take the captaincy for himself.

Once he had agreed to play, no one could accuse Seve of not being fired up. 'The American players thought we were like the third world in golf. We were always on the losing side before we started. And that was the beginning of where that challenge and motivation came from.'

Jacklin paired Seve with Paul Way, a rookie, in all four non-singles matches. Seve had thought he'd be playing with Canizares, the other Spaniard in the squad, but he was happy to be nursemaid to Way. That kind of role for Seve, with so much expectation on him and him being the undisputed leader on the course, probably explains why his singles record is comparatively ropey – overall, it's two wins, two halves, four losses. 'One of the reasons I haven't really been very successful in the singles is because usually I have already played every match,' he said. 'I am under a lot of pressure and a lot of responsibility, and most of the time I reach Sunday very tired.'

In this match, he and Way delivered the goods. After losing their opening foursomes, they won 2½ points from their next three matches. At 8–8 on Saturday night, Europe would go into the singles level rather than the customary behind.

Seve was out in the top singles, against Fuzzy Zoeller. He won the first three holes, later went 4 up, and he was 3 up with seven to play. Point in the bag. Then he lost four holes in a row. He had to win the 16th to draw level and it was still that way as they reached the par-five 18th. Seve hit a poor drive into rough and with his next could only manage to hack his ball into a bunker, 245 yards from the green. He had an uphill lie and the wind was blowing left-to-right. In normal circumstances, he would have pitched out, gone for the green in four and hoped to hole a putt for his par. In these circumstances, matchplay, and given the state of the match, he went for the green. Hitting a colossal 3-wood cut shot, with enough height to clear the bunker and enough strength to carry the extra distance that fading the ball put on his shot – it probably carried 260 yards – he made the front edge of the green. 'It was one of the best shots of my life,' he said. Jack Nicklaus, the American captain, called it 'the best shot I ever saw'. (For Jack, mind you, from a selfish perspective, Seve's 4-iron into the pond at Augusta three years later may have trumped it.)

Seve got his half with Zoeller but when it came to the crunch in the bottom of the draw, Lanny Wadkins beat Canizares at the last and Tom Watson beat Bernard Gallacher at the 17th. Europe lost 14½–13½. Seve refused to be despondent. 'This is like a victory for us,' he told his colleagues. 'Put your heads up. Next time, we win.'

Two years on at The Belfry, which was by now ready for the first of the four Ryder Cups it would host, sometimes controversially, the omens looked propitious. Bernhard Langer was the Masters champion, Sandy Lyle the Open champion. Plus there was Seve.

Everyone knew that *this* could be the year that the United States might lose for the first time in 28 years. The consequence was that The Belfry was as crammed with people as it was with expectation. At the opening ceremony, Jacklin introduced Seve as 'the greatest golfer in the world'. Few could demur. After the furore surrounding the issuing of wild cards in 1981 – or, to be more accurate, the non-issuing of one in particular – there had been no arguments in 1983. Jacklin had insisted that he alone would make the selections. What's more, he got three of them in 1985 – Nick Faldo, Ken Brown and José Rivero.

The first series of foursomes on a brisk September Friday morning did not go well for Europe. Seve and Pinero won their match but the other three were lost. In the afternoon, Seve drove the par-four 10th green for the second time in the day and earned another winning birdie three. He and Pinero won again and overnight the deficit was down to one point.

The next morning, two matches dramatically turned Europe's way. First, Howard Clark holed a 60-foot putt at the 15th and then chipped in at the 16th to win one fourball. Then, in the last match out, Lyle eagled the 17th from 45 feet to take that match down the 18th. On the last green, Craig Stadler gagged a two-footer to hand Europe a half-point that had seemed lost. Seve and Pinero were the only losers, but Europe were back on level terms. That 6–6 scoreline had become 9–7 by the end of the day, with Canizares and Rivero leading the way with a 7&5 trouncing of Tom Kite and Calvin Peete. European joy was enriched by the knowledge that the Americans were bound to feel so down.

In the singles Europe retained the upper hand, against all precedent. Seve was 3 down with five to play against Tom Kite but when he curled in a 40-footer for a two at the 14th, you just knew he wasn't going to lose. Birdies at the 15th and 17th got him the half that was his minimum due. Seven of his teammates had won or were on their way to winning.

The man of the hour, of course, was Sam Torrance. Two down after 14 holes against Andy North, he was level by the time they reached the last tee. The golf had been pretty awful – Torrance was about six over par at this point (since every putt need not be holed, Ryder Cup scoring can never be other than approximate) – but who was counting? No one. That's the point of matchplay. After Torrance had hit a great drive down the last fairway, North hit a dreadful one into the lake. Torrance knew he had the match won well before he stood over his 18-footer for a three, but since he had three putts for it, he was just desperate that North didn't concede him the putt, ordinarily the 'proper' thing to do, and deny him his moment in the late-autumn sun. Playing his best shot of the day, North courteously let him get on with it. Famously, in it went.

The United States lost by 16½–11½, their record defeat. The exultation of the crowd rammed home to Seve exactly what the Ryder Cup was all about. 'It is hard to explain,' he said, 'but I feel as thrilled with this as I did about winning the Open at St Andrews. We made so many people happy today.'

In *Sports Illustrated*, Jaime Diaz opened his report of the 1987 match with 'Seve Ballesteros had just led Europe to its second straight Ryder Cup victory . . .' Not Tony Jacklin had led, you'll note. There was no doubting the identity of the main man in most people's eyes. Nor in Jacklin's. On the Friday night, he had said: 'I think that Seve Ballesteros is the most incredible being I have ever met. In situations like this, he is almost superhuman. He is really something special, a tremendous inspiration to the whole team.'

This match was played at Muirfield Village in Dublin, Ohio, a course built in his hometown by Jack Nicklaus in order to host his own event, the Memorial Tournament. For the second successive match on home territory, he was the American captain. Against that backdrop, who else could have been? It was in these circumstances that the European side was attempting to become the first visiting team to win in the United States. Most Americans thought their chances of doing so were slimmer than Victoria Beckham. Specifically, it was felt that not only did the American players have local knowledge of the course, as the Europeans had at The Belfry, since they played it on tour every year, but its superior conditioning in contrast to what the European players encountered at home meant the guests would not feel comfortable on the course. Nicklaus himself said after the second day: 'I expected to see the Europeans wear down more on this course. But they've worn down our players.'

As it turned out, the Europeans relished a layout where the fairways were like tees, the tees like greens and the greens like snooker tables. They felt like they couldn't miss a shot or a putt. They also won because they had (notwithstanding the last two 18½–9½ wins for Europe) probably the best team Europe has ever had – major champions in Seve, Langer, Lyle and Faldo and two who would become such in Woosnam and Olazábal, plus consistently under-rated solid players like Howard Clark. (When he played – 1985, 1987 and 1995 – Europe won.)

It was a confident bunch who crossed the Atlantic aboard Concorde – even Seve. This was a guy, remember, who had blown the two previous Masters, the first of them to the man who was their host and opposing captain, the second after dogging a short putt in a playoff. This was a week in which he would go some way – whether long or short is hard to say – towards ridding himself of some of the mental baggage from those two scars and create the peace of mind for him to be strong enough to win a third Open Championship the following summer. And he was on the verge of beginning the most successful partnership in Ryder Cup history, in collaboration with the 21-year-old Olazábal, another product of a North Spanish upbringing who was also blessed with a magical touch. In particular, they were the perfect foursomes partners. They thought about the game in a similar manner and their short games were such that they could never put each other in such trouble that they couldn't escape it. In eight matches together in that format, they would win six and halve one.

On the opening morning at Muirfield Village, it looked for a while that Europe could get whitewashed. But the prospect of 4–0 became the reality of 2–2, not least because the two Spaniards beat Larry Nelson (Seve's tormentor at The Greenbrier) and Payne Stewart at the last. On the 17th, the Americans had three-putted from

25 feet and Seve had preserved the European lead by canning a 12-footer.

The beginning of their afternoon match against Tom Kite and Curtis Strange has been dealt with at some length earlier, to which should be added that Seve later holed another chip and also a bunker shot. There was another incident as well, on the 5th hole. 'I overheard Curtis Strange say to Tom Kite that José Maria was about to play out of turn,' recalled Seve, 'but they didn't try to stop him. So I told him not to play.'

This time there was a whitewash. Europe swept the fourballs 4–0. 'Our guys weren't as tough as the Europeans,' lamented Nicklaus. 'The problem is really with the American system. Because it's so difficult to win, our guys rarely get in position to contend down the stretch. Instead of being aggressive, they develop a percentage type of style. On the European Tour, there is less competition, which puts players in contention more often and makes them better; more aggressive finishers. Simply, they are more used to winning than our guys are.' He also said: 'We don't have a Seve Ballesteros on our side. I know it and the whole of our team know it. There has never been a better imagination player than Ballesteros.'

The US cause may not have been helped by some of the American team perhaps being in awe of their skipper. They knew that not only had he designed the golf course, he could play the game better than they could. And he let them know it. 'I know this course probably better than anyone,' he said, 'yet not one of my team have asked me for advice about what shot to play, where to go for or which club to use. If Andy Bean had asked me when he pulled out his 9-iron on the 17th, I would have knocked it out of his hands.' Say what you like about Seve, but when he was captain at Valderrama 10 years later, especially on the 17th hole which he had helped to redesign, he wasn't going to risk anyone shunning his advice.

In Saturday morning's foursomes, Seve and Ollie had been 3 up on Stewart and Ben Crenshaw but they lost the 14th and 17th and were in danger of losing the last – to a bogey. Seve had made a hash of the Europeans' second shot and he then knocked a six-foot downhill putt for par seven feet past the hole. But displaying all the confidence one would expect of a 21-year-old, and none of the nerves one might anticipate of a rookie, Ollie's putt was never anywhere but the centre of the cup. He was lucky the hug Seve gave him didn't crush his lungs.

Europe now had a five-point lead. Seve and Ollie lost in the afternoon – Jacklin said of Seve: 'You can get a Ferrari going at 175 miles per hour but you can't keep that speed up forever' – but the five-point margin remained going into the singles once Langer and Lyle completed victory over Wadkins and Nelson after Langer hit an 8-iron to eight inches at the last.

On Sunday Seve took on Curtis Strange, a man whom some in the States bizarrely regarded as the world's best player, this before he had won either of his two US Opens. 'Perfect,' wrote Dan Jenkins in *Golf Digest*. 'Here was a match between a European who wins majors and an American who skips majors.' (Strange had missed three of the last four Open Championships, not bothering to make the trip across the Atlantic.) Things did not go as Jacklin's team had hoped in the singles. Some big guns – Woosnam, Faldo, Olazábal – were going down. 'I was very much aware of the situation,' said Seve. 'I saw from the scoreboard that things were getting closer all the time. Too close. I knew my match would be vital.'

Seve was 3 up after four holes but only 2 up at the turn. On the 11th, he had the chance for a pay-back for Friday's incident. 'I went into the water and he played his third shot before I played my fourth, when I was away. I told the referee to tell Curtis that he had played out of turn but that on this occasion I would not do anything about it.' On the 15th, Seve made an eight-foot birdie putt to stay 2 up. With the honour on the 16th tee, he hit a perfect tee shot, eight feet from the flag. Eamonn Darcy had just beaten Crenshaw. Europe had 13 points; they needed one more to ensure the tie and retain the Cup. Seve's putt to win his match and clinch that point slid by.

'There was a lot of pressure,' he said. 'It looked like the whole thing was collapsing after we had seemed to have almost got the match won after two days.'

After hitting his drive on the 17th, dormie 2 up in this crucial match, Seve noticed Ed Sneed, a former tour pro who was commentating for American television. He went over and asked him about the exact state of play in the matches still on the course. Sneed's answer, whatever it was, failed to satisfy him. The next person he spotted was me. He came over to repeat his question. I told him that Langer was level with Nelson playing the last and that Gordon Brand Jnr was one up against Hal Sutton in the match behind Seve. But Seve wasn't thinking about that match. 'So I need to win and Langer has to halve with Nelson. Good.' Off he went.

His 8-iron second shot found the middle of the 17th green, about 25 feet from the hole. Strange was over the back in two but made his four. Seve putted his ball up to two feet. The next one went in. Seve had played his round in three under par and was the only man on either team to win four points.

More importantly, Europe had just won the Ryder Cup. Up ahead, Langer had indeed halved the 18th with Nelson, in somewhat curious circumstances. They conceded each other three-foot putts for fours, even though it was obvious this was to Europe's advantage. Nelson's only hope to at least tie the match for his team was for Langer to miss his putt. A half-point here was just fine for Europe. When Brand halved with Sutton, Europe had won by 15–13. The man who had been in the vanguard of the move to include continental players in the Ryder Cup team had become the first American captain to lose at home – what's more on his own course.

'I hope this wakes up our Tour and its archaic rules,' said Nicklaus, ever-gracious in defeat. 'I cannot see why Seve and his teammates would not be welcomed at any event they want to play in. By stopping them we are just hurting our sponsors and our spectators.' As we shall see, it's likely that the PGA Tour boss, Deane Beman, had long since turned off his television.

For the return to The Belfry in 1989, Tony Jacklin was still the European captain, for the last time, but there was a major void in the team room. His wife, Vivien, was no longer there. In April 1988, I had gone to Pedrena to see Seve for a magazine instruction shoot. The first thing he said, with deep shock in his voice, was: 'Did you hear the news? Vivien Jacklin died.' She had passed away suddenly of a cerebral haemorrhage near the Jacklin's home in Southern Spain.

The Ryder Cup was then 18 months away, but shortly before the match the captain had a sticky decision to make. The widespread assumption was that Sandy Lyle, a stalwart of the team in the last two victories but in pretty wretched form for the past 12 months, would be one of the wild-card picks. Seve assumed the same. But on the Saturday night before Jacklin would announce the team at the conclusion of the German Open in Frankfurt, he telephoned Lyle, who was playing in the States. Lyle told him he didn't want to be picked. He was playing poorly and was concerned he'd let the team down. He never played in the match again.

On Sunday night, I had dinner at his hotel with Seve and Carmen, by then his wife of nine months. 'Tony told me yesterday that Sandy was going to get one of the wild cards,' said Seve. 'I agreed with him. But after I had finished my round today, Tony told me that he had spoken with Sandy for an hour on the phone last night and he wouldn't play because his game was so bad.' He said that he agreed with Jacklin's decision to bring in instead Christy O'Connor Jnr, who had been hugely disappointed to be overlooked in favour of José Rivero in 1985, as a replacement.

By the time the match was over, *Sports Illustrated* was this time prepared to share the plaudits. 'Led by captain Tony Jacklin and inspired by the incomparable Seve Ballesteros . . .' Europe retained the Ryder Cup. But with a tie, not a victory.

At the opening ceremony, the American captain, Raymond Floyd, had introduced his team as 'the best 12 golfers in the world'. This was a ploy first used by Ben Hogan in 1967. But then it was true. Jacklin's retort was: 'What does that make Seve? 13th?' And Nick Faldo? And Bernhard Langer? (And Greg Norman, for that matter?) The fact that only three of the European team had won a major championship at that point – Woosnam and Olazábal had yet to do so, and of course Lyle wasn't there – led Mark Calcavecchia, who had won the Open at Royal Troon two months before, to suggest the European Tour was so inferior to the PGA Tour that it was a good place for struggling American professionals to play in order to increase their confidence.

After the opening foursomes, Europe trailed 3–1, as in 1985. Then, as in 1987, they made a clean sweep of the afternoon fourballs. In the morning, Seve and Chema had halved with Tom Watson and Chip Beck but in the afternoon they thrashed Watson and Mark O'Meara by 6&5. Seve finished the match with an eagle two at the 10th followed by three birdies, prompting his partner to quip: 'When Seve gets his Porsche going, not even San Pedro in heaven could stop him.' (The car analogy was amusing. After Seve had won the Masters in 1983, Tom Kite, then in more genial mood about his Spanish adversary, had said: 'When he gets going, it's almost as if Seve is driving a Ferrari and the rest of us are in Chevrolets.' At Muirfield Village, Jacklin had also compared him to a Ferrari. Motoring-wise, his compatriot didn't appear to consider him in that class.)

On Saturday, Europe retained the two-point advantage through the day. There were two more wins for the Seve and Ollie show, the first thanks to Seve sinking a seven-footer for par at the last to win their foursomes against Kite and Strange. On the first tee, Kite, hitting first, had driven his ball and then said to Seve, unaccountably: 'Remember the Alamo!' I say unaccountably because it was the Spanish-speakers who won there as well.

On Saturday night, Seve eventually volunteered to go out top in the singles, as he had in 1983. 'We had the team meeting at which Jacklin gave us the order of play. Nobody wanted to go out first. Ian Woosnam was picked to go out first but he said he didn't want to. I think Sam Torrance was the next choice but he said he wanted to be in the middle. Well, somebody had to go first, so I said I would.'

It meant he would be up against Paul Azinger, who had pleasant recollections of how much Seve had encouraged him despite being out of contention himself during the final round of the US Open the previous year. 'No wonder all the European Ryder Cup like to play alongside Seve,' was Azinger's contemporaneous thought. Strange thought differently. Doubtless remembering how Seve had got one over him at Muirfield Village, he told Azinger: 'Don't let this guy get into you. Don't let him try and pull anything. Be prepared for anything and everything.'

So on the 2nd green, when Seve asked if he could take his ball out of play and replace it because it was cut, Azinger refused. 'Seve,' he said, 'I don't think this ball is in bad shape.' The referee, Andy McFee, backed Azinger. Seve's request was refused. But what could he have been trying to pull? He holed his 12-footer for a birdie in any case. Azinger missed his from three feet. The crowd went crazy. Seve took a 2-up lead at the 4th, where he had two putts from five feet for the win. Azinger conceded the hole but Seve wasn't having that. He wanted the crowd's acclamation, so he went ahead and putted. He holed it and the fans went mad all over again.

But Seve's putter couldn't save him forever, and by the time they reached the last hole, 'Zinger' held a 1-up lead. Seve needed to win the hole to get a half, and Europe badly needed him to do so. At that point, only Mark James led for Europe and the United States led in six, including Azinger v Ballesteros.

Azinger had the honour on the 18th tee. He pulled his shot into the water on the left – way left. Seve's drive was a good one, but it just ran out of fairway and nestled down in the rough on the right side of the hole. When he saw Azinger dropping his ball, now about to be playing three, Seve said to his caddie, Ian Wright: 'What the hell is he doing? He's going to be playing a wood from the middle of the woods.' Seve went across the fairway to try to check what was happening, but Azinger and Referee McFee were on the other side of the lake. There was nothing he could do. (This anecdote is necessarily riddled with confusion, not clarified by the TV coverage. In his autobiography, *Zinger*, Azinger says he took the drop at the point Seve had wanted; indeed, he wrote: 'The place where Seve was indicating would provide me with a much better lie than the spot where the referee and I originally planned to drop it.')

Azinger played his third with a 3-wood and got his ball into the left-hand greenside bunker, a great shot all things considered. Now

Seve had to play boldly. His thinking had been that Azinger would make six and so he need not play for the green from this tricky lie. Now he had to figure that Zinger could get up and down for his five. Seve needed a par. As at the 1986 Masters, he clubbed up, from the 4-iron he would have hit to the 3-iron. From the lie his ball was in, he required perfect contact to clear the lake, let alone make the green. As at Augusta, he didn't come close to making the carry.

Now he had to drop the ball and hope to put some pressure on Azinger by getting down in two. Seve insisted Ian Wright gave him the wrong yardage for the pitch shot with a 9-iron. If so, Seve may have brought the error on himself. 'Make sure you get the yardage right on this one,' he told Wright, 'because it will be the first you've got right all day.' Hardly a remark likely to keep his caddie cool. Seve's ball finished 25 feet above the hole, on the next tier up on what is a three-tiered green – an impossible putt. 'I was very upset,' he said. 'The shot was perfect and had it finished close, it would have put pressure on Paul for the bunker shot' – the Tway/Norman, Mize/Norman philosophy.

With Seve looking set to take six, Azinger played a good bunker shot to five feet. And then Seve topped him by sinking that impossibly slick downhiller – 'truly a sensational putt', said Azinger. So good that Azinger found it in him to pat him on the backside and say 'Great putt.' But it was to no avail. Azinger followed him in for the half in five to win the match. Just as Seve's failure to close out Zoeller in 1983 had cost Europe a tied match, so this was costly, too. Europe led 14–10 at one point but they lost the last four matches.

They probably paid the penalty for celebrating too soon, when Canizares holed his putt to beat Ken Green and gain the 14th point; indeed, even before that, when O'Connor had beaten Fred Couples with a 2-iron to four feet at the last while his opponent missed the green with a 9-iron. No one went out to cheer on the outstanding matches, featuring Brand Jnr, Torrance, Faldo and Woosnam. For once, Jacklin got it wrong.

In *his* autobiography, *Woosie*, the Welshman wrote of his match with Curtis Strange, in which he was 1-up with three to play. 'We had just teed off at the 16th hole when news arrived that Canizares had beaten Green and that, officially, Europe had retained the Ryder Cup.

"Well done, Woosie," Curtis said, walking towards me with his hand outstretched. I sensed that he wanted to concede the match, so we could make our way straight back to the clubhouse.

'Thanks,' I replied, 'but do you mind if we play on and finish?'

Strange birdied the last three holes to win the match.

On the other hand, Europe only kept hold of the Cup because the Americans could not play the 18th hole. They kept going in the water – as Azinger had done, even though he survived to win – and if they didn't do that they would miss the green with their second shots or take three putts when they did get there safely. Calcavecchia, Stewart, Green and Couples all stood on the 18th tee all-square and all lost the hole and their match.

Nevertheless, for the Europeans, despite a tie meaning that as holders they retained the Cup, it was an unsatisfactory outcome. It should have been a glorious moment. Instead, it somehow felt all wrong.

One thing was certain. Dave Stockton and his team had got sick of the Americans losing in the Ryder Cup. 'Nice guys finish sickened' is one sporting aphorism. It was time to get nasty. People often say of the Ryder Cup: 'Golf was the winner.' Not in 1991. Magazine headlines about this being the 'War on the Shore' proved to be true.

Bernard Gallacher had succeeded Jacklin as captain but this week the running was made by his opposite number, Stockton. He wasn't going to razz the Europeans by calling his team the best 12 golfers on the planet. Instead, he took the mercenary route. 'This team has collectively won $50 million,' he said, 'or better than $4 million apiece.' (In the generation before Tiger Woods or Vijay Singh might win enough in a year to make Croesus seem like a benefits' claimant, this sounded like El Dorado.)

Stockton's team won the match, held at Kiawah Island, South Carolina – which was probably all they were bothered about – but in many other ways they were losers. Two of their players, Corey Pavin and Steve Pate, wore baseball caps in army-style camouflage colours, trying to invoke patriotic sentiments among the spectators as if the Europeans had been the enemy in the Gulf War earlier that year. At the opening dinner, the hosts put on a video. It only showed highlights of American successes even though Europe had held the Cup since 1985. There wasn't one shot shown of a European golfer. Ken Schofield and the players were livid. They considered walking out. 'If it's a war they want,' thought Nick Faldo, 'let's give them one.'

On his way to that opening dinner, Pate was injured in a car crash. Stockton played him in the Saturday fourballs with Pavin (stupid caps and all), where they were vanquished by Langer and Montgomerie, but Pate said he was in too much pain to play in the singles, a move made after it was known who he would play: Seve.

The consequent shuffling around of the pack, with David Gilford being the unfortunate European who had been nominated by his captain to sit out the singles in such circumstance, meant everyone else on the European team moved up a match. So Stockton got a half-point out of an unfit Pate and nothing out of Wayne Levi who was surely going to lose anyway – he had made the American team on the basis of a great 1990, not what he'd done in 1991. For Stockton, it was better for Levi to lose against Seve than against Gilford. If that was the thinking then, while totally reprehensible, it worked a treat. Four years later Gilford and Seve would get their own form of revenge.

Before the murky scenario of the singles draw, there were two days of foursomes and fourballs to be played. Friday's opening foursomes saw Seve and Ollie, of course, up against Chip Beck and – would you believe? – Paul Azinger.

This was an odd week for Seve. He ended the match as the leading points scorer on either team, with 4½ out of five, but he wasn't playing well for large periods of time. In this match, he could hardly control his ball over the opening holes, played predominantly into the wind. He hit a poor approach shot on the 1st, hooked a drive into the marsh on the 2nd, fluffed a straightforward pitch on the 3rd and hit another drive into the rough on the 4th. After those opening holes,

Gallacher and Manuel Pinero, one of Gallacher's assistants, approached Sergio Gomez, Olazábal's manager, to apologise. 'We are sorry. We don't think Seve should be playing in the foursomes, but Ken [Schofield] said he had to play.'

Before the match reached the turn, there was something else for Gomez and the gallery to ponder. On the 7th hole, Chema heard Azinger and Beck discussing which compression ball they should use, apparently because the hole was playing downwind. However, in a rules meeting before the matches got underway, it had been made very clear that players could not change the type of ball they used during the match, although experience in regular tournament play meant this was really nothing special.

Chema told Seve what he had heard, by which point they had played the par-three 8th as well. On the 9th tee, Seve saw Sam Torrance, another of Gallacher's assistants, and told him to get the captain. They and the match referees met on the 10th tee, Europe having just lost the 9th to go 3 down.

Azinger denied committing any infraction. But it seemed that once he discovered that no penalty could be applied, because only now had the Europeans made a complaint, he admitted they had switched balls. Television microphones picked up Azinger's insistence that he hadn't been cheating. 'We don't say that, Paul,' said Seve. 'It has nothing to do with cheating. Cheating and breaking the rules are two different things.' This proved to be a vital point of the match. Europe won the 10th, 12th and 13th to draw level, the 15th and 17th to win by 2&1.

One thing that infuriated Americans over the years in the Ryder Cup was Seve's tendency to cough while they were preparing to hit. Seve points out it's not his fault that he has a recurring cough; they would ask how come he didn't do it when Olazábal was set to play? After this match, Azinger – perhaps wanting to be the man who put the nail in Seve's coughing – said: 'Seve is the King of Gamesmanship.' It was not intended as a compliment and the suspicion was that Azinger said it in part to deflect from his own behaviour and because he was upset to have let slip a 3-up lead. That was certainly Seve's take on it. 'He did that to change the focus of what happened. He was very smart.' In the subsequent years, passions softened by time and by Azinger's resilient and successful battle against cancer, Seve retracted his retort of the American team being '11 nice guys and Paul Azinger'. And the title of this chapter is the same as the one dedicated to Seve in Azinger's own book.

That was one match won for Europe but by lunchtime on Saturday they trailed by 7½ points to 4½. Seve and Chema had won three of those points, two-thirds of the European's total. 'I was expecting more from the rest of my team,' said Seve censoriously. (Note the '*my* team'.) One of the American TV commentators concurred. 'One European team cannot beat four American teams.'

Not that the Spaniards wouldn't have given it a good go if the rules had permitted it. On Friday afternoon, Azinger and Beck had been zapped again by the Spaniards after Stockton had sent them out second in the draw in a doomed attempt to avoid a rematch of the morning shenanigans. On Saturday morning, the Spaniards recorded a 3&2 foursomes win over Fred Couples and Ray Floyd. Seve had been his usual extraordinary and mercurial self, albeit consistently wild – example: he never hit the 2nd fairway once in five tries all week – but Ollie had been there to carry him every time it was required. He was like Rozinante to Seve's Don Quixote, albeit no ass. 'Seve is unstoppable,' Olazábal explained. 'It did not matter where we put the ball, we always came out well.'

In Saturday afternoon's fourballs against Couples and Payne Stewart, there was a moment of vintage Seve. On the 15th hole, he was 15 feet away in three, standing over what looked likely to be a no-pressure birdie putt. Stewart was out of the hole, Couples 40 yards away in a bunker and playing four. Astonishingly, Couples holed his shot. One of the oldest adages in matchplay is that you assume your opponent will make very shot. Now Seve had to hole his putt for the win. Not only did he do so, his whole demeanour as he looked over and then stood over the shot was that no way was he going to be denied. He wasn't. The match was halved, but 'Seve's team' had come through big-time on this occasion. The other three matches had gone Europe's way. It was 8–8 going into the singles.

Seve's match against Levi was the sixth match out. The first hole was halved in par-fours. On the par-five 2nd, Seve hit his tee shot into the vegetation, dropped out in two, hit it left in three and into some other rubbish in four. Levi was in front of the green in two. The pin was cut on the back of the green, behind which was a water hazard. Incredibly, Levi went for the flag. He put a little bit extra into the shot and it went into the hazard in three. Instead of dropping near that point, he went back to the same place as before and again he hit his ball into the hazard. Seve won the hole with a double-bogey seven and was never caught. He won by 3&2, the only man to be under par in his singles when his match finished.

But the outcome of the match was out of Seve's hands. Faldo and David Feherty won the first two matches out. Mark Calcavecchia, 4 up with four to play against Colin Montgomerie, triple-bogeyed the 15th, bogeyed the 16th, lost the 17th to a double-bogey five after both men had hit their tee shots in the water, and bogeyed the last – eight over par for the last four holes. That was a half-point each. But the other matches fared less well for Europe, including Olazábal losing on the last green to Azinger.

With the score at 14–13 to the United States, it was down to the last singles – Bernhard Langer against Hale Irwin. Langer was 2 down with four to play. If he won his match, Europe would again retain the Ryder Cup in a tie. This time, with all that had gone on, it wouldn't feel like a sister-kisser. Langer won the 15th but the 16th was halved. On the 17th, a long par-three over water, both men hit their tee shots over the green. Irwin chipped to ten feet, Langer to five. Irwin missed his putt. Langer didn't: the third consecutive putt between five and eight feet he had holed under unbelievable pressure.

Langer's drive on the 18th was a good one, down the fairway. Irwin's was wild and to the left but it either got a lucky bounce or someone threw it back into play. Visibly choking, Irwin's second shot was weak and right. Langer's was just over the green. Irwin pitched poorly, to about 25 feet. Langer's effort, from about 40 feet, looked good all the way but it ran on five feet past the cup. Irwin's putt was his fourth feeble shot in a row. Langer gave him the two-footer for his five, a generous concession given that Irwin had shown every indication of his ability to miss it and that no one could accuse this match of being played in the best spirit. But spite is not one of Langer's traits.

Langer now had his putt to keep the Cup in Europe. There was a spikemark on the line he wanted to hit, on the left lip, so he decided to hit it a little firmer inside the left edge. The putt missed by a hair's-breadth on the right. Reflecting on the intense pressure Langer had been under, maybe the greatest inflicted on any golfer over a single shot, Seve said: 'No one in the world could have holed that putt. Jack Nicklaus wouldn't have holed it and nor would Tony Jacklin. And I certainly wouldn't have holed it.' Four in a row had proved one too many to ask.

It was 19 July 1993, the day after the Open Championship at Sandwich which had been won so fantastically by Greg Norman with a closing round of 64. Seve and Chema were in Pedrena for the Royal Green Match, an 18-hole exhibition that pitted them against Tom Watson and Payne Stewart, the former the American captain for the Ryder Cup match at The Belfry in two months time, the latter a member of his team. The most interesting facet of the proceedings was the total obviousness of the fact that both Seve and Ollie, and indeed Watson and Stewart, took it as absolutely read that both Spaniards would be on the European team, even though Seve was certain to require a wild card and Olazábal, in eighth place on the points table (the top-nine made it as of right) and only scheduled to be playing two more tournaments before the cut-off date, was by no means certain of an automatic place.

Seve's certainty was not ill-founded. Bernard Gallacher had told him that he was on the team unless he did a Lyle and declined his place. Gallacher was accordingly in the process of avoiding Seve over the next six weeks so it didn't look as if he was having meetings with him to discuss the situation. Their selection was not universally regarded as a done deal. Peter Alliss, the revered BBC commentator, said: 'If Gallacher picks the two Spaniards and they do well, it looks as much the obvious thing to have done as it does a masterstroke. But if they don't, all he will hear is "Why did he ever pick them? Everybody knew they were playing badly."'

Pick them he did. By that time, Olazábal was out of the automatic places, in 12th spot. In 10th place was Joakim Haeggman from Sweden, who got the third pick. The man who missed out was Ronan Rafferty, who had played in 1989. He was 11th on the points list. Seve told me that when he left the selection meeting in Dusseldorf to catch a flight home, he was under the impression that Rafferty, or perhaps David Feherty, would get the nod. Haeggman's position on the points list meant he did merit selection, but on the other hand he was a rookie. However, and behind the scenes this may have helped his cause, he was a Swede, and no Swede had yet made the Ryder Cup team to represent a Tour that had been so lavishly sponsored by Volvo since 1988. Haeggman would play a significant role in events.

In what seemed like a hangover from the acrimony at Kiawah, the first notable occurrence of the week was Sam Torrance getting annoyed with Tom Watson for his refusal to allow his team to autograph his menu at the opening dinner. What with some American wives giving Davis Love a packet of cough lozenges to give to Seve the first time he coughed in their opening match on Friday morning, things were shaping up nastily.

When the action got underway, there was no disguising that Seve was struggling with his game. On Friday morning, he and Ollie lost for the first time in six years and sustained their first-ever foursomes defeat – 2&1 by Love and Tom Kite. As you'd expect, there was the occasional spat. On the first hole, Kite had a very short putt for the half. 'That's good,' said Seve, conceding the putt, after Kite had started lining it up. Kite was visibly upset that Seve had taken so long to say anything and he stormed off to the next tee. Seve went after him.

'Tom, you didn't hear me say the putt was good before you put it [his ball] down?'

'No, Seve, I didn't. I guess the crowd was just so loud I couldn't hear.'

In the afternoon, the Spaniards got their revenge on them, winning their fourball by 4&3, and in the Saturday morning four-somes they beat them yet again. Seve and Chema changed tactics so that Olazábal would not overstretch by trying to keep up with Love off the tee but again it was Kite who appeared to be their principal adversary. In his book *A Good Walk Spoiled*, John Feinstein quotes Love about Kite over a drop the Spaniards got. 'He started running over to where they were dropping, screaming "No, you can't do that, that isn't right!" I never heard Tom curse like that in my life. He was calling these guys every name in the book.'

The 2&1 victory could not obscure the fact that Seve was playing really badly. He had missed eight fairways and one green with his nine tee shots. But a big call had already been made. With his swing almost in tatters, his back hurting and the prospect of the singles the next day, Seve told Ollie on the 12th tee that he didn't want to play in the afternoon. He sent for Gallacher and told him the same – this needing to be done before Gallacher announced the afternoon pairings with Seve in them. At Seve's suggestion, Gallacher blooded Haeggman with Olazábal.

Gallacher tried to dissuade Seve but he would not force his talisman to play against his wishes. 'I felt I owed it to him to agree to his request,' he explained. This was even though Langer had also opted out for the afternoon, in his case because he had hardly played lately through injury and was not fully fit. Tony Jacklin later said he would not have allowed Seve to sit himself out, especially with the afternoon being the more forgiving format of fourballs. Seve himself later said: 'José Maria lost with Joakim and if I kept playing with José Maria, the worst that could have happened was that we lost. So probably, looking back and seeing what happened, it was a bad decision. It's easy to say that now. It just didn't work.' Completing a trio of opinions that Gallacher would prefer had not been proffered, a few weeks later Tom Watson had his say. 'Everybody was talking about how poorly Seve was driving the ball. What I saw was Seve making every putt . . . in fourballs I have to go with a man who's putting well.' In mitigation, it should be pointed out that Haeggman beat John Cook in the singles, which probably would not have happened had he not played before Sunday.

Thus ended the Ballesteros/Olazábal Ryder Cup partnership. Together they played 15 matches, winning 11, halving two, losing two. Incredible. 'I enjoyed a lot playing with Seve,' Olazábal reflected. 'I learned a lot. It was a lot of fun. It was wonderful to watch him play. The way he performed on the golf course even though he might not be hitting the ball well. He never gave up. He fought until the end. Great matches. We won matches that looked lost. Everything was possible.' Later, he would say: 'You may think you are a competitive person, but when you play with Seve, you realise there is another level.'

Europe went into the afternoon at The Belfry with a three-point lead but the US won three of the four matches, including the one against Olazábal/Haeggman. Europe's lead heading into the singles was merely 8½–7½.

For the second Ryder Cup in succession, the envelope came into play. Sam Torrance was suffering with a septic toe which meant he hadn't played since the opening foursomes. He couldn't play the singles either. Lanny Wadkins selflessly helped out his captain by offering to sit out the singles because he had the consolation of having played on winning Ryder Cup teams before, and he had been a captain's pick rather than playing his way on to the team. Wadkins had been due to play Seve, and probably beat him. Now Seve had an easier-looking opponent: Jim Gallagher Jnr. It wouldn't have mattered if Seve had been playing one of his brothers. His game was a shambles. If it had been strokeplay, his score would have been in the 80s. The fact that he proved he was right, that his game was indeed in ruins, was obviously no consolation. He lost by 4&3. Feinstein's book recalls an American joke from the week, that there were two Scandinavians on the European team. 'Joakim Haeggman, who's Swedish, and Seve, who's Finnished.'

Only three Europeans did win their singles: Colin Montgomerie,

Peter Baker and Haeggman. From the last six matches out, only Nick Faldo, in the bottom match, when it was too late to matter, got a half. Barry Lane lost to Chip Beck after being 3 up after 13. Costantino Rocca led Love one up playing the 17th but three-putted from 25 feet and then hit a poor approach to the last to lose that as well. The USA won 15–13.

In the locker room, Rocca and Seve were in tears. At the closing press conference, Gallacher started to say: 'Unfortunately, I just felt the match and the Ryder Cup revolved around Rocca . . .' At which point, Ian Woosnam, not always regarded as the greatest diplomat, interrupted to say: 'Forget it, Bernard. It's a team event. Leave it as it is.'

'I played very badly,' said a disconsolate Seve. 'I tried my best but it was not to be. We let so many people down today. The spectators walked away like they had been at a funeral.' In a way, it felt like that.

The match at Oak Hill in 1995 witnessed one of the most remarkable final days in the Ryder Cup's storied history. To get there quickly, let's point out that Seve – who had made the team on the basis of his stellar performances at the end of 1994 – wasn't capable of hitting his visor. He played both fourballs, with David Gilford, but neither foursomes. He would have been a total liability. (Olazábal had been selected for the team but had withdrawn, in favour of Woosnam, because of what seemed at the time to be a foot injury, later rediagnosed as a serious back problem from which it took him close to 18 months to recover.)

On Friday, Seve and Gilford won, the only European victors in the fourballs. Seve told the press that he'd had a few words with David before they played because he'd be unlikely to see much of him on the course. Europe trailed 5–3 overnight. On Saturday lightning did not strike twice, and after Corey Pavin had chipped in from over the back of the 18th green to enable he and Loren Roberts to beat Faldo and Langer, the USA led by 9–7. There probably wasn't anyone in Rochester who gave Europe a prayer; maybe not even in their own team room.

'I think my feeling was very much like the rest of the team,' Seve told me. 'I read in certain magazines and papers that certain players were very optimistic. It is very easy to say that afterwards. But when we were two points behind that Saturday night, I don't think anybody was optimistic.' Nick Faldo told me: 'It was very quiet. I don't think anything was said, to be honest. There was no speech. Everyone knew, quietly, what they had to do.' Or try to do. Woosie was quoted in *Golf Digest* as saying: 'Phone it in, mates. It's time to catch the Concorde home.'

Bernard Gallacher had been on seven losing Ryder Cup teams as a player (plus a tie on his debut in 1969). Now this would be three as captain. The players got the order of play – Seve would lead off against Tom Lehman – and then they had dinner. That was it. Europe hadn't won the singles since 1985. Why should this be any different? And Seve knew nothing could be expected from him.

In the 11th century, El Cid, the great warrior of Spanish history, was preparing to lead his troops into battle when he was killed in a skirmish. To lose their leader in such prosaic circumstances was too much for his forces. He had to lead them from the front. The next day, they duly mounted him on his horse, put his sword and shield in place, and in this fashion they went to fight. Their opponents did not know El Cid had been killed, so they were not to know that the man they feared above all others was in fact dead on his steed. Led by a dead man riding, El Cid's troops prevailed.

Seve had led from the front in 1983 and 1989. Now he would do it again. But this was different. Now he had no hope of winning. He was playing horribly and the Americans had one of their strongest players at the top. 'I had a hard time sleeping that Saturday night because I was very worried,' he admitted. 'It is a tremendous responsibility to go out first and play against the best, not feeling very well at all, physically and mentally, and having no confidence.'

Seve was to be a sacrifice. He may as well take the bullet rather than risk, say, Nick Faldo getting beaten by America's Top Gun. He would, if necessary, humiliate himself for the cause. Whatever, he was ready to be a hero.

The opening hole at Oak Hill is a tough but routine par-four. It took Seve four shots to reach the green. One down. At the next, a shorter par-four, Lehman hit his approach shot eight feet from the stick. Seve was in a fluffy lie short of the green in two, a bunker between his ball and the flag. It was a tricky shot but then who better to attempt to play it? It went in for a birdie three. You just knew Lehman would miss his putt. You expected he knew it, too. He did. All-square. Suddenly, you sensed this could become bizarrely special. You also sensed that Lehman probably realised it, too – that if Seve was going to lose, he was going to go down with all guns blazing.

The par-three 3rd was unusual. Seve hit the green and got a half in pars. At the 4th, however, a long par-five, his drive hit a tree and went about 20 yards. He knocked it forwards from there. From the ridiculous to the sublime . . . his third shot with 3-wood from the rough went 240 yards and made the green. Unbelievably, as on the 3rd, both men were putting for birdies. Another half.

On the 5th, Seve's drive went so wildly to the right that it comfortably cleared the stream that's there to catch an errant tee shot. He was wider than wide. His next shot, with a 9-iron, was beyond belief. It was impossible to imagine that anyone could get a ball up so quickly to clear the trees in front of him. To see Seve not only to do that but also carry the ball far enough to reach the green must have turned Lehman's guts to mush. No other player in the world would have even thought of trying the shot, let alone actually tried it, much less pulled it off. It was so extraordinary I'm not convinced that Tiger has that shot yet. Seve's ball was miles from the pin, and his first putt left him ten feet from the cup. Lehman was eight feet away in two. No prizes for guessing what happened. Seve even made Lehman hole from 12 inches for the half.

On the par-three 6th, Seve saved par from five feet after Lehman had missed from seven feet for a two. On the 7th, Seve drove miles right. He got to the green in three, ten feet away from the hole. Lehman, who was playing spectacular golf, missed for the win from 12 feet. Seve holed for the half as if the putt was a gimme.

As he watched Seve tee off on the 8th, one presumes Lehman was not thinking about the Spaniard having held the honour since the 3rd. He may have walked in if he had. But this time, Seve could not conjure the chip-in he needed for a par; indeed, he was further away in four than Lehman was in two. Lehman, having two putts from eight feet for his four after another glorious approach shot, graciously conceded Seve's putt for a five. Seve said nothing. Lehman got over his ball. 'Do you think you can make this one?' asked Seve. Lehman pointed out that he didn't need to; he'd got two for it. 'OK,' said Seve, 'It's good.'

The 9th was halved in pars. On the front nine Seve had missed every fairway and hit just two greens in regulation. Lehman had missed nothing other than a series of makeable birdie putts. On the 10th, Seve's drive split the fairway. The cheers were resounding. Then he hit it in a bunker. Lehman was four feet away in two after yet another wonderful shot, Seve six feet away in three. You know what happened. Still 1 down.

Walking to the 11th tee, Seve said to his caddie, Billy Foster: 'You know, I am playing terrible and he is playing fantastic and we are only 1 down. If we can hang on for a couple more holes, he is going to be in a very difficult position, because the pressure will stay on and on and maybe he will play one or two bad holes.' This was matchplay, remember, Seve in excelsis – 'It doesn't matter how you play. All you have to do is beat the guy in front of you.' The 11th is a par-three. Seve might reasonably have expected to hit this target, but he couldn't. And this time he couldn't salvage the par for a half. Now he was 2 down.

On the 12th, Seve hit his second good drive in a row. As he left the tee, there was an enormous roar – not for that, but for Howard Clark making a hole-in-one against Peter Jacobsen on the previous green. (That was critical; Clark would win his match on the last.)

On the 12th green a few moments later, something else extraordinary occurred. Seve was putting for a birdie three. Even more astonishingly, he was doing so from a slightly shorter distance than Lehman, who was continuing to play flawless golf.

Lehman was 25 feet from the hole. He putted up to six inches, leaving his ball in an ideal spot for it to be marked to help give a line to Seve's putt. 'Mark the ball, please,' asked Seve. Indeed, he said it twice. Lehman responded by knocking in the tiddler.

Maybe he thought Seve was trying to razz him up – his reputation did precede him, after all – but the rules are that you cannot finish out before your opponent in matchplay if he does not want you to; your opponent has control of the ball. 'What are you doing?' Seve said, 'I asked you to mark the ball. Where is the referee?' A similar incident had occurred in Seve's match against Wayne Levi at Kiawah, when Levi had wanted to putt out against Seve's wishes. 'Most of the time, what I see with some of the American players is that they don't know the rules of matchplay,' he said.

Beside the green, Carmen Ballesteros hissed loudly: 'Seve! Seve!' She probably didn't understand the finer points of matchplay but she could tell the atmosphere in the gallery was beginning to get a touch ugly, and the subject of the crowd's heatedness was her husband. Lehman approached Seve, seemingly upset as if he thought Seve wanted the referee so that he might claim the hole. Seve explained: 'I am not trying to do anything here. I just want you to mark the ball.' Some of the crowd now began to boo. Fortunately, the sheriff . . . er, the referee came along, explained the situation to the crowd and everyone calmed down. Lehman's marker was replaced, Seve took his putt, and he missed it.

That was that. Lehman won the 13th hole and the match on the 15th green. Seve later joked: 'I hit three fairways in three days but cleared out a lot of rough for the members.' Lehman said, in the heartfelt way of a man who's just had a 16-ton weight lifted from his shoulders: 'That was the toughest guy I've ever played. He was absolutely unbelievable. I salute him.'

Amid this drama, the scoreboards reminded us that there were 11 other matches behind this one. Europe had a fighting chance of an upset victory but with Seve having lost, they required 7½ points from 11. Howard Clark won, so did Mark James. Woosnam halved with Couples. Then came match No. 6.

David Gilford was 1 up playing the last hole against Brad Faxon but he'd hit his second shot over the green. He had a poor lie in thick rough. What was worse, everyone knew that Gilford was the worst chipper on the team. He proved this by selecting his 7-iron for the shot. Seve, his match finished, was by the green with Gallacher. Under Ryder Cup rules, only the captain can advise one of his players what to do in any situation. Whether the player wants such advice or not – and Seve would liberally dispense unwanted wisdom as captain at Valderrama in 1997 – was another matter, but Seve told Gallacher he had to tell Gilford to use his sand-wedge. Gallacher decided to keep schtum.

Gilford used the 7-iron and duly left his ball in the rough short of the green. He knocked his next shot on to the green and bravely holed a 12-footer for a five. When Faxon missed from six feet for his par, Gilford had won his match anyway. If Gilford had missed his putt, or Faxon had made his, it would surely have been game over.

'The miracle of Oak Hill began when Gilford tried to chip with that 7-iron through thick rough,' Seve told me during a long conversation in Munich in March 1997. 'It was a crazy shot. It had no hope. It finished the only place it could, in the rough. Either there or over the green. Trust me – he could not have kept the ball on the green with that club. I tried to get Gallacher to go over and talk to him before he played the shot, but it was too late. But he got it up and down. That was the start of the miracle right there.' He added candidly: 'Probably we would have lost in 1995 if I had been captain. I would not have put two rookies [Philip Walton and Per-Ulrik Johansson] at the back of the field, knowing that if we were to win, their matches would matter.' In fact, Johansson lost to Phil Mickelson but it didn't matter. Walton's match against Jay Haas did matter – very much.

The points kept piling up for Europe. Montgomerie beat Crenshaw, Torrance beat Roberts. Two points were needed to complete a near-miraculous victory.

Nick Faldo was 1 down with two holes to play against Curtis Strange. Strange had been a controversial wild-card selection, his place on the team being awarded by his old pal, the US captain Lanny Wadkins. Now he had a chance to justify his selection in the grand manner. But the players having halved the 16th in bogeys, Strange lost the 17th to a par. Faldo had the honour on the par-four 18th tee but hit a poor drive into the left rough. He couldn't possibly make the green in two. Strange's drive was straight, but short.

Faldo pitched out down the fairway, leaving himself a full wedge shot into the flag. Strange's second shot was on line but not strong enough to make it home. It finished in the bank of rough just below the green. From 93 yards, Faldo played a shot of greatness, a pitch to within four feet of the pin. Strange's chip left him six feet away. His putt missed while Faldo's went dead centre. Seve rushed on to the green in tears to hug him. 'Nick, you are a great champion.' (Weeks later, Faldo wrote to Seve. 'I just dropped him a quick line to say I really appreciated that comment, to be acknowledged in that way by a fellow competitor of his stature – it was one of the highlights of my career.')

So it was down to Philip Walton, a journeyman Irish professional. He had been 3 up with three to play but Haas holed a bunker shot to win the 16th and he took the 17th when Walton missed a four-foot putt. Walton needed to halve the last hole to win his match and the Ryder Cup. His second shot was similar to Strange's but fortunately for Europe, Haas was in worse shape. Walton's pitch left him 12 feet away from the hole in three; Haas was ten feet past the hole in four. Two putts would do it for Walton; even three might. He took the two. Europe had won four and halved one of the five matches that went to the 18th green.

Seve's hadn't been one of that handful, of course. But he left Oak Hill, and quit the Ryder Cup as a player (although we only suspected rather than knew that then), with a record of having won 20 and halved five of his 37 matches. Some performance. Next time he'd be there in a different capacity.

6. 'CAPTAIN FRANTASTIC'

By the time of the 1997 Ryder Cup, six different Spanish golfers had represented Europe in the competition. Fifty years before, there had only been seven professional golfers in the country. So poor were they in the aftermath of their country's civil war that they made a plea to the British Professional Golfers' Association (PGA) for equipment so that they could resume playing the game. Now Spain's players had not only helped to revitalise the event, one of them crucially so, the country was going to host it.

The 1997 match was held at the Valderrama Golf Club, on Spain's Costa del Sol. Previously, 15 Ryder Cups had been contested on the European side of the Atlantic and only one of those, at Muirfield in 1973, had been held outside England. (Of course, only since 1979 had non-British golfers been part of what had become the European team.)

The campaign for Spain to be awarded the match had begun in earnest when it came to considering the venue for 1993. The European Tour and the Spanish Golf Federation were keen that Spain should get that match. You won't be surprised to learn that Seve was, too. In early 1990, I worked with him on a piece he wrote for *Golf World*, of which I was then editor. It appeared in the April issue. The column began like this.

'I hope that when the next European venue for the Ryder Cup is announced in the near future it will be revealed that the Club de

Campo course in Madrid [the sole Spanish candidate] will be hosting the 1993 matches. That decision is necessary in order to help boost the game in Spain and I believe it would be a fitting reward for the Spanish contribution to the competition. I think that if Spain has the Ryder Cup in 1997 instead, that will be just a little bit too late – partly, I must confess, because I believe it would help if I had the chance to be on the team. By 1997, I will probably be past my prime.'

There are clearly elements of self-absorption there, regarding his own contribution to the Ryder Cup and his desire to play in the match, as well as a wish for recognition of the number of tournaments Spain was by then hosting on the European Tour. He wasn't wrong about being past his prime by 1997, either. On the other hand, when the match did go to Spain in 1997, it helped inspire interest in the game to the extent that by 2001 it was the fastest-growing sport in the country.

The vote to decide the venue for the 1993 Ryder Cup was set for the PGA Championship at Wentworth in May 1990. The week before, Bernard Gallacher had dinner with a group of journalists at the Italian Open. He was adamant that, whatever happened, the match would not return to The Belfry for a third successive time when in Europe. 'We've been there often enough,' he said. 'They can't have it back again.'

Behind the scenes, however, The Belfry's bid was in good shape. The way the decision would be reached was that the British PGA, the body through which the Ryder Cup had been established by Samuel Ryder in 1927 and whose headquarters were at The Belfry, would have three votes. So would the European Tour. In the event of a tie, the casting vote would go to Lord Derby, president of the PGA but also on the board of the European Tour. His decisive vote was needed. He gave it to The Belfry and resigned from the Tour. For some time after that, the entire future of the event was in some jeopardy until the PGA agreed that no longer would it be their property alone but would instead be a joint venture with the European Tour. It should be said that Royal Birkdale was probably the most popular candidate among players who had played in the

1989 match, with The Belfry even having support from some of the non-British players because everything there is conveniently on site.

Whatever the respective merits of the competing claims, the bid from Club de Campo had been overlooked. The official 'Back Spain' Tour line was not wholly shared by its membership, but one player in particular was furious. 'My motivation will not be the same from now on,' said Seve. 'I understand the British PGA feel a bit resentful at what they see as everybody wanting a slice of a cake that a few years ago nobody was especially bothered about, but I would say one thing to them. Without the continental players, there would be no cake at all.' Even a year on, he was fuming. 'I felt that to take the Ryder Cup to Spain in 1993 would have been like a reward for myself. I feel that was a great opportunity to say, "Hey, we feel that Seve has done a lot for the European Tour, we feel Seve has done a lot for European golf. We feel that golf in Spain needs a lift."' No false modesty there, then.

So Seve and the Spanish Golf Federation campaigned vigorously, and successfully, for Spain to get it at the next opportunity. That it would be held in Spain in 1997 was confirmed later in 1993, but the issue had not really been in doubt. Among the ramifications of the Tour/PGA joint venture was that the Tour would have the next choice of venue in Europe. They could hardly choose anywhere else but Spain. But the outcome was still not what Seve wanted.

The next stage of his vision was for the match to be played on a course he had designed. A project called Galapagar, just outside Madrid, that he had on the drawing board was the first object of his affections. To those who questioned how the match could be designated for a course that didn't exist, Seve could respond that the 1991 match was moved to Kiawah Island, South Carolina, from Palm Springs, California, at the whim of the property company that had signed the contract with the PGA of America. There was no course at Kiawah then either. (Nor did Celtic Manor in Wales exist in the form in which it will stage the 2010 match when its proposal was approved.) But that point was soon academic; the requisite planning permission was clearly either never going to come through or else would be mired in bureaucracy for too long.

Plan B called for the match to be held at a course he had already built, Novo Sancti Petri, near Cadiz in southwest Spain. In November 1993, Seve's business manager, Joe Collet, rang to ask if I had home phone numbers for Nick Faldo, Colin Montgomerie, Ian Woosnam, Mark James and Sam Torrance. Seve wanted to call to solicit their support for Novo Sancti Petri, whose candidacy he would be announcing within the week. This being out of season, he wouldn't be seeing them on tour in the meantime. Novo Sancti Petri was up against four other courses: Valderrama, La Moreleja in Madrid, El Saler near Valencia and the La Manga Club in the southeast. There was no Club de Campo this time, which did make one wonder whether it should ever have been a candidate at all, let alone Spain's sole nominee in 1990.

The fact that he was opposed by other venues annoyed and frustrated Seve. He later told *El Pais*: 'When at last the Ryder Cup was given to Spain . . . nobody called me, nobody congratulated me, nobody asked for my opinion. I put myself forward with the course at Novo Sancti Petri before my election as a member of the Ryder Cup committee and now it seems incredible to me that people who have done nothing for golf are wrestling with me when it is I who have brought the Ryder Cup here.'

It has to be said that no one else proclaimed the merits of Novo Sancti Petri. The silence from any third party was pretty deafening. Simply, few who had seen thought it a remotely suitable venue. And Seve did somewhat compromise his own position.

Further east along the south coast, Jaime 'Jimmy' Ortiz-Patino, the owner of Valderrama, had asked Seve to redesign the par-five 17th hole. Given all that was going on, it was an odd decision of Seve's to agree to it, even if it gave him a tie-in of sorts with the likely winner. Privately, he felt the European Tour – who were controlling the Ryder Cup committee, on to which Seve was later co-opted – had already decided in favour of Valderrama, meaning that he and the other three prospective venues were wasting their money. He later said: 'Probably I would have appreciated it if the Ryder Cup committee had told me, "Seve, we

think it's better if you stay away from this", but that didn't happen.'
There was also a truth that Seve preferred to ignore. The majority of
other players, José Maria Olazábal included, felt Valderrama was
the right choice.

Valderrama is a very private club (Seve's course was open to the
public, which he felt should have counted in its favour given the
evangelical angle of the bid to promote golf in Spain) but Patino had
been a great supporter of the Tour, staging the Volvo Masters since
1988. Volvo was the Tour's overall corporate sponsor. As the Tour
has never disguised since, when it comes to selecting Ryder Cup
venues, money talks. When it does, they not only listen, they usually
agree with what it has to say. 'What we have done with the Ryder
Cup is unashamedly commercial,' said George O'Grady, executive
director of the Tour, in November 2005. 'It has to pull together the
rest of the European Tour.'

In respect of the 1997 match, Sir Ian (now Lord) MacLaurin, a
director of Valderrama, was a non-executive director of Guinness,
the owners of United Distillers, the parent company of Johnnie
Walker, the title sponsor of the Ryder Cup. Powerful company. At a
drinks party in the week of the 1994 Masters, a month and a half
before the venue for the Ryder Cup would be announced, again
ahead of the PGA Championship at Wentworth at the end of May,
Patino told me he was wholly confident that Valderrama was going
to be awarded the match. Misplacing confidence is not something
Patino routinely does. On the Sunday night after the tournament,
while Seve was preparing to join in Olazábal's victory celebrations,
Patino was with O'Grady (then the deputy executive director) and
Richard Hills of the European Tour at dinner in Augusta, somewhat
incongruously at TGI Friday's.

Seve had by now come to realise that his notional position of
influence had if anything hamstrung his attempts to get Novo Sancti
Petri chosen. He had been blindsided. 'I was excluded at the time the
committee were going through the final stages,' he said. 'I was
informed about the unsuitability of various finalists without having
previously being consulted or asked to participate in such a debate.'

He therefore resigned from the committee. Once the decision had been confirmed, he wasn't asked back.

I caught up with Seve at the Benson & Hedges International, which he would go on to win, at St Mellion in Cornwall on 6 May, 1994. I was there to cover the tournament for the *Independent on Sunday*. By Friday lunchtime, Seve had followed his opening 69 with a 70 and he was in buoyant mood. I suggested we might meet for lunch to go through a couple of ideas for *Golf World* that we had mentioned previously. He agreed, then almost immediately declined. 'I have arranged to meet Bernard Gallacher for lunch,' he said. He paused. I didn't understand his thinking but his sense of mischief was almost palpable. 'No, you come as well,' he said definitely.

It became clear that he had done this to wind up Gallacher. Seve and I were sat down before Bernard joined us and we were chatting about football. This conversation continued for over five minutes after the Ryder Cup captain had sat down, my feelings alternating between slight embarrassment and the 'What-the-hell' knowledge that it wasn't me who had double-booked lunch. Eventually, Gallacher grumpily said: 'Is *Golf World* doing football magazines now?' I couldn't blame him for being annoyed but it was soon pretty apparent why Seve had done this.

Gallacher had been anxious Seve should not cause any embarrassment for the Tour before the announcement of the venue, hence his proposal of lunch. As it turned out, it wasn't a great ruse on his part. Not only did he have to listen to more rubbish about football than he probably wished, the following week Seve had a press release issued while he was playing the final round of the Spanish Open, explaining his views on the host venue and outlining the circum-stances of the offer of an alleged bribe from Patino, worth about $1 million by way of a percentage of Valderrama's green fees or real-estate sales, for him to support Patino's campaign. It was a desperate gamble; his last shot. It missed the target. Indeed, four days after that press release, he felt obliged to issue another by way of clarification.

'I would like to express my surprise at the reaction produced after the last press conference,' he began, surely disingenuously. 'I would like to reiterate everything I said in relation to Valderrama offering me a million dollars. The fact that I, at that time, was not a member of the Ryder Cup committee, shows that such an offer could not be considered illegal. If this had not been the case, I would have denounced such an offer that very day and not waited until now.' His thinking was that if he had been offered money, who else might have been? 'In the same way that I had been made such a solid offer, there could also exist the possibility of a substantial amount of money in circulation elsewhere, [though] it would not necessarily be illegal.'

The fact that Seve was a major reason for the old GB&I team being supplemented with continental golfers in 1979, that he was an inherent part of the Spanish bid, was never going to be enough – irrespective of any shortcomings of Novo Sancti Petri – to win this competition. He wasn't simply out-fought, he was out-walleted.

Valderrama was confirmed as the venue for 1997 on 26 May. As a victorious Patino talked with journalists in the media centre at Wentworth, there was a potentially awkward moment. Seve came out from an interview and had no choice but to walk past Patino. He handled it perfectly. 'Congratulations,' he said, with no evident inflexion in his voice. 'You were too strong for me.'

While all this had been going on, it had been generally assumed that Seve would succeed Tony Jacklin (four matches: 1983–89) and Bernard Gallacher (three matches: 1991–95) as captain for the 1997 match in Spain. On 15 December 1995, Ken Schofield met him at Heathrow Airport, where Seve was on his way from Spain to look at a couple of golf-course design projects in the Far East. As it happened, I was also at Heathrow to meet Seve, to go through some initial drafts of the *Trouble-Shooting* instruction book. Seve hadn't told me that he was also meeting Schofield, and doubtless he hadn't told Schofield that he was meeting me – a kind of variation on the 'Lunch with Gallacher at St Mellion' theme. (At the Monday morning press conference on the day after the match at Valderrama, Schofield said of Seve, admittedly with some levity: 'He prepared meticulously for this since that day in December 1995 when we met in Terminal 4, gatecrashed by Robert Green.')

Schofield was aware that Seve still wanted to play in the match and he agreed that if Seve took the job, that possibility would remain open. Also, the assumption was that, as with Jacklin and Gallacher, the appointment would not be a one-off. If he was captain in 1997, he would be in 1999 as well.

As late as March 1997, Seve was talking about taking the dual role. 'I will try to make the team, and depending on how I feel and what the situation is, I will make the decision that is in the best interests of the side. I did say very clearly from the beginning that being the captain and playing would be very difficult, but not impossible.' He was to change his tune about the feasibility of that over the summer, but even then the possibility of him playing seemed as remote as Tierra del Fuego. It had taken until his seventh tournament of the season for him either to make a cut or break 70.

Seve had not accepted the captaincy immediately, with or without the rider of him perhaps being a player, too. Indeed, he said he thought he might play his way on to the team and settle for that and not be captain at all, but it is hard to believe he really thought that given the way he'd played against Lehman at Oak Hill and the fact that he was in the middle of taking a break from competitive golf, announced just after the '95 Ryder Cup, when he met Schofield at Heathrow. A likelier scenario for his scepticism about being captain is that he remained disillusioned by the political jockeying surrounding the choice of venue. In addition, or alternatively, perhaps he simply wanted to be asked nicely and often.

Any which way, given how *au fait* he was with the demands of Ryder Cup week, having effectively been the captain on the course since 1983, it is impossible to think he ever seriously thought he could cope with both playing and being captain, with the latter role demanding social functions and media responsibilities to attend and attend to, not to mention choosing foursomes and fourball pairings and making sure that all was well with the troops. In the end, his brother Baldomero convinced him he had to do it. Saying no was not a viable option. Therefore, he said yes. Then another series of problems cropped up.

He was adamant that he wanted to be able to choose four wild cards. The committee was even more adamant. He'd be stuck with the two that Gallacher had managed with. The two ended up being Faldo and Olazábal. Then Seve got a third: Jesper Parnevik, courtesy of Miguel Angel Martin.

Faldo first. Seve rang him in America in August and got him at the third attempt to impart the good news. Faldo hadn't spoken to Seve in some while and had been privately concerned Seve might leave him out for some unfathomable personal reason. That was never going to happen. Above all else, Seve wanted to win. Why leave out Europe's other genuinely great golfer?

Next, Olazábal. The injury that had caused him to withdraw from the team in 1995 had horrible consequences. The original misdiagnosis of it being a foot problem that had led to him getting the incorrect treatment not only wasted time, it wasted his feet. He got worse. The upshot was that come February 1997, Olazábal had not played competitive golf for 16 months. Subsequently receiving the appropriate attention meant he was about to resume playing tournament golf.

Seve asked him to come over to Pedrena. 'I invited Chema to my house to have lunch and play 18 holes. I told him I wanted him in the Ryder Cup because it would be important for me and for Spain, but [because of the injury] he was only going to start trying to qualify very late. I said to him, "If you don't qualify, I know you are very honest, and you will have to tell me if you are ready to be one of the picks or not".' As it worked out, Ollie's comeback began with a tie for 12th in Dubai, fourth in Portugal and first in the Turespana Masters on Gran Canaria. He was ready alright. At the European Open at the K Club, County Kildare, Ireland, in August, Seve told him that he had a wild card if he didn't make the top ten, which he didn't. And then Seve got another pick.

The Miguel Angel Martin affair was badly handled, on all sides. Essentially, his 'withdrawal' meant Olazábal moved from 11th to tenth on the points table, thereby qualifying himself automatically and leaving Seve free to issue another invitation, to Jesper Parnevik.

Martin had sustained a wrist injury at the Loch Lomond tournament in July and had an operation in early August. He intimated that he would not be able to play in the Ryder Cup – a huge shame for him because he had not played before, the match was in Spain, and he had been in the top ten on the qualifying list all year. Seve called him to commiserate. In Germany for the announcement of the team at the conclusion of the BMW International, Seve sought an assurance that Martin was out before he confirmed his wild cards. A Tour official was deputed to contact Martin. Martin told him he might be able to play and he wanted time to prove his fitness, as Olazábal had been given in 1995 before withdrawing with his injury. The announcement of the team could not be made.

Seve's view, perhaps not least because he was now on the verge of having precisely the team he wanted, although he would vehemently deny that any such expediency entered his thinking, was that Martin had to be out. How could he possibly be fit enough to represent Europe in the Ryder Cup when he would have played no golf for two months before the match? If he wouldn't withdraw himself, then he would have to be withdrawn by someone else.

It wasn't Seve who did the deed. The Ryder Cup committee gave Martin three days after the BMW tournament in which to have tests with doctors in order to prove his fitness, which he declined to do; his own doctor had ordered he wasn't even to chip balls at this stage. Martin was then sent a fax by the Tour – on behalf of the committee and captain – saying that since he would surely not be fit for the Ryder Cup, if he would withdraw then he would keep his qualifying exemption as if he had played in the match, be part of the official party, get a few free shirts, etc. It was pleasant in tone. Later that day, he was sent another fax which said that if he did not turn up on the first tee at Valderrama the next day to prove his fitness, he would be expelled from the team.

What caused that discrepancy is not clear, but Seve was sure of his own position. 'I was in favour of giving him until the Saturday, but the committee said that would not make any difference compared to the previous Wednesday. He was not going to be ready in any case. The Ryder Cup is not an individual competition, it is a team event. You do not go to the Ryder Cup to participate, you go to compete. In the past, Sandy Lyle [1989] and José Maria Olazábal [1995] have shown that by withdrawing because they were not 100 per cent ready to be on the team.'

In Switzerland for the European Masters, and the belated announcement of the team, what bothered Seve was that the press release from the Tour implied that he had been party to the committee's 'solution'. Martin blamed Seve for his abrupt omission and many harsh words were exchanged, including a threat by Martin to sue for his place. Seve did himself no favours with his outburst on this subject. 'You think Martin can stop the Ryder Cup? That little man. Martin is only thinking of himself. He must have a square head. He has had very bad advice. He's making things worse and worse. You think he wasn't welcome before, what about now?'

The latter statement does seem to condemn Seve as wanting Martin off the team, even if it wasn't strictly his decision, but anyway it had been done. Even a letter from one Manuel Ballesteros, in his capacity as president of the Spanish PGA, didn't succeed in getting the Tour to change its mind and grant Martin more time to prove his fitness. He did turn up at Valderrama with the rest of the team, hung around like an unwelcome guest and posed for the odd team picture – i.e. there was one taken with him in it but he was absent from most – but he went home to Madrid before the match got under way. It must have added insult to injury for him to read in the official programme's profiles of the teams: 'Miguel Martin: no prior Ryder Cup experience'. He still hasn't, even though the European Tour Media Guide still credited him as having qualified for the 1997 team.

With this topic out of the way for a while, Seve declared in Switzerland: 'I always thought it would take a long, long time to have as good a team as the one we had at Muirfield Village ten years ago. I think the team we have for Valderrama is better.'

After the match, mission accomplished, he admitted: 'To be

honest, I did not think the team was as good as in 1987, but I said that because I felt it was part of my obligations to help build up the confidence of the team.' And he says he has no aspirations for a career in politics? In fact, he was right – the class of '97 was not quite so strong as its predecessor. How could it be? He wasn't playing.

The Americans were pretty bullish about their chances, too. Captain Kite said: 'This could be the strongest [American] team ever.' Tom Lehman, their star-turn at Oak Hill, was moved to say: 'This team looks like the future of golf.' Afterwards, he said: 'I am still totally convinced we have the best 12 players in the world. I don't see how they could beat us,' but there you go. Probably just as well he didn't offer that opinion before the off.

On the eve of the matches, all one seemed to hear was whingeing. The terms for the two teams to stay at San Roque had not been agreed even yet; there could hardly be a worse week to hold an event in Spain since the last day coincided with the conclusion of the Tour de Spain cycle race (a bit like holding the Ryder Cup in England on FA Cup final weekend or in the second week of Wimbledon); Lord Macfarlane, chairman of Johnnie Walker, and his wife had not got their tickets; the Spaniards who had bought tickets for the match had not been allowed car park tickets whereas British and Americans fans had. Even some of the players' clothes were the wrong size.

Then there was the long matter of the par-five 17th – 'the hole that Seve redesigned/destroyed, depending on your viewpoint,' in the words of Sam Torrance. Many players were, and remain, scathing about the hole, saying it was unfair that you could hit a 300-yard drive only to find yourself in the rough that ran across the middle of the fairway. The complaints were music to Seve's ears. 'It is a great hole,' he said defiantly. 'A great hole. People say that you have a lie that is maybe not level for the second shot and I say what happens when you play your second shot to the 13th hole at Augusta? Other players say it is too difficult to stop the approach to the green if you're pitching with a wedge in there for your third shot, and I say have they ever played the third shot to the 15th hole at

Augusta and known the ball roll back into the water? And why should you have a perfect lie after a big drive? On other courses, you might be in water or a bunker.'

It's a hole that Tiger Woods has never been fond of, but then he putted clean off the green into the water during this match, so no wonder, but Ignacio Garrido and Phil Mickelson, for example, were to show that it could be tamed.

The 17th was the focal point of Seve's eager strategic advice to his team in practice. Colin Montgomerie went so far as to suggest Seve was treating him like a child, and in the match itself he got hot under the collar with the antics of his captain. 'One moment he would be pulling up in his buggy to tell us how the other matches were standing and the next he would hove to in time to tell us how to play this shot or that.' When he did the latter to Monty – on the 17th, as it happened – in his fourball match with Darren Clarke, Monty was livid. In his autobiography, *The Real Monty*, Monty said: 'I was the captain of this fourball pairing and I resented his interference.' At Seve's insistence, Clarke went for the green. He hit it in the water. Monty wasn't looking to take any advice from Seve. 'Seve, I'm nervous as hell here. Just leave me alone.' Fortunately, the Europeans won the match. Monty also said: 'There were several points about his captaincy, notably the lack of early communication with some of his players, which needed questioning. The only reason such things were not addressed was because the captain in question was Seve.'

'I think we all know how Monty can be,' Seve said afterwards. 'He is a great player and I like him very much. But sometimes when somebody asks him a question, I would like him to take a few seconds to think before he speaks. I think when you win the Ryder Cup, there should not be any complaints.'

Ian Woosnam was another critic, telling the British press during the week that 'Europe has a headless chicken for a captain'. Woosnam was not happy because Seve hadn't got it in mind to play him very often because he thought his form was shaky. Shortly after the match, Seve said: 'I was very disappointed to read that Ian

Woosnam had criticised me. The mission is to win so I don't think it was very smart for him to criticise.' In 2005, the 2006 Ryder Cup skipper told *Golf World*: 'I didn't enjoy [1997] at all. Nothing against Seve, that's the way he did it and we won. There were situations where he'd tell some players something but tell them not to tell other players. I didn't know who I was playing with or if I was going to play. [He played only once before the singles.] As one of the more senior players on the team, I was expecting to be more involved.'

In 2004, Darren Clarke said to *Golf Digest* of Seve's performance: 'I didn't have a relationship with my captain. At all. He spoke about five words to me all week. But we won. He was the luckiest man in the world that week.' Clarke, who also only played once before the singles, was asked if he thought Seve would have been 'slaughtered by the media' if Europe had lost. He replied: 'I'm not going to say that. What I couldn't understand was why I wasn't playing on the first day. I had qualified second for the team. That's his decision to make, of course. Seve is a legend and I wouldn't say anything bad about him because of that.' The unavoidable implication of that comment, which echoes Montgomerie's remark, is that if Seve wasn't a legend, he would have the odd bad word to say.

But Seve was not going to be a skipper in the mould of Nicklaus in '87: passive, crestfallen and vanquished. Being dubbed 'Captain Frantic' was better than being 'Captain Titanic'. If the Europeans were going to go down, it wouldn't be through a lack of effort on his part. 'As soon as you get them 2 down,' said Tom Lehman in wonder during the match, 'he shows up out of nowhere. He just kind of vaporizes. He's on the next tee waiting for you.'

In *Sports Illustrated*, Rick Reilly summed up the 1997 Ryder Cup like this. 'It was Seve all the way. It's was Seve's Ryder Cup, in Seve's Spain . . . Seve won the Ryder Cup and never fired a shot . . . Seve and his team were so far ahead of the Americans that this became history's only two-day Ryder Cup . . . We [the USA] can probably whip the Europeans country against country [but] we will never have a Seve. To the end, Seve was the King of Spain.' (While Seve's relationship with the PGA Tour and some American players on it could be spiteful, there was a cadre of American journalists who positively adored him for his cavalier golf and maverick spirit.)

Seve was not only active on the course, he had been meticulous in his preparations. He had decided earlier that, as home captain, he wanted to swap what had become the traditional order of the foursomes and fourballs. Perhaps surprisingly given Seve's history in the Ryder Cup – what with Strange telling Azinger in 1989 'Don't let him try and pull anything' and the latter's 'King of Gamesmanship' remark in 1991 – the PGA of America acquiesced.

Seve's logic was sound. 'We were defending the Ryder Cup, which I felt put a little bit more pressure on us. I think that starting out with the fourballs reduced that pressure by giving us more protection. In foursomes, if a player is nervous and not playing too good, it is hard for the other player. I thought it was better for us to start off with the fourballs.'

This also meant the fourballs would be contested when the players would be feeling at their strongest. For Europe, who always rely more on their core players than the Americans – the US seem positively Corinthian at times, as if since 12 players have made the team, they all pretty much deserve an equal showing, irrespective of form or class – this can be crucial. As Reilly wrote: 'Kite promised all his players they would play each day of the team matches, and they did, and everybody felt very included and the Americans got very creamed.'

Seve had already identified those who would play five times and those who would play less, though only after asking each of them how many matches they wanted to play. He also asked whom they would like to play with. Since Nick Faldo and Lee Westwood both named each other, for example, that was how one partnership arose. Above all, Seve was keen to emphasise the obvious, that this was a team game. 'There are no individual performances here. I don't care if someone wins five points and someone else wins no points. At the end of the day, the important thing is to win 14½ points.'

*

At 5.30 on Friday morning of the match, the heavens opened and decided, like English pubs since the 2005 drinking legislation, to stay that way. This was most inconsiderate. Prince Andrew had been up before 4 o'clock to join Jimmy Patino in overseeing the final preparations to the course, even though dawn was not until around 7. By then there was plenty of light – from the lightning. No other inland course in the world could have come close to withstanding such a pounding from the weather and then been ready to play the same day, but Valderrama is built upon an annually replenished bed of sand, and while spectacular is seldom a word that belongs in the same sentence as drainage, this was such an occasion. Once the rain was spent, the course was ready for play within an hour.

Seve hadn't had much sleep either. He'd been up all hours, considering who to pair with whom and which should go out first. In his most recent autobiography, *Life Swings*, Nick Faldo – well, you'd expect the most successful points-scorer in Ryder Cup history to have his book, too – recalled Seve's wife, Carmen, joking one morning: 'Another two nights of two hours sleep. If this goes on, I'll be seeking a divorce.' Obviously, not such a good joke since Seve and Carmen split up in 2004.

The weather meant the entire three days of play would be disrupted. Belatedly, the first fourball went out, Olazábal and Rocca against Love and Mickelson. The Europeans came back from 2 down with six to play to win at the last, where Mickelson missed from six feet for a birdie three that would have earned the Americans a half. It was a huge point for Europe, set up by Ollie holing his second shot at the 14th for an eagle two.

Europe's other win, in a morning where the points were shared, came from the Swedes, Per-Ulrik Johansson and Parnevik, the latter birdying the last two holes. Seve copped more flak here, though. He had decided to pair Parnevik with Garrido in the afternoon's foursomes and told him so on the 11th tee. The weather delay meant there would not be much of a break between the fourballs finishing and the foursomes starting, but Seve had told Parnevik not to tell Johansson – he didn't want him to feel down while he still had holes to play in this session. Some may call that a lack of communication; others may say good thinking.

By the close of play on Friday evening – i.e. nightfall – the teams were locked at 3–3. On Saturday, they would have to finish the last two foursomes, play the second series of fourballs, and try to complete the second round of foursomes. More torrential rain killed that idea. Saturday was Friday revisited except that the rain was heavier. But again Valderrama survived and thrived.

Concluding the foursomes, the only shot Europe had to hit in the first match was the 20-foot putt that Lee Westwood holed for a wining birdie three on the 16th green in his match with Faldo against Justin Leonard and Jeff Maggert. In the bottom match, Parnevik and Garrido got a half with Lehman and Mickelson. The overnight 3–3 had become 4½–3½ to Europe.

By next nightfall, that had become a scarcely credible 9-4. Seven matches had been completed in the day and Europe had won five of them, halving the other two. Never before, in the 70-year history of the Ryder Cup, had the United States gone a whole day without winning a point. It was, though, far tighter than it looked. At one point in the middle of the fourball session, Europe were down in the top three matches, all of which were won, two on the 17th green – by Woosnam/Thomas Bjorn and Faldo/Westwood – and one at the 18th – Clarke/Montgomerie. (Between 1985 and 1997, inclusive, of the 55 matches that were won on the 18th green, Europe won 34.)

In the bottom match, Olazábal and Garrido claimed a half against Lehman and Mickelson. They were all-square with two to play and managed to get out of the 17th with a half. Mickelson was six feet away from an eagle on Seve's fiendish hole; Garrido playing three from the back bunker. He hit a fabulous shot to eight feet. He holed that for his four, Mickelson missed, and they were still level. It looked at the last as if his effort might be wasted, but Olazábal holed from 25 feet to earn the half.

At the very end of proceedings, Europe's very great day just got better. In rapidly fading light, Lee Janzen and Jim Furyk, in the top match in the second series of foursomes, elected to play out the 18th hole when they stood 1 down to Langer and Montgomerie. The groundstaff had cut the green in readiness for the morning, thinking no one else would be putting on the 18th that evening. The Americans were about 60 feet from the hole in two, Janzen charged his putt 15 feet past, and Furyk missed his effort for a par. Europe duly won the match. Seve had apparently even got the fates on his side as well as the stronger golfers on the day. Kite conceded that he'd put out 'my A-Team, and they got hammered'.

Granted, 9–4 was a comprehensive lead, but Muirfield Village in 1987 had ended up being far more nailbiting for Europe than most people had thought on Sunday morning. Seve knew there was no space for complacency in the team room. The Americans may have inadvertently permitted it access at Oak Hill two years previously, and look what had occurred in the singles there. And there were three foursomes to complete as well; 15 points still at stake. Nevertheless, for Europe to lose from here would be dreadful. For European golf, it would be potentially calamitous. For the captain personally, well . . . living with himself might become a difficult exercise.

Nick Faldo later told the *Sunday Times*: 'Seve's team talk on Saturday evening was hilarious. In his opening speech on Monday, he'd been calmness personified – "We are here to spend a week with friends. The most important thing is that we enjoy ourselves. If we win, we win. If we lose, we lose. It doesn't really matter." Five days later, he'd been transformed into a raving lunatic. "Just remember how important this is. You don't three-putt. You don't hit it in the bunkers. And on 16 you don't hit it in the trees on the right. We *must* win."'

Seve said: 'One of the things I said in the meeting [on Saturday night] was for them not to look at the scoreboard. "Play your match. All you can do is win your match. Don't put your attention on the scoreboards because you will lose your focus and concentration and you will become more nervous if things are not going well."' Seve was horribly aware that things might not go well. 'On Saturday night, I did take two pills to sleep, but I couldn't sleep for the whole night. I was very worried that we may have a bad day and lose the Ryder

Cup; going into Sunday leading by five points, that would have been a total disaster.'

The final series of foursomes had to be completed on the Sunday morning. This day, the weather started out gloriously before taking a huge turn for the worse. After the three matches had been finished, the 9–4 scoreline had turned into 10½–5½. The five-point margin was still intact. Surely it couldn't go wrong now? It didn't. Narrowly.

Given this was the Ryder Cup, with its special pressures, home advantage may not ordinarily count for much. No one could feel too comfortable out there. But requiring just four points from 12 to win the match, a measly three and a half to retain the Cup (although for Seve that would have felt worse than it had at The Belfry in 1989), on a course the European golfers all knew so well from their annual pilgrimages for the Volvo Masters, this was surely as invincible as it could feel.

It proved to be far from easy. Losing was definitely on the agenda during certain segments of the afternoon, when the scoreboards seemed to drip with the red that indicated matches to the advantage of the United States.

Seve led off with Woosie who was up against Couples. It was a reprise of his two singles matches against the American in 1993 and 1995. Those matches had ended all-square and that would be a good start for Europe now. Couples, seven under par, won by 8&7. No one could think the Americans felt they were chasing a lost cause.

In the aftermath of that, the news wasn't scintillating for Europe, either. Leonard won the first four holes against Bjorn; Mark O'Meara was quickly in command against Parnevik; Maggert shot 31 on the front nine against Westwood; Lehman shot 30 on the front nine against Garrido.

However, Europe won both the second and third matches out. Johansson beat Love by 3&2 and Rocca, almost fantastically, beat Woods by 4&2, a massive point. Rocca had told Seve he wanted Tiger and he got him, helped by the fact that Woods didn't make a birdie until the 11th, by which point he was 3 down. Of equal merit from a European perspective, Bjorn halved with Leonard after that dreadful beginning. (The three American major champions of 1997 – Woods, Leonard and Love – played a combined total of 13 matches in the week and only had one win between them.) Europe had won 2½ of the first six points available, leaving only 1½ more to win the match. That's precisely what they got.

Olazábal seemed in control against Janzen, 2 up through 15 holes. It would be almost a fairy tale if he could capture the vital point in his home country on his comeback to the competition. But he lost the 16th to Janzen's par. Back to only 1 up. Both were on the 17th green in three, Olazábal some 20 feet away, Janzen 15. If Chema could halve the hole to go dormie one, Europe would have retained the trophy, because in the match behind, Langer was now dormie two against Faxon. In these nervous times, that would at least bring some respite, some room to breathe. If Ollie could win this hole, Europe would have ensured the 14½ points required to win. He missed, Janzen holed, and they went down the 18th all-square.

Langer had not won a singles match since 1985 and had inevitably been the focus of Europe's loss in 1991. When Faxon missed a ten-foot putt for his birdie at the 17th, Langer had two putts for the match from six feet. As Harry Vardon would have suggested, he prudently used them both. He had beaten Faxon 2&1; Europe had won 14 points.

That was not enough, of course. Seve desperately wanted the victory; not a mere retention of the Ryder Cup. 'A tie for me would be like a loss,' he said later. A half-point was still needed. Janzen had by now made a marvellous birdie three at the last to beat Olazábal; he'd won the last three holes to keep briefly alive his team's hopes. Those hopes were now extinguished as regards winning the Ryder Cup but the US could still frustrate Europe – and Seve.

That twist against Olazábal didn't look good if you believed in destiny – and Seve does. Meanwhile, Faldo had lost to Furyk, who had chipped in for a half at the 14th and holed a bunker shot for another at the 15th. What were the fates trying to do to him?

What they were doing was making it all come down to Montgomerie. He had squared his match with Hoch at the 14th and gone 1 up with a par at the 16th. At the 17th, Hoch made a birdie four to get back to level. If Europe were going to win the match, rather than only earn the tie, Monty needed at least to halve the 18th.

The Scot had Hoch marked the whole way down the last. Monty hit a terrific drive and then an admirable second shot to be on the green in two, 20 feet from the flag. Hoch was more adventurous, as in incompetent. He was in the rough off the tee, in trees with his second and consequently on the green in three. He was 15 feet from the flag. If Monty could two-putt, it was all over. Monty's putt duly finished a concession away from the cup. Europe had won the Ryder Cup.

Monty rather wanted the full point for himself but there was no doubt who would be the leading character in this scene. 'I dearly wanted to finish on a winning note myself,' Montgomerie wrote in his autobiography. 'No chance. Along comes Seve. He walks on to the green and picks up the American ball, thereby leaving me with a halved match rather than a win.'

'I thought to ask Hoch to make the putt would have been a little bit cruel,' explained Seve. 'I thought we should show a bit of sportsmanship.'

Not long after the match was over, the grey skies lived up to their promise and the rain bucketed down again. And kept on for another 24 hours. Even given Valderrama's drainage, there could have been no play on the Monday.

'If we had come to Valderrama to win the Ryder Cup, that would have been much less pressure,' said Seve. 'Because we won last time at Oak Hill, it was even more pressure on me. To have the Ryder Cup in Spain and be the captain and have to defend it – there cannot be any more pressure than that.' He had become the first man since Dai Rees in 1957 to have both played in and captained a winning Ryder Cup team against the United States.

At the team press conference on Sunday evening, the most stirring moment came after Seve had asked each of his players to say a few words. 'This has been very special to me,' began his old partner, Olazábal. 'A year ago I could not walk . . .' At that point he welled up with emotion and couldn't talk any more. There was a silence for a full half-minute until Costantino Rocca took his hand and the audience began to clap.

After he had taken a call of congratulations from the man who does reign in Spain, King Juan Carlos, which must have been barely audible above the sound of the rain from God, Seve made a surprise announcement. 'I'm not going to be captain in '99 [the original intention], for the simple reason that I want to get my own game back. Things haven't been going too well for me for the last two years, so I'd like to be playing in '99. I would like to be captain again, but maybe in Ireland or some time after that.' That's one wish that didn't happen and one that surely won't. In essence, though, Seve had quit while he was ahead. Who could say he was wrong?

'He was rewarded with the result he craved,' said Nick Faldo. 'I was happy for him. In my 20 years as a Ryder Cup player, nobody ever wanted it more.' All in all, a perfect epitaph.

Seve has had nothing further to do with the Ryder Cup in an official capacity since. That doesn't mean he has been bereft of opinions about it.

The 1999 match was at The Country Club in Brookline, just outside Boston, Massachusetts. The United States overhauled a 10–6 Saturday night European lead to win by 14½–13½. The decisive moment came in the singles between José Maria Olazábal, the reigning Masters champion, and Justin Leonard. On the 17th green, Leonard holed a 45-foot birdie putt that seemed to win the match for the United States. Half their team invaded the green, along with assorted well-wishers, to celebrate. In their excitement, they had overlooked the fact that if Chema holed his 40-footer for a matching birdie, the match would not be over. It took several minutes for calm to be restored. Olazábal's effort was commendably close, especially given all that had just gone on, but it didn't go in. The US had indeed won.

Seve had uncharacteristic sympathy for the Americans' behaviour in light of the huge fightback they had achieved. 'I'm not trying to excuse them but the same thing probably would have happened in Europe,' he said.

He was less charitable about the tactics of the European captain, Mark James. First, James had given one of his two precious wild cards to Andrew Coltart, a rookie. This had come as a complete shock to most people, who thought the experienced Bernhard Langer, who had also been close to qualifying for the team, should have been chosen instead; if not, that the place would have gone to Sweden's Robert Karlsson, who was ahead of Coltart in the points table.

'I think it was an insult to Bernhard Langer not to pick him,' said Seve, 'the way he was playing and after all he has done for European golf. And why would James pick Coltart ahead of Karlsson? What has he done more than Karlsson? And Bernhard was only two places behind Coltart in the table.'

James compounded the apparent folly of this decision by then not playing Coltart – a player he had gone out of his way to get on to his team – until the singles. He did likewise with Jarmo Sandelin and Jean van de Velde. 'It was crazy to play on Sunday with three players in the singles who had not played before – and they were rookies!' said Seve. 'Really, on Sunday morning, we were only one point ahead. Those three had no chance to win.'

To get four points ahead on Saturday night had been an amazing effort, but it had required one as well. Seve knew better than anyone, since he had been asked many times to play all five matches, that it had come at the price of most of the European team feeling exhausted and the rest ill-prepared.

The 2001 Ryder Cup took place in 2002. The catastrophic events of 9/11 meant there was no way the American team wanted to leave home shores to play at The Belfry (yes, for the fourth time). Indeed, to act out the mock battle that is the Ryder Cup would have seemed crude and wholly inappropriate set against the backdrop of what had happened in the real world less than a fortnight before.

The European captain was Sam Torrance. 'Sam asked my advice about some things,' said Seve. 'I suggested he set the course up to suit our team, obviously. He said he was going to put some new bunkers in. I asked why – that would take away the biggest advantage we have, that our players know the course so well.' Nevertheless, new or repositioned bunkers compared to the previous Ryder Cup at The Belfry, in 1993, featured on 12 of the 18 holes.

Torrance's two wild-card picks were Sergio Garcia and Jesper Parnevik. 'For the wild cards, I would have picked Garcia and Olazábal,' said Seve. 'Why? Compared to Parnevik, Olazábal is more respected by the Americans, he has won at The Belfry, he has much more Ryder Cup experience, he is a tougher competitor . . . you need any more reasons?'

In Europe's 15½–12½ victory, Parnevik played only twice, losing a fourball and halving his singles against Tiger Woods in what was, at the end, a dead match. Overall, though, since Europe won, it's hard to knock Torrance for anything.

Seve wasn't there to see it in person. He had been invited to attend as part of the 75th anniversary celebrations of the match but that didn't interest him. He was asked by Rob Bonnet of the BBC why he would not be going.

Seve: 'Nothing to do. I am not the captain. I am not the [previous] past captain.'

Bonnet: 'All the other former captains are going.'

Seve: 'You think so? I don't know.'

The latter response was obvious dissembling. What had piqued Seve was that he had not been treated with due deference. He'd been invited as if he was any old Ryder Cupper. It might not be a charming attitude but Seve knew, especially when it came to the Ryder Cup, that he deserved more.

Despite that, though, he rang Torrance's mobile while Sam was celebrating beside the 18th green on Sunday. 'Enjoy it,' Seve told him, 'because there are not many moments like the one you are living right now.' Torrance's version of their conversation in *his* autobiography (yes, yet another one) was a briefer 'Fantastic, Sam. You did a great job.' Torrance added: 'I so wanted to hold the phone up to the spectators and tell them that the great Seve Ballesteros was on the line' – a nice sentiment given that Torrance had been disappointed in 1997 that Seve had not bothered to contact him to say he wouldn't be getting a wild card. It probably never occurred to Seve that Sam might think he was in the running.

On to 2004, and Europe's hammering of the United States at Oakland Hills. The scoreline of 18½–9½ was the exact reverse of that at Walton Heath in 1981. This European team didn't have a single major champion in its ranks, although it was led by one in Bernhard Langer.

In the build-up to the match, Seve told BBC Radio 5 Live that he was disappointed not to have been invited as an official guest. 'Some people have short memories,' he told Iain Carter. 'It is a little bit sad, but what can I do?' This was a great example of Seve's posturing. It seems he wanted to go to Birmingham, Michigan, in 2004 more than he had to Birmingham, West Midlands, in 2002.

The following month, October 2004, Seve had lunch with Colin Montgomerie – who had been outstanding at Oakland Hills – and persuaded him that he should not be looking to be the captain in Ireland in 2006, as he had intimated he might. Monty would then be 43, three years older than Seve had been in 1997, but he could still make it as a player. Seve told him: 'You're a long time away from the game when you retire, so keep playing for as long as you can.'

Ian Woosnam was the captain in Ireland and Monty was once more a leading light as Europe yet again won by 18½ to 9½ points. Astonishing. It was the first time Europe had won three matches in a row. Seve was there, invited by the European Tour, to see Olazábal – back in the team after seven years – win three points out of three in this demolition job.

When Seve announced his retirement from competition in July 2007, he said, grinning: 'I think I just would like to see the Americans win the Ryder Cup again. It looks like there's only one side. There's no competition. On Sundays, it's not fair anymore.' He added: 'But that's one of the legacies I am leaving behind me, I think.' Indeed, one of several.

7. AMERICAN ANTIPATHY

Jonathan Swift (1706): 'When a true genius appears in the world, you may know him by this sign, that the dunces are all in confederacy against him.'

Severiano Ballesteros (1983): 'In the United States, I'm lucky. In Europe, I'm good.'

Aside from his (happily) unsuccessful trip to the PGA Tour qualifying school in 1975, Seve's first tournament in the United States was his Masters debut, in 1977. His second was the Greater Greensboro Open in North Carolina in late March 1978. He won it. The tournament was the week before the Masters, and this was part of his preparation for Augusta. It worked out well, but things did not get off to a smooth start; a really bumpy ride, in fact.

On the flight out from Madrid to New York, he noticed El Cordobes, the famous bullfighter of the day and the man who would hog the headlines in Spain when Seve won the 1979 Open. He was up front in first-class; Seve in the back in economy. They had been in the air for two hours when the pilot came on the tannoy to say they had a problem and the plane was going back. When they returned to Madrid, Seve spoke to his manager *du jour*, Jorge Ceballos. 'I told him I was considering not going. By the time I could get to America, it would be too late to get to the tournament.'

He was persuaded otherwise; it had taken a great deal of effort

to secure a sponsor's invitation. After a six-hour wait, he set out in
another plane bound for New York. There was a further four-hour
wait on the ground there before the connection to Greensboro. He
arrived on Monday morning, 24 hours late and exhausted.

Given that, it was no surprise that after two days of the
tournament, he was 10 shots off the lead. One shot worse and he
would have missed the cut. On the Saturday, playing in very strong
winds, Seve shot 69. That halved the gap between him and the
leaders.

On the Sunday morning, a misunderstanding over his courtesy
car – the forerunner of Baltusrol – meant he got to the course too late
to practise. No matter. He shot 66. Legend has it that as he
approached the last green, the on-course announcer, doubtless
intending this as a convivial Southern greeting, declared: 'In this
group is the tournament leader, Severiano Ballesteros from Spain.
Let's give this spic a big Olé!'

Seve's total of 282, six under par, held up despite the best efforts
of those behind him. When Jack Renner's eight-foot putt for par
slipped by the hole on the final green, he was the winner. 'I don't
know how I win the tournament,' Seve said. 'When I came here, my
game was not so good and I didn't feel confident. I try to do my best,
but never think I will win the tournament.' He was the first foreign
non-PGA Tour member to win since 1966; the fourth youngest Tour
winner ever.

The PGA Tour commissioner, Deane Beman, offered him a
tour card, enabling him to play the circuit as a full member. This
annoyed several seasoned professionals, who felt he should have to
go to the Tour school to prove he could really compete. He infuriated
the critics even more when he subsequently declined the offer – he felt
it was unfair that PGA Tour rules meant that his home tour was
designated as Spain, not the European Tour. As of right, he would
then only have been able to enter three tournaments in Europe, plus
the Open Championship.

After witnessing at first-hand Gary Player winning the Masters,
Seve accepted the invitation he got into the Tournament of

Champions at La Costa, California, as a consequence of his win at Greensboro. With a round to play, he had a five-shot lead. Seven shots back, as he had been at Augusta a week previously, was Player, who would again be the winner.

Seve posted a shocking 79 on Sunday. He double-bogeyed the 1st, drove in the water at the 5th, went out in 40 and came home in 39. It wasn't just the resentful players on the PGA Tour who would have been pleased to see Seve's game unravel. In the final pairing, his playing partner was Lee Trevino. Trevino's caddie had been on Seve's bag at Greensboro and, for by no means the last time in his career, Seve found himself at odds as to what financial arrangement had been agreed. Seve had paid him four per cent of his winnings; the caddie thought five per cent was his due. The presence of such a recent adversary throughout the final round may have helped to unsettle Seve, although you'd never get him to admit that he'd been unnerved by a caddie. What did get to him, however, were the players who consoled him when he knew they were glad to have seen him collapse. 'They pat me on the back now, but when I was leading they didn't want to talk to me,' he mused.

Some sports writers, on the other hand, loved him. In the *Los Angeles Times*, Jim Murray noted: 'He goes after a golf course like a lion at a zebra. He doesn't reason with it; he tries to throw it out of the window or hold its head under water till it stops wriggling.'

In late 1978, aware that it would help his career if accommodation could be reached with the PGA Tour for him to play more regularly in the States, Seve said: 'We are trying to arrange the whole thing with Mr Beman . . . I think it will work out alright. I'm hopeful that I can get the type of deal which will enable me to become a transatlantic golfer without tiring myself out.'

Beman had been the commissioner of the PGA Tour since 1974. Pre-Seve, pretty much all the best players in the world played on his circuit. It was *the* Tour. Gary Player, for example, didn't have to try to reconcile playing commitments in America with those in his home country of South Africa, which staged only a handful of events on its Sunshine Tour and then, it being the southern hemisphere, mostly outside the PGA Tour season. Seve had the European Tour, as well as himself, to think of.

When American golfers came over to Europe to play, they got appearance fees, which were prohibited in America. One of the aspects of his relationship with the PGA Tour that irked Seve most was that he was made to feel he was stealing from the American players by winning prize-money in their country whereas in Europe they collected fat fees simply for turning up. In the land of the free, or at least the supposed free market, Seve was astonished to find that many of his peers only wanted the market economy to operate in line with their own interests. From the American side, there was a suspicion that Seve was only interested in playing in America when he couldn't count on $100,000-plus by way of an appearance fee in Europe. That sentiment was not an accurate description of Seve's modus operandi, but it was no surprise that scepticism, and jealousy, existed in the States as to his motives.

Beman was only doing what most of his members wanted in respect of Seve. It wasn't the Nicklauses or the Millers or the Trevinos (maybe Trevino's caddie, though) who didn't want him over there. When they didn't know he was around, he'd pick up on what was being said. 'I hear several times in the locker room,' he said. 'They say, "Here comes the Spaniard to take our money".' They also found a way to rile him to his face. As if by mistake, they'd call him 'Steve' (like, per that post-1988 Open headline, *Sun* readers might.)

Those supporting Seve included Johnny Miller, the man who had beaten him at Birkdale in 1976. 'Seve has a talent that comes along every 20 years,' said Miller. 'He would make me look pretty mediocre [in record terms] if he played the PGA Tour full time. Seve's conflict is that he needs to play in the US but he wants to play at home.' Miller added, in a tough assessment: 'He has to win 25 US tournaments and he has the ability to win 10–12 majors, maybe more. But majors are not enough. He has to win those tour events and it's very difficult to win in the US.' When the maths were done at the end of his career, Seve had won six times in America – twice at Augusta, twice at Westchester, once each at Greensboro and New Orleans.

That ties the European record (as at March 2008) alongside Nick Faldo, José Maria Olazábal and Sergio Garcia, the latter two being capable of breaking it.

By 1983, the year of his second Masters victory, even the more blinkered Americans could see that Seve was an asset the PGA Tour would be better off having than being without. The manner of his victory at the Westchester Classic in New York in June had underlined his appeal. Needing a birdie four at the 18th to win, he'd hit a 3-iron to 15 feet and made the putt for an eagle. Accordingly, it was announced that with effect from the 1984 season, Europe – not just Spain – would be designated his home tour. He joined the PGA Tour as a full member, which meant he could play more in the States than when he had been relying on sponsor's invitations (none of the three major championships in America are run by the PGA Tour, so they were not an issue in any case) but it also meant he had to commit to play at least 15 tournaments on the PGA Tour each season. He had at last got his way over Beman.

It didn't take long for the realisation to kick in that this wasn't nirvana. He was mostly travelling alone with no other Spanish speakers regularly around for company. He was living in a culture with a language he could handle but was not comfortable with. It was almost impossible for him to read a newspaper, difficult to watch television or go to see a movie. His English was competent enough to cope with press conferences but it wasn't sufficiently satisfactory for him to be able to conduct a relaxed conversation with people he encountered outside a golfing environment. He found he was constantly having to explain himself, and he couldn't relax because he was having to concentrate so hard in an effort to ensure he didn't miss any nuances in the language.

'It is much easier for, say, Nick Faldo in America than it is for me,' he told me in 1985. 'Although I speak the language well enough, I can't read the papers as well as I wish, I don't understand the television as well as I would like, and I can't express myself as well as I can in Spanish. That gets very tiring because I have to think all the time.'

Ben Crenshaw, who won the Masters in 1984, Seve's first season as a full PGA Tour member, said graciously: 'Seve is the most gifted golfer in the world. He relishes playing a different shot to other people. As Bernard Darwin [the most famous British golf writer] said, it's tough playing in the other fellow's country. He has a good command of English but it's still tough for him in America.'

Seve has an almost schizophrenic attitude to playing in America, depending on the time-frame he is contemplating it from. Contemporaneously, he often thought it was a horrible experience, partly because of the attitudes of some other players towards him – a negativity that was not only fuelled by resentment of him 'stealing their money' but also by scepticism that he was lucky rather than gifted, a legacy perpetrated by the outlandish way in which he had won the 1979 Open – and partly because he found the cultural assimilation too difficult. With hindsight, on the other hand, he will frequently say it's where he should have based himself, to enjoy its better facilities and higher prize-money. In the March 2006 issue of *Golf World*, for example, he told Paul Mahoney: 'I did not compete enough in America. I would have won the USPGA Championship and the US Open to complete a Grand Slam if I had played there more. I am 100 per cent convinced of that.' Hmm, but it's not an argument anyone is going to win against him.

In his first full season as a PGA Tour member, in 1984, he finished in 52nd place on the Money List but failed to win a tournament. In 1983, doing things his way, he'd won at Augusta and at Westchester. To Seve, it was a no-brainer. He wouldn't repeat that mistake. In 1985, he played only nine times in PGA Tour events instead of the stipulated 15, won the USF&G Classic in New Orleans, won more money per event played than anyone else on the PGA Tour and finished 26th on the Money List.

Not surprisingly, Beman was none too chuffed to see the olive branch flung back at him both so rapidly and with such vehemence. After all, as far as he was concerned, it was just too bad if Seve felt isolated by the language and had trouble following the plot of *Dallas*.

(Hey, who didn't with that 'Bobby-back-from-the-Dead' series?) Seve was duly banned from playing on the PGA Tour in 1986.

The upshot of that meant he could play only in the three American major championships and defend his USF&G title in New Orleans. We've already seen what impact that may have had at the 1986 Masters. He wasn't even permitted to receive sponsor's invitations, which hurt them, too. Beman was no fool. He knew Seve would get several of those, just as Seve had anticipated he would when he declined to fulfil his obligations, and Beman was not going to allow his authority to be undermined in that fashion.

'Seve has set himself on a course of confrontation with us,' Beman declared. 'Now we have gone back to the old rules after his failure to comply with the new ones.' Just to rub it in, he had Seve's name obliterated from the Money List. As if he were on the wrong end of an Iron Curtain coup, Seve had become a non-person. *Sports Illustrated* wrote that 'the PGA Tour has told the best golfer in the world to get lost, and we agree with Ballesteros who says "It was a thoughtless decision that can only harm international golf".'

In fact, Seve later extracted some measure of revenge. In 1987, his one-year exile having been served, he was able to play the PGA Tour as a non-member. He won £305,000 from the maximum eight starts he was permitted (five tour events plus the three American majors) – again, more money per event played than anyone else – and finished 32nd on the Money List. He had come very close in the Masters, quite close in the US Open, had blown the USPGA and been runner-up in two regular tournaments.

'It was almost a great year,' he said ruefully. 'I missed three or four important putts that changed everything.' He also intimated that he'd be prepared to commit to 12 PGA Tour events per year, but that was forlorn. The rule was not going to be changed again.

In September 1987, Dan Jenkins wrote in *Golf Digest*, lamenting the lack of Seve in America: 'Beman and his policy board . . . try to ensure that every touring pro gets rich though he may not know any more about golf than how to hit a mediocre iron into a soft green, drive a courtesy car, wear a visor with a silly logo on it and smile only at people who look like they might be executives from Nabisco [the Tour's major sponsor].'

Gary McCord, now a full-time broadcaster on CBS television, was on the PGA Tour policy board when the 15-tournament minimum rule for membership was invoked. In spring 1988, he explained: 'You can't put one player above the game. Even though the Tour needs the magnetism Seve brings so bad that it's unbelievable, we can't devalue the privilege of playing for $32 million by changing a good rule.' Jack Nicklaus was among the few who felt Seve should be allowed an unlimited number of sponsor's invitations – 'I mean, have you ever heard of Seve hurting a tournament?' he asked *Sports Illustrated*, presumably rhetorically.

In 1988, Seve went even better than he had in 1987, by winning again. First, though, a hint of the sort of thing he didn't like. After Hale Irwin had been outgunned by Curtis Strange at the Memorial Tournament in May 1988, he sought consolation by claiming he had been beaten by the best golfer in the world. 'You can talk all you want to about Mr Ballesteros,' said Irwin, not Seve's biggest fan for the past nine years. 'He doesn't play over here regularly. Greg Norman does and we just saw Curtis beat him in a playoff not long ago.' Seve's (admittedly somewhat self-inflicted) enforced absence from the PGA Tour was another stick he could be beaten with.

But not among the elite. At the US Open at Brookline in June, Nicklaus was asked for his views on the topic. 'I think Greg, Seve and Sandy Lyle, coming off the Masters [which Lyle won], are probably the three strongest players that I can think of.' Strange didn't get a mention. He then beat Nick Faldo in a playoff at Brookline to win his first major.

As in 1983, Seve's 1988 PGA Tour victory came at the Westchester Classic. In 1987, he had lost this title by butchering the first playoff hole against J.C. Snead. This time he was up against Greg Norman, David Frost and Ken Green, although that was possibly thanks to the oft-maligned Vicente. His brother was his caddie this week and it was he who insisted Seve lay up with his second shot to the last, a 535-yard par-five, after his drive had landed in the rough. Seve eventually agreed, hit an 8-iron instead of the wood, and pitched on and holed his putt for a birdie.

The first extra hole, the 10th, is a shortish par-four, the green reachable with a perfect drive. Seve's almost was and his ball finished in a greenside bunker. It had a downhill lie and his stance was horrid. He'd have to stand with his right foot out of the trap. He didn't have much room to work with but the shot was a beauty; typical Seve. The ball sat down just three feet from the hole and none of the others could match his birdie three.

'We all look for the kind of pressure where you are one shot ahead or one shot behind,' enthused Seve afterwards, 'and you try hard to hang on with all the excitement. That's what competition is. [Today] is what we all are looking for. It is why we play golf.' Jack Nicklaus famously said that his ultimate kick in golf was three holes to play in a major championship, a birdie and two pars to win. So it was with Seve, still close to the peak of his powers.

'I won the Majorca Open this year,' he added. 'I was six shots ahead [playing the last hole] and I didn't have any feelings at all.' He once explained: 'I am happiest when I am in the hunt for the title. I am like the gambler. The great moment is not when the roulette wheel has finished spinning, and the gambler knows if he has won or lost. The great moment comes while the wheel is spinning, and he does not yet know the outcome. That's what I live for.'

After Seve won the Open at Lytham in July, he hoped – but did not expect – that Beman might make further overtures to him about rejoining the PGA Tour full time. But Beman was secure in the knowledge that his job was about looking after the interests of his members, who then were overwhelmingly American, rather than worrying whether he should be persuading some European golfer to join, much less alter the regulations – again! – to suit him. At the USPGA Championship, Seve ventured the notion that players and sponsors review the regulations regarding the minimum number of tournaments required to retain a tour card. If he really thought Beman would take the bait, it's a rare instance of naivety on his part.

That overwhelming emphasis on American players is much less

so today under the regime managed by Beman's successor, Tim Finchem. People used to say Beman ignored the rest of the world; they now say that Finchem, who was the prime mover behind the creation of the World Golf Championship tournaments, wants to run it. But this is now; that was then. In November 1989, the PGA Tour did consider a proposal that golfers would only have to play a minimum of 12 tournaments, rather than 15, to be eligible for membership. It didn't get considered for long.

I think Seve's intermittently voiced regrets about not playing more in America were coloured by his deteriorating relationship with the European Tour. The fact is that when Seve was making his career choices, he was unhappy with the prospect of being in America for most of the year. Europe was the best option for him as well as for the European Tour. However, given the way the PGA Tour has become more amenable in its outlook towards international golfers since Finchem replaced Beman in 1994, history may tend to show it was simply unfortunate that Seve – the most international of golfers – was ahead of his time.

8. . . . AND NOT WHOLLY HARMONIOUS AT HOME

Samuel Butler: 'Genius . . . has been defined as a supreme capacity for taking trouble . . . It might be more fitly described as a supreme capacity for getting its possessors into pains of all kinds, and keeping them therein so long as the genius remains.'

It's like a multiple-choice question on *Who Wants to be a Millionaire?* – which of these four phrases is the most apposite:

A/ Seve Ballesteros and the European Tour

B/ Seve Ballesteros on the European Tour

C/ Seve Ballesteros with the European Tour

D/ Seve Ballesteros versus the European Tour

The answer could be any of them but you'll probably have guessed that we're going for D.

When Seve took up golf, he did it because he loved the game. By the late 1970s, he had some idea of his value to the nascent European Tour. And he wanted to be a millionaire.

The subject of appearance fees – the payment of money to a golfer as an inducement for him to play in a tournament – as a divisive topic has already been raised here in connection with Seve's omission from the 1981 Ryder Cup team. As a phenomenon, it was nothing new. In one guise or another, appearance money is as old as the professional game itself. Being paid for taking part in exhibitions, which is how they earned money before there were tournaments, is what the professional golfers of Scotland would do in the 1800s, before there was such a thing as the Open Championship. That was only begun in 1860 after the death of Allan Robertson. In 1858, he had gone round the Old Course at St Andrews in 79. It was the first time anyone had broken 80. Robertson was the best player in Scotland – which was the same thing as being the best player in the world – and when he died of hepatitis in 1859, one R&A member was moved to say: 'They may shut up their shops and toll their bells, for the greatest among them is gone.' The Open was inaugurated to establish who was the best player now Robertson was no more.

Just over a century later, with tournament golf now part of the sporting culture, Tony Jacklin started to be paid appearance money in Europe after he won the Open in 1969 and the US Open within a further 11 months. By the mid-1970s, the rule was that European Tour members were eligible to receive appearance money if they had won at least one of the Open, the Masters or US Open (not the USPGA Championship, a snub for the garish blazers of the PGA of America) or if they had topped the Order of Merit the previous season. Non-members were able to get as much as they could command.

Seve was therefore eligible for appearance money beginning in 1977 – he had topped the Order of Merit in 1976 – and he would never lose the right to ask for it under the regulations that pertained at the close of the 1970s.

However, at the turn of the next decade, the European Tour announced that members could receive no more than $10,000 by way of what were euphemistically called 'expenses'. This was a fraction of what Seve might be able to command by way of an appearance fee but the Tour was emphatic. Ken Schofield, its executive director, wrote to Seve in early 1981, saying 'no one player can, from this day forward, expect to clear $250,000 in appearance fees before teeing off on the European Tour'.

At this time Seve was, with Jacklin no longer a serious

competitor, the only European golfer with a major championship to his name – two, in fact. The rules had originally been implemented to reward Jacklin – i.e. to keep him from playing all his golf in America. It seemed to Seve, seldom reluctant to embrace a conspiracy theory if he might be on the wrong end of it, that the regulations were being amended to punish him. What compounded his outrage was that non-Europeans could try to charge whatever they liked, even though by this time Seve was the biggest attraction in world golf so far as European tournament sponsors and promoters were concerned.

'I never said "No pay, no play." My attitude was let's leave it to the sponsors,' he said. 'If they want to pay, that's fine. If they don't want to pay, then that's OK, too. But I didn't see a reason why there should be a rule to stop the payment of appearance money. And why should the Americans be paid and not me? I was as much or even more valuable to the Tour than the American players were. It was a very unfair situation.'

Looked at from one perspective (OK, from Seve's), this now meant that tournaments in Europe could save money on Seve, because of the financial limit imposed by the rules, and use what was effectively surplus money in that part of their budgets either to pay more money to non-Europeans or pay for more of them. Either way, he was not happy. And with good cause.

In 190 tournaments in the 15 years from 1976–90, Seve missed just eight cuts in Europe. During that period, he won 46 times. He seldom failed to give great value for money. Conversely, it was not unknown, more than once, for an American golfer to come over to Europe with his wife, get his appearance fee and then miss the cut. The disappointment of the unhappy couple would sometimes be seen to have been assuaged when it was found out they'd earlier booked into a hotel in Paris or Rome or Madrid (insert as applicable) for the weekend.

With Seve, you got what you were paying for – a thoroughly committed competitor, the most thrilling draw in the game, the near nailed-on certainty that he'd be around on the weekend and the great probability that he'd be in contention come Sunday. To his way of thinking, all he wanted was his due, his market rate, to enable him to maximise his earnings while he was at the peak of his game. 'I was the one carrying the Tour on my shoulders,' he said, 'all the hospitality, the promotion of the European Tour.'

In his marvellous book, *Brilliant Orange*, about the eternally enigmatic nature of Dutch football, David Winner quotes the country's greatest-ever footballer, Johan Cruyff, saying: 'When my career ends, I cannot go to the baker and say: "I am Johan Cruyff – give me some bread."' Thus it was with Seve, and so it was that, frustrated and annoyed to distraction, he 'provisionally' resigned from the European Tour in April 1981. (He treated all tours alike; it didn't have to be an American tour for him to resign from it.) Although this decision was born of a culmination of factors, the actual trigger for it was the assumption that he would not be granted a release from the Madrid and Italian Opens to go to play in Japan. This was the step that led to him being left out of the Ryder Cup team.

As far as Seve was concerned, there was a significant principle involved in this. As far as the Tour was concerned, his significant principle was principally money. The dispute grew increasingly rancorous. On 25 June, Seve sent the following letter to some friends and associates, copying it to Schofield and Beman, his chum across the Atlantic.

The past few months have been both difficult and confusing. Many things have been said about me and until this time I have made no statement in my defence. It is my sincere hope that this letter will clarify all your questions and concerns and close the book on any further speculation . . .

. . . Having read in the press that I would be fined and/or suspended should I choose to play the Japanese events, and wishing to avoid any problems, the ETPD was contacted a third time and advised of my plans and respectfully requested to approve my release request. When no response was received, a further communication '. . .

provisionally withdrawing my ETPD membership' was sent.
Had the ETPD chosen to approve my request, I would have
returned to Europe and signed my ETPD membership form
and the issue would have been closed. Instead they chose
not only to leave my request unanswered but to issue a
release which was further damaging to my career and was
written in the press 'Ballesteros stripped of ETPD membership and Ryder Cup standing'. This was totally untrue. I was
not even an ETPD member [by then]; I did, however, make
every effort to conform to regulations which were unclear
and changing daily so as not to cause the ETPD any
embarrassment or loss of stature. These efforts were met with
a series of new regulations aimed directly at me. I was very
disappointed.

There are two issues which are very distinct and separate,
although many have attempted to mingle them together. I feel
I have responded to the first issue: the question of a release for
my Japan trip. I would now like to respond to the matter of
guarantees on the ETPD Tour.

I have been repeatedly quoted as saying 'golf owes me a
living'. I have devoted my life to golf since I was nine years
old, forsaking my youth and teen years. While I believe my
success and achievements are ample reward for this
dedication, I want it clear that I was in reality only responding
to an ITV interviewer's question: 'Do you think golf owes you
a living?' I responded: 'I think golf owes me something . . . or
maybe we're even?'

The above was an interview with the late Brian Moore on London
Weekend Television in April 1981, just before Seve's defence of the
Masters. Dudley Doust's book quotes this relevant excerpt from the
transcript.

BM: May I put it to you then, that I think a lot of people will
be saying at this moment, that golf has given you a lot, maybe

you should give golf something back by not requiring appearance money.

SB: Do you know how much I give to golf? I start since I was nine, and since then I live until I am now 23, that way all for golf. You think that is not enough? I think it is enough.

BM: Your life?

SB: My life, and the life is more important than anything else, right, so golf owes me something, or maybe . . . but I don't owe anything to golf. You agree with that?

BM: I agree with that. How do you feel finally on the money side? If appearance money were abolished, how would you react to that?

SB: What do you mean?

BM: If appearance money was ruled out.

SB: Appearance money will never disappear. Will never disappear. How can you . . . let me explain to you. How can you bring Hale Irwin, Tom Watson, Lee Trevino from America to play in Europe if they have three times more prize-money in America? How will they come to play in Europe and fly 10–15 hours?

As you will note, Seve's summation of this in his letter was a little, as Alan Clark once said, 'economical with the actualité'.

Back to the letter . . .

The only problem I have with the ETPD regulations relating to sponsors' guarantees is that they have changed without notice and appeared to be aimed directly at excluding me. In the past, specific regulations were passed to *include* British pro's who have had exceptional successes. I would rather not think that the ETPD action is related to the fact that I am Spanish. However, rational reasons for such behaviour are difficult to find. I did not invent guarantee money – in fact, it is the invention of the ETPD and the sponsors. As far as I'm concerned, guarantee money is unimportant to me; it is merely an indication from the sponsors of their recognition of my achievements and my value to their event.

I have played in many ETPD events for minimal expenses or little or no guarantee. However, I feel it is unfair for sponsors to pay large fees to foreign players while expecting ETPD pro's who have equal or better credentials to play for expenses.

The past six months have been very confused by numerous changes in the ETPD regulations affecting me alone. Following each of my major victories I chose to remain loyal to the European Tour. This has not been the case with most ETPD players who have achieved any degree of success.

Having been the object of apparent intentional efforts to portray me as disloyal, mercenary, and then further being discriminated against in specific ETPD regulations and finally to be *excluded* from the ETPD Order of Merit while other non-members were included, I can only say that it has hurt my feelings very much. Where I once felt very much at home, recent actions by some have made me feel very uncomfortable.

At the present time I am not a member of any recognised tour organisation. The remainder of this year I plan to participate in from four to six European events and an additional three US PGA Tour events, and three to five tournaments in Japan, Australia and possibly Latin America or South America. This, together with the events I have already played, is certainly a full schedule. As a member of no golf tour and having won major events in five continents, I feel I can best serve golf and my own career objectives by participating on the international circuit. It is therefore my decision not to accept membership in any tour organisation for the remainder of this year. While I greatly regret that this will exclude me from the Ryder Cup, I see no other alternative.

I would like to thank those members of the press, associates and sponsors who have stood by me during this difficult period and have not responded or reacted to the rumours and innuendos which have been so hurting. I have received great encouragement from your support.

As far as I am concerned, the subject is closed. While I will be pleased to discuss any other subjects with any members of the press, I will not have any further comment on those matters covered in this letter. The responsibility is now yours to set the record straight. I have no ill feelings for the ETPD or the sponsors who have been involved; in fact, I have great admiration for their efforts to build golf in Europe. While I feel a great injustice has been done, I feel it was simply the result of growing pains in developing and sophisticating the ETPD regulations. I sincerely hope the final outcome is a universally applicable set of regulations which will serve the best interests of all members, even those whose achievements deserve special consideration.

I am encouraged by my recent play and trust that with your help this matter can now be put behind us and that the second half of 1981 can be an opportunity for growth and achievement.

Sincerely
Severiano Ballesteros

It will be apparent that an adviser's hand was behind the drafting but that doesn't negate the fact that Seve felt deeply aggrieved at the way he had been and was being treated. Indeed, over 20 years later they were part of the picture he saw which caused him to say the Tour was 'nearly like a Mafia'.

The outcome back then was that come August 1981, the only tournaments Seve had played in Europe all season were the Open Championship and the French and Scandinavian Opens. The latter two had been able to pay him a fee in line with his demands because those deals had been signed before 1981. But this was a battle he couldn't win, not least because he had used up his allocation of exemptions into PGA Tour events. On 11 August, he rejoined the European Tour. On 23 August, as we have seen, he learned that still wasn't enough to get him a wild-card place on the Ryder Cup team.

Of course, what he told Brian Moore was absolutely correct. 'Appearance money will never disappear.' The European Tour has made repeated efforts to do something about it, but really it's always been an obfuscation. Players can legitimately get the extra by doing a clinic, attending a dinner, making a speech. On the PGA Tour, that's how they have long got round the problem and continue to do. In Europe, this strategy reached its zenith (nadir?) when for a few years the Tour ran an exhibition event called the Champions' Challenge in the week of its own flagship tournament, the Volvo PGA Championship (now the BMW Championship). Featuring the top names only, appearance fees were paid according to what the champion in question had won. That went down better with the recipients than it did with some other tournament promoters, tired of being berated by the Tour for paying appearance money themselves.

In later years, Seve had a rather nifty loophole he could exploit himself. When his company, Amen Corner, promoter of the Spanish Open, paid him appearance money for playing in the tournament (oops, sorry, remunerated him for playing in a shoot-out and attending a cocktail party), he would have been eligible to take a dividend as well.

Ultimately, in what is a capitalist pursuit, playing an individual sport for prize-money, it is foolish to try to tell companies what to do with their money. No amount of hectoring by the Tour, insisting that a tournament budget has to be invested in the purse rather than some of it being siphoned off into appearance fees, is going to work. People can always take their money elsewhere, like tennis.

(In light of the PGA Tour's self-righteous abhorrence of appearance money, it was hilarious to learn that at the Ford Championship in March 2005, IMG was, with the PGA Tour's knowledge, offering to sponsors the availability of such clients as Vijay Singh, Ernie Els, Retief Goosen and Sergio Garcia to play in Monday outings for fees ranging from $50,000–$200,000 apiece, with the promise that 'these professionals will look favourably upon staying for the tournament'. If that's not appearance money . . . well, the PGA Tour probably uses a fairly thin thesaurus.)

While all this was going on in the 1980s, it was not as if the sponsors' interests coincided. They had no incentive to band together in support of the Tour's wishes. If you were running the Irish Open, your concern was to get the best field you could at the best price. At the time, that meant getting Seve. He couldn't play every week, which meant his participation had to come at a premium – or it would have done had the Tour not moved the fiscal goalposts.

Seve was magnificently defiant on this subject in 1985. 'Everybody was against me then and I still think everybody was wrong and I was right. I believe that since tournament sponsors are the ones who put up the money, they can do what they want. They can choose to pay top players whatever they wish.'

Schofield played his hand to the hilt and, in the short term at least, he could feel vindicated. The prodigal son returned to the fold. However, if instead Seve had opted to join the PGA Tour and play in America full time, and had later stuck to his guns and not bowed to the entreaties of Tony Jacklin to give the Ryder Cup another chance, then both the European Tour and the Ryder Cup would certainly have fared differently, and to the detriment of both, throughout the remainder of the 1980s, a decade which saw prize-money in Europe rise more than six fold.

While Schofield & Co would rightly claim some credit, few would dispute the identity of the man primarily responsible for that growth. An unequivocal Seve told John Huggan in *Golf Digest* in 2000: 'My success then was not really promoted to the advantage of the European Tour. Not as much as they should have, anyway . . . [but] the European Tour would not be as big as it is today if not for me. I'm not trying to give myself all the credit. I'm just trying to be realistic and say what happened. I could have gone to the US very easily. The money there was five times more. But I stayed in Europe.'

What stuck out for Seve in all of this was his isolation. It would be a few years yet before Messrs Langer, Lyle, Faldo and Woosnam would be in a position of similar financial bargaining power as Seve was then, as the undisputed Master of his Universe. Therefore, they weren't there, right behind him in the trenches. Within a few years, this would alter – hugely.

Nick Faldo told me in 2004: 'Appearance money was a big issue way back [in the mid-1980s]. It would burn some guys to think that I was getting bloody £100,000 or whatever – I got an awful lot of money in that era – simply for teeing it up. [So much for Schofield's dictum.] In some tournaments, I think I was getting pretty much the first prize for teeing it up. No wonder they felt cheesed. But it's very simple. If you want it, join the club. Go and hit a million balls and get in there and compete. It's very competitive, our sport.'

And at that time, Seve was peerless in Europe. He could comfortably clear in excess of £750,000 a year in appearance money, three times what anyone was making in official prize-money. Not until Seve won just over £500,000 in winnings in 1986 did anyone break the half-million pound barrier. At some continental tournaments, he might get £175,000 by way of an appearance fee. He'd play for less in Spain, and also in the UK and Ireland, the former because it was home and the latter because he loved the enthusiasm and support of the galleries in those countries. In those cases, there was incentive beyond money. As for why the sponsors paid so much for him, in Britain and Ireland he brought more people through the gate, increasing revenues; on the continent, where actually selling tickets has never been as easy, he aroused media interest, without which the sponsors might find coverage of their tournament relegated to the small print in the press and no one near a television screen.

Faldo added: 'Without appearance money in Europe, we [he meant himself, Seve, Langer, Lyle and Woosnam] would have all gone to America full-time. It was triple the prize-money. Appearance money saved the Tour.' In other words, the Tour's star players felt the European Tour didn't understand the deal.

How the world has changed. It may not be strictly true to say that the European Tour now embraces the payment of appearance money, but the words 'tacit approval' come to mind. Events like the inaugural Abu Dhabi Golf Championship in January 2006, with a purse of a comparatively meagre $2 million, wouldn't have been on the schedule at all if the sponsors weren't able to shell out shedloads of money in appearance fees to lure Vijay Singh, Sergio Garcia and Chris DiMarco from the riches and comforts of the PGA Tour.

While Seve was damned for demanding appearance money, he was also condemned when he didn't play. In 1987, he declined to defend three titles he had won the previous season – the French and Irish Opens and the Dunhill Masters. The promoters of the first two – Lionel Provost and Joe Flanagan, respectively – were relatively sanguine about the situation, feeling that Seve had supported them well in the past and no doubt would in future, but IMG, which ran the Dunhill, was upset to the point of being in denial about his non-participation. A day or so after the news leaked out, they admitted Seve would not be there and began the process of redesigning their promotional materials without his image. Bernhard Langer, an IMG client, was among those who chastised Seve – 'There is an unwritten rule that you should always defend titles' – but Seve was adamant.

'I will play less in order to prolong my career. I have decided to play no more than three events in succession.' What's more, of course, Seve won so many titles in the 1980s that it was almost inevitable that changes in either his or the tournaments' schedules would mean it was not practicable to expect him to make a defence every time – although doing that three times in one season did seem to be rather over-egging it.

Golf tour politics can be a labyrinthine business. A tedious one, too – especially if you're involved in it. The players are represented on committees which help to shape the development of the circuit, but it is self-evident that a golfer is more likely to be worried about his swing or his putting stroke than whether the players' hotel in Berlin the week after next is going to be up to standard. As Tiger Woods said of being involved on the PGA Tour Policy Board: 'Thing is, about us having more input, it's tough enough to play out here, besides getting involved in issues. That's two jobs.'

Seve has at times paid the penalty for not shirking the battle. He told me in 1997: 'The problem seems to me that over the last 20 years, it is always me who makes the first step. So all the bullets get fired at me. Right now, there are many people who say things but they always stay in the background. In one way it is good to say what you think but, on the other hand, people read what you say and that makes some people unhappy.'

It follows that with the players being more preoccupied with their golf, a great deal of trust and reliance is placed on what the tour officials do on their behalf. In some respects, and this does not only apply in Europe, the whole set-up is weird. Ask anyone for whose benefit the tours are run and the answer you are most likely to get would be 'the players'. Other words mentioned may be 'sponsors' and 'fans' but players would be the first word you would expect to get. But the players are transitory. They qualify for the tours, they have their careers, then they do something else, which may involve playing a senior tour once they have reached 50. But the process is essentially a matter of 10 years or less in most cases, up to 15 or maybe even more for the exceptional, such as Europe's Famous 5.

Ken Schofield, on the other hand, was chief executive of the European Tour for 30 years, from 1975–2004, until he handed the reins over to his erstwhile deputy, George O'Grady, in 2005. The staff at the Tour's Wentworth headquarters in Surrey numbers more than 120, employees who not only draw salaries amounting to around £7 million in total but also have pensions. It's when the rank-and-file tour players board their flights to Malaga and see some tour staff turning left into club class – obviously, they're on expenses, too – while they are herded into zoo-class that a question gets asked. 'Just who is working for whom here?'

Among the more exalted tour players, those who use private jets, such as Seve did, there is a different perspective on this, but nevertheless a heartfelt one. Why is it that the players are regarded as free agents when it suits the tours (i.e. they get no salaries, pensions, etc.) but as contracted individuals when *that* suits the tours (i.e. players have to play a minimum number of events per year in order to maintain membership of a tour and they can't play elsewhere without getting permission)?

Retief Goosen, the South African who has won two US Opens (2001 & 2004) and twice topped the European Order of Merit (2001–02), told *Golf World* in America in late 2004: 'When I play over here, I have to get releases from there [Europe]. When I play in Europe, I have to get releases from here.' Tiger Woods had told the same publication in March 2002: 'It's our tour? When I hear that, it makes me chuckle. If we're so-called independent contractors, why do we have to play a certain number of tournaments? Why do we need releases to play elsewhere?'

Dissatisfaction with the civil-servant class is the lot of many employees around the world, who tend to think they are doing the real work while a bunch of parasites get rich off their efforts. Most pro golfers have not been in Seve's class in terms of income – he was the first player to reach £1 million, £2 million and £3 million in career earnings on the European Tour, and his prize winnings will pale in comparison with what he could make away from the golf course – and they perhaps feel such bitterness more keenly than the elite of the Tour. But not necessarily more keenly than Seve.

In July 1994, Seve played an exhibition match at the newly opened London Club in Kent with Jack Nicklaus, who had designed the main course there. On the subsequent flight to Scotland for the Open at Turnberry, Seve expressed his dismay at the way Schofield had done a poor job for the European Tour, failing to exploit the opportunities the Famous 5 had created and being in too close a relationship with IMG, the biggest single player in the sports marketing business. Over a decade later, his views hadn't mellowed. Indeed, hardly a shock, they had become more strident. In March 2006, he told *Golf World*: 'I think Ken was really bad for the Tour. Ken never listened to the top people. He listened to the players at the bottom. He divided the players to win. He did the minimum to develop golf in Europe.'

Back in September 1996, Seve had instigated the calling of a players' meeting at the Trophée Lancôme in France. The catalyst for this was the appalling state of the greens during the British Masters at

Collingtree a fortnight before. The following week, the Tour had been at Crans-sur-Sierre in Switzerland for the European Masters. Schofield and his colleagues went into damage-limitation mode. The boss admitted that 'Collingtree was a disaster' but he was frustrated in his attempt to meet with the player he was most eager to talk to. 'My efforts to see Severiano did not meet with success,' he said.

At the Lancôme event the prospect of a clandestine-inspired mutiny alarmed the Tour's hierarchy sufficiently enough for Bernard Gallacher to tell the press that such 'cloak-and-dagger' meetings were damaging to the Tour and any complaints should go through official channels. Seve was later reported by the *Daily Mail* to have hinted to a couple of members of the press at Collingtree that 'It is time for revolution'.

In the January 1997 issue of *Golf Digest*, it was written of Schofield that 'he has said privately that Seve Ballesteros is out to get him'. Asked about the veracity of this, Schofield told me: 'It insults both of us.' Whether true or not, the fact was that Europe was heading into a Ryder Cup year with its captain and executive director barely on speaking terms.

At the Overseas Players' Dinner at the Masters that April, Seve watched Schofield spending the evening schmoozing people with a regularly replenished glass of red wine while Tim Finchem worked the room with the well-honed political finesse that indicated his Washington legal background. Seve was not amused – nor amazed. It made him more determined to do more about the way the Tour was run.

We shall get to that in a moment. First, however (although he also brought this into his disputes with the Tour), he wanted to establish his own legacy on the Tour which he had played such a crucial role in bringing along.

In the wake of Europe losing the 1999 Ryder Cup to the United States in Boston, Seve decided the timing was right to institute a new event on the European Tour calendar – a match involving the Continent of Europe versus Great Britain & Ireland. This had been the format of the old Hennessy Cup, the event in which Seve had driven the 10th green at The Belfry in his match against Nick Faldo in 1978, but that was no longer part of the schedule. Seve would revive it under the name 'The Seve Trophy', a biennial match between 10-man teams to be played in non-Ryder Cup years. Well, there'd be no doubt as to who was behind it.

In January 2000, I was in Orlando for the annual PGA Merchandise Show, the biggest trade fair in golf. Also present was John Simpson, who had been Nick Faldo's long-time manager, first with IMG and then on his own. He told me that, at very short notice, Seve was looking to get this new event under way that spring. Seve had asked Nick to be the GB&I captain. Simpson hinted that Faldo had declined because of the late notice, although there may have been a question of ego and also the matter of money. Faldo told me in 2004: '[The captaincy] was talked about. I don't know what happened; I don't know who cocked that one up. I was told by John Simpson that it was going to be me and Seve as captains, but it never happened. John was dealing with my affairs at the time. I don't know what he over-negotiated on that one.' (Though Faldo would be the GB&I captain in 2007.)

With Faldo out, Colin Montgomerie was in. The first match was played at Sunningdale, near Wentworth, Surrey, in April 2000. Rain came close to ruining the week but the event climaxed with a memorable day for Seve. The format called for the opposing captains to face each other at the top of the singles draw on Sunday. This put Seve, world ranking No. 590 and no tournament wins for the last five years, against Monty, world ranking No. 3 and winner of the last seven Orders of Merit. Seve beat him 2&1, leading his team to a one-point victory. His one point. He even played good golf, being three under par when he closed it out.

'I have to be honest with you,' said Monty. 'This was a point we felt was secure.' One of his team, Lee Westwood, had this to say. 'For a long time the gallery didn't seem to know who they wanted to win. Seve is loved around the world and he has such a strong fan base here. In fact, if I were in that crowd, I'd be cheering for him.'

The 2002 match was at Druids Glen in Ireland. In the fourballs with José Maria Olazábal, against Padraig Harrington and Paul McGinley, Seve had been pretty much out of things and out of sorts until he birdied the 14th and 16th and then holed a 60-foot bunker shot to win the match on the 17th. 'Of all the matches José Maria and I have played, I think it was the best of all time,' he lied.

The only other match he trusted himself to play in was the one he couldn't duck, the top singles against Monty. Again, even more against the odds than at Sunningdale, Seve won. Monty shot an approximate 73 and contrived to lose to a 78. That's matchplay, folks. In the *Guardian*, David Davies noted: 'Seve sallied forth as he always has done, slashing and burning, hitting more horrendous shots in one round than Montgomerie is liable to hit in a season . . . he also hit so many miraculous recoveries, solved so many insoluble solutions, that the thoughts of deals with the devil occurred.'

It was reckoned that Seve received three free drops, had been compelled to hit two shots left-handed, had – due to rebounds from wayward drives – twice failed to reach the ladies' tee, and had to chop out sideways or backwards from the undergrowth three times. He hit one fairway and had 26 putts. He beat Monty on the 18th – 'I was a little bit lucky to win' – but GB&I won the overall match.

'It was amateur hour, to be honest,' said Montgomerie. 'But Seve is magical. Just when you think you're going to win a hole, you lose it. I've never seen anything like that; it was quite unbelievable. Seve is remarkable.' He'd done to Montgomerie what he'd threatened to do to Lehman in the 1995 Ryder Cup.

Thomas Bjorn had been in the match behind. '[Darren Clarke and I] watched them all day. That's Seve for you. Every single young player could learn something just from his hatred of losing. Every time we looked up, Monty was in the middle of the fairway, Seve was somewhere else, and then we would see him halving and winning all those holes. It must be horrifying to play against.'

The next Seve Trophy took place in November 2003 at El Saler in Spain, having been shifted forwards 12 months because of the post-9/11 Ryder Cup switch. The continentals lost this one by 15–13, which could unfortunately be put down to Seve. This time he played in three of the four pairings matches, losing the lot, and in the singles, again against Colin Montgomerie, he was 2 up after seven holes and then lost the next seven, playing them in six over par, to lose the match by 5&4.

By 2005, some players on his team no longer wanted him to play, feeling it devalued the event. One player anonymously told the *Daily Mail*: 'What's the point of playing, of taking it seriously, when we're two points down before we even start?' That is, assuming Seve only played twice. Seve was therefore a non-playing captain at the Wynyard Club near Newcastle, even though this was less than a month before what would be his first tournament appearance for two years. Olazábal was the obvious candidate to step into his spikes.

Great Britain & Ireland won again, although the occasion was further marred for Seve by an unscrupulous tabloid twist put on his press conference comments about modern-day players, which meant he was branded as having said that he did not respect the competitors in his tournament and that only Tiger Woods of the contemporary generation impressed him. So hurt was he by this treatment that he signed a letter to every competitor, explaining what he had said and how it had been misinterpreted. This was unusual in that the British press has generally been generous to Seve for 30 years. He wouldn't say the same for the European Tour, not least because the 2007 Seve Trophy in Ireland was generally dogged by an air of ennui that must make its future uncertain. Players withdrew like it was being staged in Baghdad, and spectators were almost non-existent on the first day. As Derek Lawrenson put it in the *Daily Mail*: 'The European Tour want to be seen to be doing something to honour their greatest ambassador. But, perhaps bruised by all the wars they have had with Seve Ballesteros in the past, they don't have the inclination to plough serious muscle into it.'

In March 1997, around the time that Seve and Ken Schofield were hardly talking to each other, Seve told me: 'I think it is time for other people to speak for everybody else. I think it's about time I stayed back a bit more.' Wise words, perhaps, but ones he chose not to heed.

In 2000, the European Tour had to deal with the 'Gang of Four' – not an attempted oriental coup (coincidentally, Mao Tse-Tung died in 1976, the same year that Seve rose) but a desire by four of Europe's most eminent golfers to examine the way the European Tour was conducting its business. The four were Nick Faldo, Bernhard Langer, José Maria Olazábal and, of course, Seve Ballesteros.

On 27 September, the four men wrote to Neil Coles, chairman of the European Tour (and Seve's old pal from the 1981 Ryder Cup selection committee), asking for 'permission to conduct a financial and legal audit' of the Tour for the years 1995–2000. They added that they 'would respect the confidentiality of all information made available to us'. They would also pay for the audit. As the winners of 15 major championships between them, and countless money by way of other tournaments and endorsements, they could afford the fees.

The Tour was not happy at the suggestion of possible malpractice inherent in the request, even though Olazábal insisted they simply wanted to look at the books. 'We just want to see where the money is going and where it has been spent,' he said. Told that they required the signatures of 10 per cent of the Tour's membership in order to serve notice on the Tour that a meeting be called to vote on their proposal, the advisers of the Four persuaded 53 other players at the Volvo Masters to sign a petition to that effect. Colin Montgomerie's signature was the most notable absentee; Sergio Garcia was among the most vocal of the backers. 'In America they tell us what they are doing, but here we don't know anything.'

Among the areas of concern was the fact that in 1999, PGA European Tour Productions – a 50/50 joint venture between the Tour and Trans World International (TWI), a wholly-owned subsidiary of Mark McCormack's IMG – made a pre-tax profit of only £50,000 on a turnover of nearly £16 million from producing and distributing television programmes featuring the European Tour. One didn't need to be a financial wizard to figure this might be down to a sensible allocation of management fees that legitimately kept most of the money away from the Inland Revenue, but as Garcia said, 'we want to know where the money has gone'.

On 30 November, the Tour, inevitably reluctant to accede to this request, made counter-proposals which in part presented the request of the Four as an attempt to gain access to information that would be denied to other players. Under the Tour's control, it proposed, an audit would be undertaken at its direction, not that of the Four, although that meant the whole Tour – i.e. all the players – would have to foot the bill. A meeting and vote would be held at Wentworth on 21 December.

I was with Seve in Spain that December, and he was convinced the Four would prevail. 'How can the players not back us?' he said. Surely they would go for the greater independence of the Four's more comprehensive audit than have the Tour effectively investigate itself? Within 10 days, they hadn't.

Perhaps the biggest surprise was that Seve didn't bother to attend the meeting (maybe he had indeed decided to apply that philosophy of 'I think it's about time I stayed back a bit more') but Olazábal made the flight from Spain; Faldo the three-mile drive from home. It was a hopeless cause.

'We were totally outmanoeuvred,' said Faldo. 'Totally. It was bizarre. Ollie and I went to the meeting and they'd already had the vote. How the Tour reacted was amazing. We had wanted an audit on a few areas for a bit of transparency. Simple as that. But they put together a team of guys to call around the players. Basically, they trashed us and the vote was done. They had the names and numbers [of the players], we only had the names. So we go to the meeting and they're sat on the podium up there, knowing the vote was 3 to 1 against us and we were wasting our time. As I walked out the door, I just thought "Fine, forget that one." Those people had totally got hold of the wrong end of the stick. I was thinking of the Nick Doughertys of the Tour. I've had 25 years on the Tour and look what we've done with the Ryder Cup. The players have given the Tour the backbone to go out and sell, marketing-wise. I wanted to make sure that for the next generation, all our work was going to bear fruit.'

From Spain, Seve said: 'I was very surprised at the vote. It is difficult to understand that over 50 players signed the petition and then changed their minds. What we did was try to help everybody.'

Ultimately, Schofield himself saw some benefit in the exercise. The original contract under which Tour Productions had been set up was effectively unbreakable by the Tour (it may even have been illegal under European Union law) but the changes made as a consequence of the audit by Arthur Andersen led to the Tour having the right, under specified circumstances and with three years notice, to terminate the deal. In early 2004, Schofield said: 'When you have a third party [the Andersen Report] saying this deal has been here since 1986 and it could go on and on, and don't you think there should be something to deal with the eventuality that the people involved might change, then that adds an impetus for change.' Maybe he should have sent Seve & Co a thank-you note. But then again, in light of other goings-on, that was never going to happen.

The genesis for Seve's 'nearly like a Mafia' quote – which did him possibly irreparable harm, not so much when it occurred as by its ramifications – was at the Madeira Island Open in March 2003. Seve was returning to competitive golf after a six-month sabbatical. After rounds of 76–75, seven over par, it seemed likely he would miss the cut, but that wasn't what made him incandescent. He accused the tournament administrator who had been timing his group of failing to take account of the difficulties his threeball had encountered with the strong winds, as if they had been playing in a microclimate all of their own. When the official said he didn't care, Seve retorted: 'That was a very rude way to answer a professional like myself who has been playing this game for 30 years. I am the only star here this week who has won a major. For the people of Madeira, it is important I play well and make the cut.' So there.

The tournament director, José Maria Zamora, backed his official and said that Seve's version of events was incorrect. In other words, he accused Seve of lying.

'My only comment would be that Seve's group finished 27

minutes behind the group in front,' said Zamora. 'If we take off 10 minutes between matches, he has finished 17 minutes out of position.' Seve confronted Zamora in the car park with a finger-stabbing display of annoyance, which mostly served to turn memories of the Car Park Champ 1979 into the Car Park Chump of 2003. Surprisingly, Seve did made the cut, which must have thrilled the local populace, but he could do no better than 71–76 on the weekend. His total of 298 beat his nephew Raul, Baldomero's son, by three.

By this stage of his career, although he disputed it, Seve was a slow player. It didn't help that he was unwillingly hitting the ball more frequently, and the demons that occasionally infested his mind and regularly his swing were of no assistance either, but that was the fact. In the first round of the Masters that April, Seve's threeball had fallen two holes behind Sandy Lyle, Tommy Aaron and Charles Coody – the no-hoper grouping – after just five holes. And Seve wasn't the quick guy in his three.

Seve next teed up in Europe on 1 May, in the Italian Open at Gardagolf Country Club near Brescia. As in Madeira, he just made the cut. In the third round, a minor form of hell broke loose. Seve was penalised a shot for slow play. He refused to accept the penalty, which would have meant adding a shot to his score, and so was disqualified for signing an incorrect scorecard. 'Ballesteros and Gregory Havret were found to be approximately 12 minutes out of position after the 5th hole,' said the chief referee, John Paramor. 'On the 14th tee, Seve was allowed [under the regulations] 50 seconds to hit the tee shot but took 64 seconds. On the 16th tee, where he was permitted 40 seconds, he took 51 seconds. I informed him after both those shots that each was a bad time.'

The elements of Seve's defence included the fact that Havret had to go back to play a second tee shot at the 2nd, that he lost a ball himself on the 10th (the only time they held up the group behind) and on the 17th he had to replace his ball. Those points, however accurate, can only have a bearing regarding him being out of position on the course on the 5th hole (Paramor had arrived on the 4th), that being due to Havret replaying his drive. But Seve's sense of injustice was fuelled beyond control with the realisation he had been penalised even though he and Havret had finished on the 18th green before the group behind had reached the 18th tee. They were not holding anyone up. (This fact, and that Seve was no threat to the leaderboard, dismayed people involved in running the tournament – Seve remained an attraction for the promoters and to lose his presence over a matter of seconds seemed a constipated application of the rules.)

Following the imposition of the one-shot penalty, Havret duly marked Seve down for a five rather than a four on the 16th, which turned his 75 into a 76. Paramor was in attendance. 'I was in the recording area to make sure the penalty had been added. I said to Seve, "I just wanted to make sure that [Havret] had included the penalty. I didn't want you to get disqualified."' Seve rubbed out the five, reinstated the four and signed his card with a lower score on a hole than he had in fact taken, the penalty for which is disqualification.

'You want to disqualify me, go ahead,' he told Paramor, and with that he left the recording area. Paramor said he made repeated requests for Seve to return, and at one point even told Havret 'Let's give this two more minutes', which strictly he should not have done. Seve never came back. Paramor subsequently agreed that if he hadn't got involved, trying to make sure Seve did the right thing, thereby invoking Seve's notoriously stubborn pride, he might have signed for the penalty. As it was, he was left with no option but to disqualify him.

Paramor had been the rules official who had refused Seve the drop he thought he deserved on the final hole of the 1994 Volvo Masters, when he came up one shot shy of a playoff. The five-minute altercation there while Seve disputed that decision would surely have seen anyone else excoriated by the press and other players. After the third round there, Bernhard Langer, a notoriously slow player, complained about Seve's pace of play, saying: 'Players should not be fined money. That sort of money means nothing to Seve. They should introduce the American way: time them, fine them, take shots off, more shots and then disqualify them.'

Earlier in 1994, Seve had complained that two slow-play warnings in the final round of the BMW International Open in Munich had hurt his concentration and possibly cost him the tournament. He finished a shot behind Mark McNulty. 'I feel I am being driven off the Tour,' he said. In 1997, he clashed with another official, Tony Gray, after being warned about slow play in the German Masters. Seve was no stranger to antagonism with authority on this topic.

In Italy following his disqualification, Seve held a press conference and threw it all back to the Gang of Four. 'It showed we were right. The situation [between IMG and the Tour] is really hard to say, but it is nearly like a Mafia.' Oops. 'Not the Italian Mafia, of course, I mean the PGA Mafia, IMG and the Tour. They [IMG] have the television, the players, the exhibitions, the course design, everything. When somebody is against the system, they are the No. 1 enemy. This is a personal problem that comes from Ken Schofield and all of his staff. This Tour is a dictatorship. There is no freedom. When someone goes against the system, he is in the sights at all times. Most of the players are against the regime but they are afraid to speak out.'

He also threw this in. 'The Tour had dates for [the Seve Trophy] for this year's event but because we didn't have the sponsor confirmed, they took away the dates. It will disappear because Mr Schofield is against it but after 30 years on Tour, what am I supposed to do? Am I supposed to take nothing, go home and disappear?'

He didn't command much support. As the manager of another player put it: 'The trouble is, Seve mixes the two things: that he doesn't like the Tour and that he can no longer play competitive golf.' Langer, one of the Gang of Four, said: 'I told Ken Schofield that I don't feel the way Seve does. We did it [the Gang of Four] for the good of the game and for everybody's interests and I think it was good because some of the stuff that came out moved the Tour in the right direction.'

Langer added: 'There is no reason to act the way he has. We have rules and we must obey them, otherwise you'd have 150 guys out there all arguing, and where would you end up? He knows the rules and he should abide by them. It's not proper.' Even Olazábal refused to back Seve's conspiracy theory on this.

Judgement day was set for the week of the Volvo PGA Championship at Wentworth. Padraig Harrington summed it up like this. 'Seve has done everything that can be done in the game and he is a hero to so many. There is not a current player who would not give his arm for a career like his. It is like he is trying to prove something when he's proved it all.'

Seve wanted to prove that whereas once he was great and graceful, he didn't now want to be remembered for being slow and embarrassing. He told the *Sunday Times*: 'It was persecution. The referee [Paramor] decided he was going to penalise me, basically for what happened in Madeira.'

Ernie Els pleaded on his behalf. 'I'll probably get fined for saying this, but I think there was an overflow of feelings there. I think Seve knew he was timed for 14 holes and felt that was unfair. He shot 75 or whatever and he wasn't going to let anybody put a stroke on his card. It was just an emotional thing.' Els urged the Tour not to 'kick him too badly when he's down' given that Seve was the man 'who kept this Tour alive in the 1970s and 1980s'.

A typically generous and thoughtful comment, but not one that swayed the minds that mattered. On 21 May, Seve was fined £5,000 and severely reprimanded by the European Tour's players' committee. The fine was for being rude in his dispute with Paramor, the reprimand for altering his scorecard. The chairman of the committee, irony of ironies, was Mark James, who said Seve had 'put his side of the story eloquently and with intensity'. He also said: 'It is with reluctance that we would fine anyone like Seve.'

For his part, Seve had said: 'I will accept what the committee decides because they represent the players.' When he learned the news, however, he was distraught. He withdrew from the tournament, citing illness but actually suffering from a temporary broken heart.

The obvious inclination is to see this unhappy episode as indicative of Seve refusing to accept his declining prowess and perpetually seeking someone else to blame for his failings. He does have a tendency to see life as a complicated conspiracy against him, maybe partly as a motivational force and maybe partly because he is somewhat paranoid. Of course, just because you're paranoid, it doesn't necessarily mean they're not out to get you. And how he hated being judged by people not really fit to be called his peers; whose wealth he so contributed to by what he had done for European golf.

Later in 2003, in an interview with the website GolfOnLine, Seve was quoted as saying of the decision to fine him: 'It was disrespectful to me. It was hard to sleep and I cried because I thought the players' committee judged me without regard for the big picture and my contributions to the European Tour. I wonder if the members can sleep with the decision to judge me as they did.'

Any slumber deprivation the committee members may have suffered would probably have been alleviated by Seve's brazen statement, reminiscent of Madeira: 'The crowds are there to see me. I am the attraction.' Obviously, it would have been better for Seve if someone else had said that on his behalf, since it's true, but it may have been advisable to leave it unsaid rather than try to rectify matters himself.

In January 2004, Ken Schofield told me for an interview in *Golf International* that in respect of Seve's 'like a Mafia' remark: 'I think we sensed at the time that here was a man, in terms of charisma who's Europe's Arnold Palmer, in a continuing low moment . . . thinking that the world, and that included the Tour and at that specific moment John Paramor – "yet again he's out here and he's all over me" – was against him.' He added: 'The sadness of that moment and of Seve's playing traumas is something that we all suffer . . . I've seen him at his best and there was no better company than Seve when he was winning.'

Then Schofield got nostalgic. 'I prefer to remember the early days, when he was leaving a tournament in Europe that he'd yet again won and he was going off to Akron for the World Series. He asked if I was coming and I said I was. "When do you arrive?" he asked. I told him and he said he'd be there for dinner. Our plane was delayed so we were late, but he was still there for dinner. That's the Seve I prefer to remember.'

The Tour was manifestly not always out to get him. In April 2004, Seve helped to organise a 'Sportsmen Against Terrorism' golf day in Madrid. It clashed with the first day of the Seville Open – i.e. in conflict with Tour regulations. The off-the-record line from the Tour was emollient – 'We don't want to pick any more fights with Seve.' So Seve decided to pick one himself.

On 12 September, the rules official from Madeira, José Maria Zamora, was competing in the Spanish Amateur Championship at Pedrena. Seve saw him in the clubhouse there – on his home ground! – and approached him. Words were spoken and, allegedly, there was some physical confrontation.

The Tour asked for a report; the Spanish press sat on the news. However, once the story was broken by Lewine Mair in the *Daily Telegraph* on 27 October, during the lead-in to the Volvo Masters, the Spanish media had to run with it and the Tour had to act more urgently. In fact, there was a deadline that meant endless procrastination was not an option – O'Grady wanted this out of the way before he formally took over from Schofield at the start of 2005.

On 10 December, the Tour issued a statement regarding the 'alleged incident at the Spanish Amateur Championship on 12 September at the Real Club de Golf de Pedrena, involving Severiano Ballesteros and European Tournament Director, José Maria Zamora'.

> George O'Grady, who becomes executive director of the European Tour on 1 January 2005, today announced that, following inquiries with regard to this incident, no further action will be taken.
>
> O'Grady said: 'There was an incident. Both Seve and José Maria regret that it took place. Words were spoken in the facilities of a private golf club and Seve accepts that he should have talked to José Maria in private so that the issue was left between the two of them.

Among friends. The four Spaniards who helped Europe win the 1985 Ryder Cup – from left to right, Manuel Pinero, Seve, José Maria Caniazares and José Rivero.

Seve holes from two feet to beat Curtis Strange in his singles at the 1987 Ryder Cup and Europe have just beaten the United States for the first-time ever in America.

Despite this gesture, theirs was the greatest partnership in Ryder Cup history. With fellow Spaniard José Maria Olazábal, Seve won 11 and halved two of the 15 matches they played together.

Spot who's missing. Amid some great controversy, Seve's three wild cards for the 1997 Ryder Cup were Olazábal, Faldo and Parnevik – no place for Miguel Angel Martin.

Prince Andrew may have been an interested onlooker at Valderrama but there was no doubt who reigned supreme at the 1997 Ryder Cup.

Seve is usually on the other end of the lens but here he takes the camera from photographer Dave Cannon during a session for the *Trouble-Shooting* instruction book on the 17th hole at Valderrama, which Seve redesigned to less than universal applause.

More used to taking courtesy cars to the course, Seve opts to become a cameleer in Dubai.

Seve on site at Pont Royal in the South of France in 1990, one of the earlier golf-course design projects in which one of his companies, Trajectory, was involved.

Pedrena 1988. Seve with nephews Ivan and Raul, the sons of his eldest brother, Baldomero, then aged nine and seven, respectively. Ivan now manages Seve's business affairs; Raul is a sometime player on the European Tour.

At Pedrena Golf Club. However much wealth he has accumulated over the past 30 years, Seve remains loath to lose a single golf ball.

The ultimate highlight. Twenty-one years after he enthralled everyone at the 1976 Open, but with his own game by now in comparative tatters, Seve captained Europe to victory in the Ryder Cup. It was, and is likely to remain, the last great hurrah for one of the game's greatest players.

'I have had a full and frank talk with Seve and I am now aware how bad he feels about the whole situation he has been going through. We do not condone what took place but there are mitigating circumstances for an incident so totally out of character during a career stretching more than 30 years.

'Seve has expressed how upset he feels about the incident. I have accepted this and Seve has assured me that is the end of the matter. Earlier this year Seve offered total support for my new role as executive director of the Tour. He has reaffirmed his commitment to me and his allegiance to the European Tour. He remains a true champion and he has an important and influential role to play as an ambassador for the Tour and our sport.'

Seve Ballesteros said: 'I talked to George O'Grady to whom I offered my account of what happened at a private golf club in Spain. Being a very reasonable person, George understood my thinking. I am aware who I am and what I represent and thus regret what happened. During my extensive professional career, I have always respected the noble rules of this game both on and off the course. As far as the incident is concerned, my apologies to the European Tour and to those affected by my wrong manners.

'I am a passionate character and the high tension of the moment were detrimental to the situation. Neither as a player nor an individual do I hide away from my responsibilities.

'I would like to express my annoyance over the incident in the clubhouse at Pedrena last September which has attracted so much recent media attention. I can only say that I am distressed about any uncomfortable situation it may have caused the European Tour and my fellow professionals with this private matter being brought into the public domain.

'In talking with George O'Grady I stressed to him that I have the utmost respect for the rules of the Tour and the standards we set ourselves as professional golfers. In my 30 years as a professional I have prided myself on living up to those high standards while entertaining golf fans across the world to the best of my ability.

'I am extremely proud of the part I have been able to play in making the Tour such a success and introducing the Seve Trophy event which helps our best young players prepare for the unique challenge of the Ryder Cup.

'I have formally conveyed these words in a letter to George O'Grady which I believe provides both George and the tournament committee of the European Tour with evidence of my true displeasure and genuine regret.'

José Maria Zamora said: 'What happened at Pedrena should never have been taken to the level that it has. Seve and I had our differences in Madeira where as the tournament director I was obliged to discuss with him, no different to any other member of the European Tour, a ruling on which we disagreed. But it would be wrong to imply, as has been the case, that there is on-going friction between us, and as far as I am concerned I look forward to Seve being able to compete again. He remains one of Spain's leading sportsmen, let alone the greatest golfer we have ever produced, and he is an inspiration to all our young players because of his achievements.'

That was the end of that but it won't be the end of the saga. As recently as January 2006, Seve was robustly sticking up for himself. He told CNN Television: 'I speak up always very clearly. I speak up in defence of many people. As time went by, I've had proof that I was right at least 50 per cent of those times. And as time went by, that showed me that a lot of people don't really appreciate . . . [they] let me down a little bit. I think that's not what I deserve or what I expect. But I guess that's life.'

By the tail-end of 2006, Seve was talking up his imminent new life on the senior tour in America. 'Recently there has been a lot of speculation about whether I am going to retire or not, so to make it clear, I am going to continue. I am going to compete on the Champions Tour in the USA and aim to play 14 tournaments there next year.'

His first foray into this new, gentler, environment came just over a month after his 86-80 outing at the 2007 Masters, at the Regions Charity Classic in Alabama. It was also his final fling. He opened with a double-bogey, shot 78-81-73 (albeit, in what was a nice touch, finishing with a birdie) and tied for 77th – also known as dead last – with Lee Trevino.

Seve had chosen to make his senior debut in a low-key setting because he hadn't wanted to begin in the more high-profile situation of the Senior PGA Championship the following week. He withdrew from that event and returned to Spain. Within two months, he had confirmed that the Regions Charity Classic had not only been a debut of sorts but also the definitive swansong. His career really deserved better than that.

Looking back, one of the great shames is that Seve has not really been the Arnold Palmer of European golf. Right up until his last appearances on the PGA Tour and in the Masters, even though he couldn't play a lick, Palmer was greeted with reverence and warmth. Seve's several run-ins with the European Tour have tended to erase sympathy that might otherwise have been felt for his decline. The attitude of some younger players seemed to be that not only had he become a loose cannon, shooting off at anything that moved, he was also a waste of space, occupying someone else's spot in the field; the loony no one wanted to sit next to on the bus. An alternative view is that he was rendered an irrelevance by a bunch of ingrates.

What the foregoing has shown is that Seve's disputatious relationship with the European Tour was no recent phenomenon. It had been going on for almost as long as his career. The sad truth is that his own sometimes unsavoury part in the more recent rows had not been ameliorated in the public perception by the redeeming quality of his wondrous golf.

As Bjorn, Westwood and others have acknowledged within these pages, Seve deserves better than that, even if it has been his own behaviour that has contributed to the situation.

Bjorn again: 'You can't put into words how good he was.'

While I've tried, he's right.

9. FLAWED GENIUS

George Best, late flawed genius (died 2005): 'People prefer loveable rogues to Mr Nice Guys. The real heroes are the mavericks, the people who play sport with a glint in their eye.'

Seve has been a wayward genius on the course and a wayward man off it. He has a distinctly dark side to his character. It's a part that the public seldom saw, or at least didn't until the 'nearly like a Mafia' incident and other manifestations of unfortunate behaviour, perhaps brought about by the misery inflicted on his psyche by the comparative wretchedness of his golf game.

This does not mean he is bad; it shows him to be human. Seve was a professional golfer, not a saint, a man driven to glorious successes in his heyday and driven later in a desperate bid to fight against the dying light of his own brilliance. There was more than a hint of desperation evident when he said such things as this, to *Golf World* in March 2006. 'I was the Tiger Woods of Europe. I was Tiger Woods before Tiger Woods was Tiger Woods. I was even more spectacular than Tiger Woods. I don't think there has been any player who brings more showmanship to the golf course than me. I was a real crowd-pleaser . . . I really believe that Tiger is incredible. But at my best against his, in this time with the new clubs and new balls, I am convinced I would be right up there next to him.' Seve may be right, but it would have been better if he hadn't said it himself.

Seve is like a marriage (even if his is over) – for better or worse. His capriciousness is an essential part of his make-up, as is the 'impenetrable' mind that Dudley Doust wrote about. In 1988, Peter Dobereiner, the finest British golf writer of his generation, wrote: 'He is the subject of demonic possession. Ballesteros's demon is justice.' He fought with the European Tour about being discriminated against over appearance money because he was a European (i.e. he was penalised for being 'one of us'); he initially fought with the PGA Tour because to them he wasn't a European, he was a Spaniard.

In an interview in *Golf Digest* in 2005, one of Seve's old rivals, Curtis Strange, said: 'Some pros are harder to play with than others, and the worst was Seve Ballesteros. To say he was difficult is an understatement. To a man, every player who went up against him in the Ryder Cup had a run-in with him. His gamesmanship was irritating, and he never let up. He'd do outrageous, childish things, like coughing as you got set to swing, and if you objected, he'd act wounded and escalate the situation. When he put himself into the role of victim, that's when he'd play his best. Just knowing he'd use a nasty incident to play well made me so mad that I'd play worse.' From Seve's perspective, that's quite brilliant, if you think about it.

Strange added: 'There was only one Seve, and a little of him went a long way. But I'll tell you this, he could back it up. If you were 0–5 against a guy [as Strange was against Seve in the Ryder Cup], that stuff would hack you off, too.'

That was an adversary's perspective. Over lunch at the Spanish Open in 1986, one of Seve's Ryder Cup teammates, Howard Clark, related an anecdote from the Madrid Open four weeks before, in which Clark had beaten Seve down the stretch. At one point, Clark sought relief from casual water. He asked Seve for permission to drop his ball elsewhere in the fairway. Seve came over and saw Clark agitating the water by rocking his feet. Seve lightly did likewise, but not in the same spot. No water was forthcoming.

'I see no water,' said Seve, simply being cussed. 'If you want a drop, ask the referee.'

A frustrated Clark asked: 'What's the problem, Seve?'

'The problem is that you're too heavy.'

Alistair Tait talked to Clark for his book, *Seve*, in which Clark spoke of Seve's gamesmanship that day. 'When we were going down the 9th, all of a sudden he told his caddie to put the hood on his golf bag. The inference was that he thought my caddie was looking at the clubs he was using and giving me that information.'

If the tactic was to unsettle Clark, it didn't work. After a three-shot swing on the 12th, where Seve took a double-bogey six, Clark led by one, which was his margin of victory. On the 16th, Clark recalled Seve standing so close to look over the line of Clark's putt, which was on a similar line to Seve's, that 'I could smell his after-shave'. On the 17th, Seve went off at a photographer by the green – 'From what I could see,' said Clark, 'the photographer had done nothing wrong, but Seve just lost it completely. I think he was trying in his own way to do a [John] McEnroe . . . [and] upset somebody else in the hopes of upsetting his opponent.'

Three years later, Seve won the same tournament by a shot from Clark, who told the press: 'He tried to intimidate me. He continually walked around while I was putting.' Seve retorted: 'The best way to concentrate is not to watch the other player.'

It maybe that no one has got closer to Seve than the mercurial Mac O'Grady. Formerly a fairly successful PGA Tour player, O'Grady's relationship with Deane Beman and the PGA Tour was more confrontational than Seve's. That tempestuous streak somehow made him a soul-mate of Seve's; two loose cannons, if you like. Mac was also a great student of the golf swing and latterly had become a teacher of some repute. Seve, who'd try any teacher at least once but seldom twice, eventually gravitated towards him. He even got possessive. After Vijay Singh beat him by two shots to win the Trophée Lancôme in 1994, Seve told Vijay that he could tell from the way he played the shot to get up and down from a bunker at the last that Mac had been teaching him how to play the short game like Seve. Within minutes, Seve rang O'Grady in America to complain about two-timing him.

There followed a lover's spat after which O'Grady refused to speak to Seve. He relented over Christmas and Seve spent time in Palm Springs, California, where O'Grady lived, practising for the 1995 season under Mac's supervision. He flew back to Europe in early February – Los Angeles–London–Madrid–Las Palmas – for a tournament in the Canary Islands. I joined Seve at Heathrow. He was in animated mood, charmingly getting the stewardess to arrange a seat-swap so that we could sit together – 'I think your friend is very famous,' said the uprooted woman passenger – and earnestly singing Mac's praises, going so far as to say that David Leadbetter had nicked a lot of his teaching methods off O'Grady.

The time he had just spent with O'Grady gave birth to an oft-repeated anecdote of the day, that he and Mac had gone out into the desert to bury photographs and videos of his old, now unwanted, swing. It was a tale fabricated to tease the press. 'It's just a story Mac made up,' Seve told me later. 'It's just one of those crazy things he does sometimes.' Mind you, Seve did his bit, too, telling journalists: 'It was a very happy funeral.'

But even on that flight there was a hint of the big chill to come between them. Seve remarked how odd he thought it was that Mac had not once asked him to dinner at his house that week. Within a few months, Seve was saying in answer to any polite enquiry: 'It's best not to speak of Mac.' By July 1998, O'Grady was telling *Golf Digest* that Seve was 'emotionally bankrupt . . . a collapsed star, a black hole'. For good measure, he told the *Los Angeles Times* that their relationship had terminated because 'I finally found someone more neurotic than me.' A telephone conversation I had with O'Grady in February 1999 perhaps summed it up most succinctly. 'I love Seve 100 per cent,' he said, 'and I trust him zero per cent.' I wouldn't go to those extremes but from my experience of working with Seve, I have an idea what he means.

The first significant step (well, it seemed at the time that it might be) I took towards working on a book with Seve was in 1993. My agent, Sonia Land, and I met with Joe Collet, Seve's then manager, at the

1993 Open at Royal St George's, after which a draft contract was drawn up for me to ghostwrite his autobiography. There followed desultory spasms of enthusiasm from Seve during 1994 and 1995, notably while I was at Valderrama with him in November 1995 to work on the *Trouble-Shooting* instruction book – a project that Seve's next manager, Roddy Carr, had approached me about during the Ryder Cup at Oak Hill. Shortly after that, Seve cooled on the idea again, at least partly because Baldomero thought the timing was premature. In fact, of course, the timing would have been perfect, leading up to the 1997 Ryder Cup, when Seve was captain.

In February 1996 I flew to Spain to meet Seve to go through the proofs for *Trouble-Shooting*. I got to Pedrena just before 4 o'clock. It was quickly apparent that the omens were not good. Dave Cannon of Getty Images, who had taken the photos for the book, was there, having worked on a photo shoot for Sunderland waterproofs that Seve had shot earlier in the day. He said that Seve and Roddy Carr had pretty well done all they could with the Sunderland promotional work and were waiting for me so that they could get on with the book. I didn't like the sound of that: it struck me as one of Seve's efforts to cram too much into one day so he could get on with what he really wanted to do, i.e. practice, notwithstanding that he was being extremely well paid for the book by most standards.

Actually, it was worse than that. Seve had read hardly any of the text I had sent. He said he wanted me to read through the copy and he would make comments on it. This laborious way of working meant we had done just two chapters by 6.30 and Seve, who had been up since 5 a.m, had had enough. We agreed to reconvene in the morning.

The next day was substantially more frustrating. Carr rang me at the hotel at 10 and asked me to go to the club. His brother, Manuel, would be along soon and he would get hold of Seve. In the event, none of them turned up until 2.30.

Seve pitched up first, just. 'Bored?' he asked with a slow grin, as if he knew I must be. I was totally hacked off. Roddy turned up with Manuel and suggested to Seve that maybe the best way would be for

Manuel to go through the text with me on Seve's behalf. With almost admirable hypocrisy, Seve said: 'I think that would be unprofessional.' The truth was that he really didn't want to spend any more time on it than the two days he had already. He then said to Roddy that he had not got enough money for it and could have made more by doing a couple of exhibitions.

In fact, it suited me to have Manuel do it; much less hassle. We made good progress. At one point, Manuel offered: 'It saddened me to walk into this room and hear him say he did not want to do this book because it did not pay enough money. Seve does not need the money! He should do it because his fans and other people would like to see this book.'

He also said: 'Seve has a bad attitude because his game is bad. But his game is bad because he has a bad attitude. He is never happy. He does not appreciate all he has and how lucky he is. I bet he never sits back and recalls his life and thinks what happy memories he has.'

In respect of the stalling autobiography project, Manuel said: 'I could tell a story that would be much more interesting than Seve's' – I was sure he wasn't kidding – and 'It should be done now, while he is still active in golf, not wait until he retires. He could do a bit every month.'

That was what I thought, too, but there was only one opinion which really mattered and he had no interest in doing it. Three years passed until I was at the 1999 Italian Open in Turin. Seve noticed me while he was on the practice putting green and called me over. 'How is the book going?'

It was the first time he'd mentioned it since February 1996, and then it had been to express no interest in proceeding. He had given me no time since; he evidently just assumed I had been putting stuff together, which intermittently I had been doing even though we had no formal agreement. I reminded him of this and he said:

'But how far along are we?'

'How do you measure that?' I replied.

'If it was a round of golf, are we on the 10th, the 15th or what?'

I paused for a moment. 'It's a bit like we have teed off on all 18 but not holed out on any of them.'

This nonsense answer seemed to satisfy as much as intrigue him. He said that he wanted the book out by the 2001 Ryder Cup – 'That would be a good time' – and, with that, he was off to play with one of the Agnelli family in the pro-am.

So I started to do a bit more. In September 1999, I rang him from Boston, in the early part of Ryder Cup week, to fix a date to go out to Spain to see him. He was back into slow mode. He said he wanted more time to work on it himself so the book was as good as it could be. He was vaguely defensive, but he did reiterate – without prompting – that he would be sending his notes, etc. on to me. The next month, we spoke again and he said: 'I will be writing things down over the winter,' he said. 'I don't want any pressure. I have been under pressure for 25 years.'

In September 2000, *Golf Digest* published an interview Seve gave to John Huggan. In it, he said: 'I am going to start a book. If I tell you everything, nobody will be interested in the book.' And by now, it did seem we were getting somewhere. That autumn, he agreed we should go with it. A contract was drawn up and signed between us for me to ghost his autobiography. The publishers were later identified as HarperCollins, although the contract between them and Seve was never actually signed.

I went to Pedrena for three days in December 2000. He was in good form, a good mood, and we seemed to get a lot done. We were working to a fairly loose timetable but, given the amount of work to do, the idea was for the book to come out in 2002. On my last night there, Seve had a better idea – he wanted it out in September 2001, to coincide with the Ryder Cup; the idea he had floated in Turin. 'I know it will be very much work for you to do,' he acknowledged, 'but that would be best.'

I figured it would be just about manageable. HarperCollins were delighted as this timing was even better for them. So I got on with it. Seve arranged to see me at Heathrow in January when he was on his way to play in the Far East, but instead of talking about the book, we watched the television as his team, Racing Santander, beat Barcelona 4–0. Seve kept calling Carmen, who was at the match, on his mobile. I should have known then it wouldn't end in cheers.

Seve pulled the plug on completing the book in March, though we were behind schedule by then anyway. With excruciating timing, I had to communicate the bad news to HarperCollins a day or two after they had informed the trade about the book's imminent publication. That might have been that if not for the postponement of the Ryder Cup because of the subsequent horrific events in New York, Washington and Pennsylvania. Despite the earlier setback, the publishers were keen to do the book to tie in with the rescheduled match, in September 2002. So was Seve, now that the timeframe for completing the job was inevitably more generous. I went out to Pedrena in January 2002 and worked on the book, completing the manuscript by early March. We were back on track and HarperCollins were ready to go with it.

During the ensuing few weeks, stuff happened. I got a generally complimentary e-mail from Baldomero about the manuscript. (The volume of e-mail correspondence on this may be bigger than this book.) Then Seve wanted the manuscript translated into Spanish, the better to understand what I'd written, but he didn't want to pay for that task, which was eventually undertaken by Spanish publishers who were known to Baldomero. There was more back and forth. Then, on 29 April, another e-mail from Baldomero – 'we have decided to postpone the launching of Seve's book until next year'.

With the whole project facing extinction, it was agreed, after much toing and froing, that I would go to Pedrena in June 2002 in a bid to salvage the deal and the September publication. I would spend two days (missing the England v Brazil World Cup quarter-final!) incorporating the material that Seve apparently wanted to add, some of it anecdotal about his mother. Teresa Bagaria, a Spanish golf journalist, would be there to help express to me in English what Seve allegedly had difficulty explaining except in Spanish.

Within an hour, it was clear this wasn't going to happen. Seve and Baldomero were still talking about 2003. They had no intention of hurrying this along to honour the intentions of HarperCollins. I left the next day – which meant I was home in time to see England lose to Brazil . . .

On 17 July, Charlie Sale's column in the *Daily Mail* carried the following item.

> Sports publishers Collins Willow [the sporting imprint of Harpers] may be celebrating the successful launch of Ian Woosnam's autobiography this week – but they have been left exasperated by the mood swings of Seve Ballesteros over a similar project. *Woosie* . . . had been planned to follow the Ballesteros book into the shops. But the Spaniard has prevented the sale of his life story for two years running, much to the dismay of Collins Willow, who have twice promoted the book in trade publications.
>
> The manuscript was ghostwritten by Robert Green, editor of *Golf International* . . . it has long been in the possession of Collins Willow, who need the player's go-ahead for publication. Ballesteros . . . wants his official autobiography to be released only when he is back at the top. Collins Willow, having missed their 2001 publication date, were hoping to launch the book for September's Ryder Cup. But Ballesteros refused to co-operate and now September 2003 is the new target – if Ballesteros can start hitting the fairways again or accept he never will.

I'm not at all sure that Seve's motive for the repeated delay was down to some vain hope of rekindling his prowess as a golfer, but one thing was certain – HarperCollins were not interested any more. They had been burned twice. Why go for the hat-trick?

More London/Santander e-mails were exchanged, expending a lot of words to no purpose. At some time in early 2003, Seve (or maybe Baldomero) was evidently in contact with Sir Alex Ferguson, the Manchester United manager, whose own autobiography, written with the matchless Hugh McIlvanney, had been a hugely successful book. Seve, or his people, must clearly have said something to the effect that 'You won't believe this but no one will publish my autobiography.' At Ferguson's suggestion, Baldomero called Roddy Bloomfield of Hodder & Stoughton, who published the Ferguson book. Bloomfield called me to ask if this was true. I explained the situation – Ferguson had obviously not been told the story behind the apparent stupidity of no one wanting to publish Seve's book; why no one was interested any more. Seve believed that the publishing industry would do whatever was needed to publish his book on his terms and in his time. He was wrong. What Sir Alex should have mentioned to Seve was that he did something like 25 days' publicity for his book. Baldomero had said Seve would do only two at most.

It was sad to deal with Seve in this way. The more prolonged the interminable discussions and negotiations had gone on, the more it was rammed home that while Seve was not dishonest, he wasn't straight; that he wasn't a cheat but he was cheap – 'who would pay for Teresa Bagaria?', 'why were the royalty percentages like this?', 'who was getting what?' It was desperately dispiriting.

In April 2003, I saw him for the first time in a while. It was after the Masters, where Seve had shot 77–85 to comfortably miss the cut and then gone on to do commentary for the BBC on the weekend. I was in the BA lounge at Atlanta Airport when Seve appeared. He broached the subject of reaching a settlement with regard to the intellectual property rights in the manuscript. 'I know you have spent a lot of time and money on this. If you want, *if* you want, I will pay you now what you deserve.' I said I'd think about how I saw things. As I went for my flight, he asked: 'So how do we take our conversation forward?' I replied: 'I don't know if there is a way to take it forward.'

But eventually we did. We reached an agreement for him to acquire the copyright in the manuscript, but soon the book that was written was not only out of date, it had quite a bit missing – like his stand-offs with the European Tour and his divorce, neither of which are topics any publisher would want ignored and neither of which cast Seve in a light he would be happy about. Absent from the book you are reading, unfortunately but necessarily, are many stories about his growing up and several entertaining anecdotes about his brief period of military service. In September 2007, several of these surfaced when Seve eventually published his autobiography.

I also recognise now that many of our discussions took place against the background of Seve's disenchantment with his game, and therefore with life itself. After all, in many respects, he lived his life through golf. It wasn't only me with whom he could be offhand or act unusually. At the golf club at Pedrena, before the 'incident' with José Maria Zamora, Seve had perturbed officials by turning up to practise at 2 o'clock in the morning, as if to relive being the rebellious kid sneaking on to the course to play by moonlight.

Such behaviour could hardly be called normal but maybe it wasn't entirely out of character. Seve's mind can be a dark place. In July 2000 a Dublin-based psychologist specialising in performance management wrote an open letter to Seve saying that if he wanted to recover his career, he needed to start by acknowledging his weaknesses. 'At your peak anything was possible,' he said, 'because of your unshakeable belief and tendency to see yourself as "bigger than the situation". The Catch 22, however, in which you now find yourself means that the harder you try to prove that you are still strong, the weaker you will actually become.' Among the character traits he identified in Seve was his need for control and fear of being harmed or controlled by others. Also lust.

Depicting Seve as a latter-day Don Juan has never been difficult. In 1980, just after he had won the Masters, in a laughing response to stories that he had four girlfriends, he told the press: 'I don't know, maybe more. It is very boring when you play the same course every day.'

An inclination towards philandering may be part of the make-up of a genius; a belief that fidelity is lethargy masquerading as integrity. Well before he was married, Seve was very aware of the sex appeal he had. In a previous biography, *Seve*, by Lauren St John (in 1993), the former tour pro Simon Hobday is quoted as saying: 'You cannot

believe how women loved that guy. There were 600, 700 groupies at
every tournament. They were just after Ballesteros. All ages, too!'
After Seve had won the 1983 Masters, he was asked if he intended to
play more in America and less in Europe. He said he didn't. 'I love to
be an international golfer. I love to play in Japan and Europe and the
US. I love to travel because I meet different girls.'

Seve was a bit like George Best in this regard, too: men wanted
to be in his company, women wanted to be in his bed. In Britain, an
alleged relationship with a former Page 3 model, Liz Hoad, made the
tabloids, but those were the days when the sports press tended not to
go looking under the covers for stories, so what he got up to at night
seldom saw the light of day.

But Seve has never tried to downplay his interest in the opposite
sex. In an interview in September 2002 on one of the BBC's more
obscure channels, Rob Bonnet suggested to Seve that in the way he
played and the way he looked, he had 'made golf sexy', an echo of the
famous Ruud Gullit quote about 'sexy football' at Euro '96. Seve,
however, seemed to take it as a comment about sex. 'Obviously I like
girls very much,' he said, 'like most normal people. Arnold Palmer
used to say that every time he was on the golf course and he saw a
beautiful lady, it was a tremendous inspiration for him. It was a little
bit my case, too. It's good. It's always nice. It makes you feel good
there are beautiful ladies following you. It makes you try even
harder.'

In late September 2001, when we had just decided to press on
with the previously postponed autobiography, I met Seve at Harrods.
He was over to do something for Hugo Boss, his clothing sponsor, at
the store. The Boss representative was a fairly striking-looking
woman whom Seve had clearly met before. Afterwards, I gave him
and her a lift to Heathrow (separate terminals). At one point in the
conversation, Seve remarked how he had noticed her in his gallery at
a tournament in Germany the month before. Whatever happened to
his legendary focus, to tunnel vision?

He once told Mac O'Grady that it was hard to concentrate at the
Lancôme – where the spectators were generally dressed to the nines

– because of the good-looking women in the gallery. Since Seve's main source of personal vanity/appearance concern has long been the prospect of losing his hair, one wondered if this explained his errant golf. How could he expect to hit the ball well if at the top of his swing he's worried that his hair might not look right and, coming down, he's trying to ogle the women in the crowd? When I once asked if he wanted to say anything in his autobiography about female interest, his only answer, with a sly smile, was: 'It's very delicate.'

In October 2004, he gave an interview to Paul Kimmage of the *Sunday Times* under the headline 'In Bed With Seve', named after the Madonna film of that title (that is, if you swap her name for his) and because he was lying on a king-size while it was being conducted.

'Why don't we start with all the women you've slept with during your career?' suggested Kimmage. 'When was the first time?'

'I don't remember,' Seve replied. 'It was a long time ago.'

As the interview was drawing to a close, Seve asked: 'Have you any more questions?'

'How much time can you give me?' replied Kimmage.

'Five minutes.'

'You haven't told me about the women yet,' he pressed.

Kimmage wrote: 'He flashes me a grin that needs no translating. *That would take more than five minutes, my friend.*'

One favourite of his was apparently a French woman whom I suspect (but don't know) he met at the 1997 Ryder Cup. I say this because, somewhat bizarrely, she was staying in the same apartment as me and a French friend of mine – he had fixed my accommodation at Valderrama and he was a business associate of her stepfather, hence why she was there. Five years later, she was at the Ryder Cup again. I had sometimes seen her at tournaments in which Seve was playing – such as the 2000 Open at St Andrews – and she was in the bar at The Belfry on the Saturday night of this Ryder Cup, although Seve couldn't be accused of being in attendance on that occasion. His name came up, though. A mutual friend introduced me to her. She understandably didn't recall meeting me before but had an instant reaction when our friend mentioned I was probably going to be writing Seve's book with him. (There was no point in explaining the project was already effectively dead.) 'I should be in it,' she said. As if on cue for a cliché, she added: 'His wife doesn't understand him.'

At the Open Championship at St Andrews in July 2005, I saw the American golf writer, Jaime Diaz. He and some other journalists had been talking with Seve earlier in the week. Seve had repeated a piece of advice he had been given many years before by Roberto de Vicenzo. 'Seve, to be a champion, you must be able to do three things. Sleep in any kind of bed. Eat any kind of food. And make love to any kind of woman – but not too well, or else she will follow you.' Among Seve's other troubles has been his inclination to follow them.

Carmen Botin, Seve's ex-wife, comes from one of Spain's wealthiest families. The Botins control the Banco Santander Central Hispano, the largest financial institution in the country, so big that it gobbled up what was then called Abbey National. Her father, Emilio Botin, head of the bank, is one of the richest men in the country and Spain's most powerful businessman. He inherited control of Banco Santander from his father, who in turn had succeeded Emilio's grandfather. The bank was established in Santander in 1857 to finance trade between Spain and Latin America. In this regard, under the direction of Carmen's grandfather, the family acquired banks in Panama and Argentina in the 1950s, during which time they had strong connections to the Franco government. Since Carmen's father assumed control of the business in 1986, Banco Santander has made major acquisitions in Chile, Venezuela, Colombia and Mexico. One of Carmen's elder sisters, Ana Patricia, is a highly regarded banker in her own right, the chairman of Banesto. In 2005, she was ranked by *Forbes* among the top-100 most powerful women in the world.

As mentioned before, Seve and Carmen first met when Seve was giving golf lessons to her and other members of her family. He started going out with her in 1981, while she was living in England, studying at college in Ascot, Berkshire. He was playing in the World

Matchplay Championship at nearby Wentworth and she went along to watch him. He beat Ben Crenshaw in the final to record the first of his five wins in the event. They met up afterwards and the relationship blossomed from there.

People have long said there were problems about them getting married because she is from an aristocratic Spanish family. In the April 1988 issue of *Golf Digest*, Peter Dobereiner characterised their romance as like Romeo and Juliet. 'In his office at the bank, father Botin studies the statement of Romeo's account. Each figure is followed by a seemingly endless row of zeros, like the wheels of freight trains rolling across La Mancha bearing treasures to his vaults. An eminently suitable son-in-law, he concludes. But mother Botin, the blue blood of the Capulets rising in her gorge, has a proper scorn of money, especially new money. You can, she asserts with vigour, take the boy out of the caddie shack, but you can't take the caddie shack out of the boy. I will never permit the most fragrant flower of the Capulets to be united with a Montague.'

Excellent stuff, but not true. Instead, the issue was to do with their respective upbringings. We have seen how Seve's formal schooling was halted after his tipsy altercation with a teacher. Carmen, on the other hand, was at Brown University on Rhode Island for five years. 'The problem between them,' said one friend, 'was that her parents were worried about his comparative lack of education. And in the end, you have to say they were right to be concerned.'

Nevertheless, before 1988 was out, united they were. Their eventual marriage attracted great interest in the gossip pages of the *prensa rosa* in Spain. Every day the fact that they had not got married spawned stories that therefore they must be splitting up. When they did get married, they went to great lengths to keep it from the press.

The wedding was on Friday 25 November 1988. Seve was 31, Carmen 23. Only 23 people were invited to the ceremony, so determined where they to keep it a secret. The more friends and relatives they asked, they knew the more likely it was that the news would get out, even if not for malicious or greedy motives. The ceremony was held at Carmen's parents' house in Santander. Joe Collet was among the uninvited. They hadn't even told him, so that he wouldn't have to lie to anyone who might ask him what was going on.

One thing did go wrong, though. Having gone to great lengths to keep their lives out of the public domain, they didn't sell their wedding pictures. Instead, someone else did. Seve and Carmen took the one roll of film that a guest had snapped with them to the Caribbean for their honeymoon and got the pictures developed there. The man in the photo lab recognised what he'd got and flogged extra copies to a news agency. This was sad for them. They had never entered any deals with the media and morally they had some right to expect their private life would remain private. It didn't happen.

So began the next phase of Seve's life: marriage. One of the first things he had done when he could afford it, in 1980, was to build a house for his mother and father to live in with him. He did this, with his mother alone after his father's death in 1986, until 1988, when he and Carmen began to live together following their wedding. The house where they lived immediately prior to their separation is about 500 yards from their first marital home. They moved into it in 1994. It is large but not ostentatious, with generous grounds affording glorious views across the bay to Santander, to the Cantabrian hills from which the *montaneses* take their name, or on to the golf course.

They have had three children together. Javier was born in August 1990. His first name is Baldomero, after Seve's father, but Javier soon became the preferred name to use within the family. Miguel followed in 1992, their daughter, also Carmen, in 1994. Seve once said to me, with what I thought was unwarranted emphasis: 'She's called Carmen – after my mother.' In fact, he was right. His wife would have chosen a different name. However, at the 1984 Open, when both mother and girlfriend were there, he had publicly said: 'I'd just like to say I won this for my mother. This is the first time she has seen me play in an Open.' (His mother passed away suddenly, while he was at a tournament in Madrid in 2002.)

Seve would take his family with him to tournaments at times. When he went from Madrid to the Canary Islands in February 1995, Miguel had been so anxious that his mother and Javier would not go to see his father without him that he had sat in the car at home for 45 minutes before they left.

That week, Seve said to me: 'The hardest thing was that after I got married, I could not be so selfish. For the first time, I could not do everything for me, when I wanted to. At times I would forget there was Carmen as well and I would do things that I wanted. It's hard being a player's wife. You are at the course all day, then he wants to practise, then he is late because he needs to practise for longer than he said, and when he does get back, he is very tired.'

John McEnroe highlighted the essential selfishness of a top sportsman's life in *Serious*. 'If I was going to be committed to just one girl, I wanted her to be with me, and since my job required a lot of travel, that meant she had to travel with me. If it ran counter to her needs . . . well, I wasn't thinking about anyone else's needs at that point. Nobody will be surprised to hear that No. 1 in the world requires major-league ego. You need ego to get there, and ego to stay there . . . When you're No. 1, you're not thinking that much about tomorrow. As for the outside world – what outside world?'

But as Seve's golf deteriorated, his family provided a sense of perspective. 'I would not change my wife or my three children for any British Open or Masters or whatever,' he said in 1997. On the weekend before the 2001 Open at Lytham, where Seve had won the Open twice, he caddied for Javier while he played 10 holes of the course with his first full set of clubs. Seve would watch videos of his triumphs with his children. 'Is that really you?' they would tease. One can imagine that behind the smiling acknowledgement was a sadness that the only greatness they have seen of their father as a golfer has been via old footage.

In the summer of 2003, accepting that his declining powers were a fact, not a recoverable accident, he told the press: 'I have a great record over the years. I have nothing else to prove. I've been spending time with my family. It's the best place to be, going to the beach and enjoying life as much as I could. From now on, I'll play when I feel I want to play.' Within 18 months, he wouldn't be spending so much time with his family.

In October 2004, the rumours began to spread outside Spain that Seve was having an affair with a woman from Pedrena. As one friend said, it would be bad enough if the woman lived in Madrid, but this would make it utterly intolerable. It wasn't as if Carmen hadn't got enough to cope with. That same month, her father was charged with tax and documentation fraud by a Spanish court. He and his also-indicted colleagues had to put up nearly £60 million in bail. Carmen was completely confident that nothing would come of it – her confidence was not misplaced; all charges were subsequently dropped – but it had to be unsettling. (At the World Matchplay Championship at Wentworth later that month, I popped into the BBC compound to see Peter Alliss. Seve was in the cabin with him. 'You're well?' I asked. He said he was. I then asked: 'Is Carmen well?' He said she was, too. After he had left, Peter said rather archly: 'I notice you didn't ask about her father.')

The following month, I met Jimmy Patino at his London office. He had heard that Carmen and Seve had separated. 'He's brought it all on himself,' he said.

Before Christmas, Seve had left home and it was announced that he and Carmen would be getting divorced. Seve was staying in their home in Pedrena; Carmen and the children had moved out to Santander. In defiance of reason, Seve felt their separation was her fault.

Seve has intimated that he thought his career had become 'cursed' after he got married to Carmen, because he hadn't won a major championship since then. While that is a clearly preposterous notion, there may be truth in the suggestion that Carmen's regular presence at tournaments may have had an unsettling effect on Seve and played a role in his declining golf. With her nearly always there, he was never free to be selfish and it restricted his opportunities for playing around.

I think in common with most people who have met Carmen (I have never heard anyone have a bad word to say about her), I have been struck by her charming personality. It would not be overly harsh to characterise some tour players' wives as vain and arrogant – nothing to do but spend his money and display the consequences. Carmen's upbringing and education have helped to make sure she is not like that, but the fact that she is as independently wealthy as she is brings an extra and admirable dimension to her invariable courtesy and respect for other people.

In October 2005, a 'friend' of Carmen's was quoted in the *Daily Mail* saying: 'She gave everything up for Seve. She would never have divorced him. Now she's trying to rebuild her life, seeing friends she hadn't seen for 16 years.' Another friend of Carmen's said: 'He means nothing to her now. She wants him to be happy so that he leaves her alone. It's like he's someone she never knew.' They also said that Carmen had never known about Seve's possible dalliances with other women until after the split. If she had, she would have left him. 'He used her,' the friend said, 'used her to have kids.' She is even contemplating seeking an eventual annulment of their marriage, on the grounds that when she got married she was too young to understand what she was letting herself in for.

For Seve, life apart from her has not been devoid of heartbreak. In spring 2007, a woman with whom he was living left home in a hurry for work one morning. She was late. She went through a red light, expecting the road to be deserted as usual, and was killed in a collision with another vehicle. It was this tragic incident that spurred the rumours, vehemently denied, that he had attempted to commit suicide.

Whatever the future holds, Seve and Carmen obviously have to maintain some sort of relationship, at least for a while, because of their children, but as strained as it was before, I'd suggest that Carmen's mood is unlikely to have been improved by Seve's remarks about her in that autobiography.

10. 'WHAT'S HE LIKE?'

People don't bother Seve much when he is at home. Mostly, he likes it that way. Sometimes, though, he is proud when the opposite occurs. A few years ago, he was in a village close to Pedrena. An old man, walking with the aid of a stick, approached him. 'Thank you for all you have done,' he said, 'for putting our region on the map of the world.'

The reason for this comparative anonymity of the man who, for the rest of the world, is surely the most famous son of the Santander region may lie in the fact that a) golf is not that big a sport in Spain and b) when Seve was at his peak, it was a smaller deal than it is now. As we have seen, they didn't see – there was no television coverage of his greatest triumphs in his homeland.

When they did write about golf, the Spanish press routinely did so in the expectation that Seve would win. When he didn't, which obviously happened more often than he did, he was criticised. By the mid-1980s, when his name was increasingly linked with that of Carmen Botin, reports of his golfing exploits were merely a sideshow to the story the press really wanted, which was anything to do with his love life – Would they marry? When? Would her parents veto the union? – and how much money they had between them.

Golf was Seve's overriding passion: playing and winning. The consequence of his being successful at it was fame and the trappings that brought – for better or worse. In 1985, he told Sarah Ballard of

Sports Illustrated: 'When I was beginning, I was enjoying everything so much. It was exciting going on airplanes, being in different places all the time, meeting different people. For two years I was happy just to play. I had nice clubs and enough balls and gloves and shoes. Golf was everything for me. It still is. But [you knew they'd be a but] after 1976, when I knew I had a good chance to be a champion, that is when I started to have big ambitions. Now, nine years later, it is different. I don't like flying. I'm tired of hotels. It's tough to be alone most of the time and also difficult to live like a little star. People are always coming to you with the same questions. Last year I played in 29 tournaments. I spent 34 weeks away from my house. I made 93 flights and I spent a total of 11 days inside an airplane.'

(One such occasion was quite harrowing. After Seve had won at Sun City in 1983, he and Vicente changed their plans, flying home through Lisbon and Barcelona rather than Madrid and Santander. The latter flight crashed in fog, killing everyone on board. It was announced that Seve was expected to be among the dead. Even though he was safe at home by the time that happened, the broadcast of his own demise was a shocking experience for him and his family.)

It was hardly surprising that Seve found it difficult to make the adjustment from nonentity to celebrity. As Manuel Pinero told Lauren St John for her book: 'He was put in a situation where, when he was 16 he was caddying for 100 pesetas a day and when he was 19 he wouldn't pour the tea for less than £10,000. You cannot go from one extreme to the other in that time [and remain unaffected]. It's impossible.'

Seve did add to Ballard, though, that 'I like this way better than the other way around', i.e. having no career as a tournament golfer. His career has been full of contradictory statements, such as he wishes he'd played more in America or he's glad that he didn't. But there is no doubting the truth of this statement he made in his prime. 'The biggest mistake I ever made was to start playing professional golf when I was only 16. I lost all my growing-up years. I haven't lived a normal life.' As he later put it to me: 'When you become famous, the first thing you lose is your freedom. I think it is good to be recognised but not to be famous. You cannot go into a restaurant without people wanting your autograph or to talk to you. It gets really tough.'

Having said that, he would occasionally be the one disrupting other people. The British golf writer, Tony Stenson, recalled having dinner in Switzerland with some other British journalists. Seve saw them, wandered over, sat down and eventually began to talk about how his life was similar to the late Princess Diana. In one respect, it was.

I was with him, Carmen and their two boys at Madrid Airport in February 1995. Shortly before we were due to go through security, Seve noticed a couple of guys hanging around. He went off for a little wander. His suspicion was correct – they were paparazzi. He went to explain the situation to the security staff, ahead of what he was about to do. When it was time to go, he took Javier, Carmen took Miguel, and they each hugged the child close to them so their faces could not be snapped by the photographers. Sure enough, the two paparazzi tried, there was a volley of flashlight, but they got through having succeeded in keeping them largely hidden from the cameras. Even as a peripheral figure in this, it was easy for me to understand how intrusive it must have felt.

That is one downside of fame. Mostly, though, Seve has enjoyed an excellent relationship with the press, especially in Britain, something he acknowledges. The British media were fascinated by and fantastic to him, in part because he wasn't one to duck a question. Why would he? When he was at the peak of his estimable powers, he felt so fireproof that he never worried about whether he was being diplomatic or not – on the contrary, he has a very likeable love of mischief as well as a darker mood of menace – or if anyone else agreed with him. He was Seve. He could say anything he wanted. 'Controversy can be a good thing,' he once said. 'It's boring if everyone thinks the same thing.'

When he was named Golfer of the Year by the Association of Golf Writers in Britain in 1991, for being the player who had done most for European golf that year, he was presented with the award at a dinner during the week of the 1992 Open at Muirfield. He thanked the assembly 'for making me more famous than I really am'. This remark was all the more timely for coming at the beginning of a week that ended with the new champion, Nick Faldo, making his widely excoriated joke about thanking the press 'from the heart of my bottom'.

Bill Elliott of the *Observer* wrote: 'More than any other player before or since . . . he included we hacks in his special world. He knew we were important to him but, more than this, he appreciated that, for better or worse, we were on this ride together; that he had his job to do and we had ours and that together we could be so much more than apart.'

It was rapidly easy to see why Seve had such a good rapport with the British press, a relationship forged all the stronger by the lack of interest in him at home. After he won the Open in 1979, he gave a bottle of champagne he'd been gifted to, the now late, Michael Williams of the *Daily Telegraph*, saying: 'Have a drink with all the other writers for all the nice things they've said about me.'

The first occasion I spent any degree of time with Seve was at the Sun City Million Dollar Challenge tournament in South Africa in December 1984. It was an hour-long interview, just after he had won by six shots from Nick Faldo. Seve returned on the same flight to London as we journalists, he then to catch a connection to Madrid. In the airport bus on the way to board the plane in Johannesburg, he noticed the holdall being carried by Renton Laidlaw, then of the (London) *Evening Standard*, now of The Golf Channel. At that time, Renton bore absolutely no resemblance to a sylph. (He doesn't now.)

'What's in that?' Seve asked cheerily. 'Your dinner?'

After we had got to Heathrow, as Seve made his way towards the transit lounge, he said: 'Have a good Christmas all of you, and don't drink too much wine.' Pause. 'Especially you, Peter.'

Peter Dobereiner's affection for *vino tinto* was well known. So was his and Seve's reciprocal affection. Shortly after Peter died, in August 1996, I saw Seve at the Lancôme. He had written to Peter, knowing he was ill, and had received a letter back from him. 'It was wonderful,' he said. 'It brought tears to my eyes. He was a great man.' In his letter to

Peter, Seve had written that he knew 'you have a big battle in front of you'. He continued, endorsing the philosophy of the relentlessly beleaguered hero outlined on the first page of this book: 'As you know as well as most people, much of my life has been spent fighting battles. They have said I am finished many times now and all I get from this is the fire to fight.' He signed off '*Un abrazo*' – 'A big hug.'

In Britain, the media helped build Seve into such a big deal – more so than, say, Nick Faldo or Sandy Lyle – that he was chosen to present the team prize at the BBC Sports Personality Awards to the Manchester United captain, Roy Keane, in 1999, the year United won their historic Treble. Once he had acquired even a rudimentary grasp of English, Seve became one of the best interviews in the sport. The nature of the European Tour in those days meant that, say, Seve and Bernhard Langer might be the chief protagonists in the French Open. Although not the native tongue of either men or the country they were in, English was the spoken language because it was the only one anyone had in common, to some degree or other.

Seve developed an excellent sense of humour in English, although it did require constant maintenance. The instruction video shoot in Dubai that I referred to in the opening chapter took place in February 1990, before Seve had been on tour that season. No one had thought about the impact this might have on his delivery, and the shoot took longer than expected because Seve's English was rusty through lack of use. He'd probably hardly spoken it for over two months. I think that was one of the reasons his spell as a BBC commentator for a couple of years (2003–04) was difficult: not being on tour any more, the only time he was speaking English was during his BBC work.

One word that regularly crops up in association with Seve is 'mercurial'. No wonder. As Herb Wind wrote: 'His moods are as changeable as a matador's or a Trollope heroine's.'

As a competitor, he was formidable. 'I look into their eyes, shake their hand, pat them on the back and wish them luck,' he once said of his attitude to his opponents. 'But I am thinking "I am going to bury you".' In his book, Dudley Doust recalled something Seve said about Arnold Palmer as he was on his way to overhauling him at the Trophée Lancôme in 1976. 'Out of the corner of my eye I saw Palmer lowering his eyes and shaking his head. I knew his morale was gone and that made me feel good.' Seve added: 'If you ever feel sorry for somebody on a golf course, you better go home. If you don't kill them, they'll kill you.'

To quote John McEnroe again, obviously about tennis but still wholly applicable. 'It's dog-eat-dog out there. You can be friendly off the court, but when you're all chasing the same dollar, you feel you can never totally let down your guard. It's screwed up, but that's the reality of it. You're basically on your own . . . it's easier to have enemies than to have friends – especially if your friends happen to be fellow professional tennis players and you're on your way to being No. 1 in the world. It may be a cliché that it's lonely at the top, but just because it's a cliché doesn't mean it's wrong.' When Langer said of Seve in 1984, 'He never speaks to me so why should I be nice to him? If you only say he's good, he thinks you're putting him down,' Seve probably took it as a compliment of sorts, even if, with reference to McEnroe, a backhanded one.

Not only was Seve relentless, he had his reputation for games-manship, as Paul Azinger and Curtis Strange would testify. After his singles loss to Azinger at the 1989 Ryder Cup, Seve said to him: 'We were very hard on each other today.' That's part of why he got to the top. I remember hearing Nasser Hussain, the former England cricket captain, on the radio one afternoon, plugging his autobiography, saying that gamesmanship was part of sport 'except for golf . . . and even in golf Seve Ballesteros would do certain things that constituted gamesmanship'. What was that about the King of Gamesmanship? But while he might take it to the edge, Seve knew there were limits. At Sun City in 1984, I saw him call a penalty shot on himself, at a critical time in the tournament, when his ball moved while he was addressing it in the rough and no one else could have seen the infraction. He did likewise at the German Masters in 1988 – 'It was only a little hit but they all count just the same.'

In a metaphorical sense, his caddies were certainly used to getting little hits. There was doubtless an intentional touch of mischief in the decision of Julian Barnes, in the final chapter of his novel, *A History of the World in 10½ Chapters,* to give the name Severiano to his caddie.

Being Seve's caddie has been described, more than once, as the worst job in golf. But Seve is rather like Arnold Palmer in this respect, too. To play his best, Palmer had to believe that any mistake was not his fault. To think otherwise would be to admit to an element of vulnerability that was a stretch too far. If he had hit a rank bad shot, then the blame must lie with the fact that the wind had just got up, that he had a flying lie, that the ball was in an imaginary divot, or even that – to borrow from the P.G. Wodehouse character, Mitchell Holmes, in *Ordeal by Golf* – he was disturbed 'because of the uproar of the butterflies in the adjoining meadows'. Alternatively, and certainly if none of the foregoing seemed like an appropriate excuse, there was always the hapless caddie. It's the same with Seve.

On the course, Seve was never wrong. If his caddie called his judgement into question, that would put doubt in his mind, and there is no room for doubt when you are playing golf at the highest level. And self-blame is not an option. Mutual recriminations might be acceptable after the round is over but, while the heat is on, one of a caddie's functions is to be the mule who's a fool; the cat that gets its butt kicked; to be (completing an anti-anthropomorphic hat-trick) the scapegoat for anything that goes wrong, even if the perpetrator is the other guy on the team.

One of Seve's former caddies, Peter Coleman, who later teamed up to great success with Bernhard Langer, told me in 1984: 'I liked his remarks after the World Matchplay – "I only talk to my caddie to complain." That's very apt. Four years ago he was a hard guy to work with but he's different now. Much mellower. He talks to me during a round but only to discuss clubbing, etc. And it's not just Langer that he doesn't talk to. He doesn't communicate with other people. I mean, Greg Norman may come up to Seve and chat and he'll respond, but it won't be *vice versa*.'

Coleman had hacked off Greg in Australia shortly after he had left Seve's employ to work for Norman in 1982. He told an Australian journalist: 'Seve's a better player but Greg's a better payer.' Not surprisingly, Norman wasn't thrilled at that. But Coleman knew what he was talking about. Greg paid top whack; Seve had been paying him two per cent below the average. By way of justification, Seve used to say 'five per cent of nothing is nothing.' Being on Seve's bag in those days was a guarantee of dosh as well as grief, but then Norman spent most of his life on the leaderboards, too.

Whatever the rights and wrongs of Seve's sometimes less than glorious treatment of his caddies, the downside could usually be attributed to meanness. Sarah Ballard wrote in 1985: 'British golf writers point out that he has fared best when he has used British caddies such as Dave Musgrove and Peter Coleman. They speculate, half-seriously, that the tight-fisted Seve would use them more often if his brothers were not cheaper.' I'm not sure about the 'half-seriously' bit in there.

Ian Wright, who got an earful for supposedly giving Seve the wrong club on the last hole of his Ryder Cup singles against Azinger in 1989, had this to say after the 1990 USPGA Championship. 'On the 17th he had blown up again when he put his ball in the water. It had to be my fault, of course, but whereas in the past I had just learned to keep quiet and take the medicine, this time I had had enough.' Coleman had warned Wright that he'd find caddying for Seve very difficult and Musgrove, who had won the 1979 Open with Seve, told Wright: 'Don't take the job, Ian. You don't know what you're letting yourself in for.'

It wasn't all bad, though. Seve gave Wright a Rolex watch that he got for shooting the low round of the week at the 1988 German Open, a closing 62 which won him the tournament. However, more emblematic of his attitude is the tale Michael McDonnell of the *Daily Mail* reported of Seve talking to his caddie at the 1986 Open after some shot had gone awry. 'It's not your fault. It's my fault because I listen to you.'

If Seve being munificent to his caddie was an aberration, he is more than capable of acts of generosity away from the course. At the 1989 French Open at Chantilly, my wife, Jane, and I had dinner one night with Seve and Carmen – a journalist on expenses and a millionaire; two if you count Carmen. Doing the decent thing, Seve offered to pay. He couldn't – the owner insisted it was on the house. It wouldn't have happened the other way around.

He also had a kind of running joke with me that I only had one jacket, a blue one. This wasn't true – I must have had at least two blue jackets – but when I met him in Spain for a photo shoot in 1991, he arrived with a pure-silk olive green Hugo Boss jacket for me. 'Here, another colour for you,' he said. It had probably cost him nothing but it was certainly thoughtful. He gave the British cartoonist, Tony Husband, a golf club in return for one of Tony's drawings of Seve – 'Like having a guitar off Keith Richards,' said Husband. Seve was an ambassador for the Barcelona Olympics in 1992, and through Joe Collet arranged tickets for the last three days for Jane and myself.

The cover of the first issue of *Golf International*, published in July 1997, depicted Seve in old-style military uniform – dressed as a captain, as he would be at the forthcoming Ryder Cup. The idea for the pose was his, and we went ahead with it despite objections by Baldomero that wearing the uniform might make Seve a target for ETA.

Some of my most pleasant memories of Seve came from that meeting in Pedrena in December 2000, when we were working on the autobiography: dinner with his friends at a local restaurant, where the proprietor cooked the geese that Seve had shot, and going to watch his team, Racing Santander, beat Alaves 2–1. For Seve and his family, there's no executive box or reserved car-parking space, no special treatment. They are fans, pure and simple. It was refreshing to see and enjoyable to be there.

For all his testy relationships with instructors and caddies, and for all his flaws and the all-consuming straining for excellence in his sport, Seve may be a better-rounded, worldly-wise and more generally aware person than the majority of professional sportsmen. In 1996, he told Derek Lawrenson, then of the *Daily Telegraph*: 'I look at the flowers on the trees at this course in January and I think that never used to happen . . . I honestly think that one day someone is going to blow up the world.'

In 2004, he said to Paul Kimmage in the *Sunday Times*: 'I'm curious about dying. I've thought about it a lot. You know sometimes you sit down and look at a sign, or maybe you close your eyes in bed. It's just one of those things that comes to your mind. What will happen when I die? Will it be a fantastic life there? Or will it be nothing? This is the same curiosity I have about my game, and in a few years' I will be able to say "I was right" or "I was wrong".'

By then, of course, Seve was probably the only person on the planet having that sort of debate about the prospects for his golf. The debate about the other matter is likely to continue among a wider congregation.

Also in 2004, Seve said to Gordon Thomson of the *Observer Sports Monthly*: 'I was born to win. And I still have goals. Dreaming doesn't cost very much, you know. If you have no dreams, you are dead.' Sometimes they made him feel like death. In 1999, after Jean van de Velde had spectacularly lost the Open by taking seven on the last hole at Carnoustie when six would have won it, Seve was so distressed that he had woken up three times that night, having dreamed it had happened to him.

Three months before that, I had walked a couple of holes with Carmen at the Masters while Seve was on his way to missing the cut. It was his 42nd birthday and he had palpably given up any hopes of being around for the weekend. Carmen had been instrumental in getting Seve to start working with a well-known sports psychologist, Bob Rotella, because she believed his problems were mostly in his mind. 'He needs to change the way he is,' she said. 'He needs to concentrate better on the course and not think so much of golf when he is away from it. He cannot spend all his time thinking about how badly he is playing. He could before, when he was younger [i.e. not married and no kids] but not anymore. People change. Life changes. I believe in him. He has a strong mind and he is physically strong. He will come back, but he has to see it will not happen in a week. He has to make cuts, get into contention, and maybe realise that it might be two years before he is ready to win another major.'

At the time, that seemed an optimistic assessment but not wholly fanciful. Time would tell that, the odd few weeks excepted, such as his golden autumn in Europe in 1994, Seve's game was in terminal decline. During the Open that poor Jean van de Velde would hand over to Paul Lawrie after a playoff, I walked a few more holes watching Seve, this time in the company of Mac O'Grady. O'Grady said one of the problems of working with Seve was that he temperamentally felt compelled to be tough on people who got too close to him, and this tendency could be exacerbated the worse his golf got. 'For Seve, this is trauma,' he said. 'Playing golf is traumatic for him. All his bad experiences of shots going wrong in the past mean he cannot relax.'

When he was in his prime, or fighting to climb at least some way back towards where he was, relaxation wasn't something that came easily to Seve. Although he has always lived close to the sea, which played a big part in his father's recreational life, Seve isn't interested in fishing and he finds swimming boring. The latter may be because he has to swim in order to help alleviate the stress on his back. Cycling is something he does enjoy, however, both doing it and watching it. It's great exercise for him and the Spaniards share the same love of the sport that is to be found in France and Italy. At the Lancôme in 2000, Seve played a practice round with José Maria Olazábal and Miguel Angel Jiménez. Seve was first to leave the lunch table to go to the practice range. Olazábal laughed. 'He's going now because he wants to finish by 4 o'clock so he can watch the Tour of Spain on TV.'

Despite the back injury he suffered as a teenager, Seve retains an affinity with boxing. Muhammad Ali is something of a heroic figure to him, and he was understandably thrilled in 1980 when Ali called him the week after he had won the Masters. 'He talked a lot and called me "The Greatest,"' Seve told Dudley Doust. Seve has kept the tape recording of that conversation. As well as the sweet science, Seve has always been keen on football. In 1992, he was in the royal box at

Wembley to watch his 'second team', Barcelona, beat Sampdoria to win the European Cup. But leisure time is not one of his priorities. A great deal of his non-playing, non-business time is taken up with exercises to try to ease the pain in his back. He hardly reads books, seldom buys CDs.

As for golf itself, as much as Seve has loved playing it, it's the competition he craved. I once asked him if there was anywhere in the world he had contemplated going to play golf just for fun – Pine Valley, perhaps? He hadn't. Lee Trevino once said: 'I don't know if Seve has ever really enjoyed it [playing golf]. He loved to compete and win, but I don't know that he loved to just play.' Not that friendly games are completely out of the question. He has played with American basketball stars Michael Jordan and Charles Barkley. During the 2004 Madrid Open at Club de Campo, he wanted to fix a game with the rally driver, Carlos Sainz, on the host venue's other course. The club said no. Seve contacted the mayor's office – the club is owned by the city – and got approval. That's the sway he holds.

By and large, however, the trappings of celebrity are not for Seve, even if he does sometimes show up as a guest at the Spanish Grand Prix and he and Carmen were invited to the Spanish royal wedding in May 2004. For some contemporary sportsmen, fame doesn't seem so much a logical extension of their ability and notoriety, more the apotheosis of what they do. Not so for Seve. Accepting fame did not come easily or naturally. He played golf to be the best player in the world. If asked about the consequences, he would have realised that money and fame would surely follow. But those weren't the reasons he was in the game. He was in it because it was the game he was raised on.

In 2002, he said: 'At the beginning, I enjoyed it on tour. It's like when you fly for the first time – everything is fantastic. But you get tired of it. You eat in wonderful restaurants and stay in 5-star hotels, but it's a weird world. You are not living like a normal person. When I come home, I feel happier. When I go to tournaments, everyone shouts my name and idolises me. I feel embarrassed. To be honest, I'm tired of that. I don't like it.'

Seve has often and genuinely professed his admiration for players like Arnold Palmer, who are willing to devote hours signing autographs for their fans. Phil Mickelson is perhaps the most eminent current player who has a reputation for generosity in this way. Seve does sign, and he's happy with the adulation and understands that it is his duty to satisfy his public with this small if time-consuming ritual, but he finds it a bind. He learned one particularly practical tip off Nicklaus in this respect: as you sign, keep on walking. If you don't, you'll be out there forever, the target of a thousand biros.

Such can be the allure of his presence that it isn't just fans who can be captivated by him; feel themselves drawn to the charismatic force field of his personality. An illustration of this occurred after our conversation at Atlanta Airport in 2003. Seve drifted off to get a glass of water. When he returned to his seat, people flocked to him like bees round a honey pot – as they do. He had as his main audience Peter Dawson and his predecessor as R&A secretary, Sir Michael Bonallack. Among other things, Seve told them the rule that had enforced a two-shot penalty on Jeff Maggert at the Masters the previous day after his ball rebounded on to him from the face of a bunker was 'ridiculous – there should be no penalty'; there should be a limit of 54 degrees on wedges ('It's a good point,' said Dawson); the tournament ball should be increased to 1.72 inches; grandstands at the Open should be considered as regular obstructions and be in play – 'Everyone knows they are there' (Dawson said: 'Actually, I agree with him'); and the long- and belly-putter should be banned – 'I was thinking of using one this week but the greens at Augusta are too undulating, but within seven years everyone will be using one or the other'. It was hugely entertaining banter. It was also very noticeable that whereas the R&A types were all around him, Ken Schofield, John Paramor and Andy McFee from the European Tour stayed away, on the other side of the room.

But it has been the staff of the Tour, not the gentlemen of St Andrews, who have been on the receiving end of Seve's combative behaviour for so many years. It wasn't just that Seve was in the vanguard of any conflict because he was Europe's first world-class golfer. Those incidents arose in part because of what he's like.

In January 2006, Mac O'Grady told *Golf World* magazine in the States that he was writing a book of his own, called *Seve, the Commissioner*. 'He should be the commissioner,' Mac said. 'Seve knows the game better than anybody.'

Perhaps Schofield got out in time.

11. SWINGS AND ROUNDABOUTS

Until Tiger Woods emerged on the tournament scene with the impact of a meteorite, Seve was the youngest Masters champion ever, just past his 23rd birthday. Tiger had two shots at beating that mark once he turned professional and he took it at his first attempt.

Tiger won the 1997 Masters by 12 shots with a record-low total of 270 as he set about rewriting the tournament's record books in a way that Seve seemed he might in 1980. Seve had been derailed by the 12th and 13th holes but he'd won the tournament anyway. On the first day of the 1997 Masters, Seve approached the par-five 13th at one over par, not great but not bad. (Woods played the front nine in a four-over-par 40 before tearing the course to bits.) He had parred the preceding 12 holes. He then played 13, 14, 15 in 6-6-8 – bogey, double-bogey, triple-bogey – and finished with an 81. Previously, it had seemed he almost owned the place. Now it was like someone else had possession of his swing. Even at his beloved Augusta, he couldn't find the semblance of a golf game that had been largely missing since he'd mislaid it some time before his Ryder Cup singles against Tom Lehman in 1995. He wasn't really passing the torch over to Tiger – it's doubtful he could have hit that target.

At the end of the 1997 season, in which Seve was the non-playing Ryder Cup captain, he was asked how many more times he thought he might be capable of playing in the match. 'I think maybe three more times. It just depends on my desire and how I feel physically.' After that, he never finished in the top-100 on the European Order of Merit. If his illustrious past hadn't secured his playing rights on the Tour, only in 1998 would he have retained his player's card.

It may be that Seve's belief in his own ability to analyse his swing and how to deal with it was flawed because he failed to take account of the ageing process. Certainly, golf-wise, his defied logic. For most professional golfers, the short game goes first. The touch shots, the ones that require greater feel, are the ones professional golfers no longer have at their beck and call. Putting can present near-insuper-able difficulties. They may get the dreaded 'yips', the inability to control the small muscles and nerves in the hands, but in any case they have seen so many short ones go past the hole that the sense of invincibility they had in their youth – when the very notion of missing a three-foot putt was frankly preposterous – has given way to a deep, abiding certainty of their vulnerability. The miss is no longer the exception; it's the expected.

With Seve, it was the other way around. As he so decisively demonstrated in his match against Tom Lehman at Oak Hill in 1995, his short game was outstanding. However, the shot Seve could not rely on is the one that 99.9 per cent of pro golfers, probably including club pro's in that figure, know they have in their locker – the safe bunt down the fairway. It may not go very far but they can be sure they can steer it on to the short grass and then get to work in earnest. Seve, who has had no superior as a shotmaker in this infernal game, could not manage that. 'I always thought it was strange that he couldn't be as precise from the tee as he was from the trees,' his old adversary (well, one of them), Hale Irwin, told *Golf Digest*. His confidence was fragile not around the greens but when he was on what should be the sanctuary of the tee, a perfect lie guaranteed off a peg.

In September 2000, I was talking to him about how Tiger seemed to play so aggressively all the time. 'Yes,' agreed Seve, 'but when I had my new BMW, I was very confident with it at first. But then I had an accident, and the confidence is not the same. You know what I mean?'

You have to laugh. In *Golf World* in 2007, Jock Howard wrote of Seve's reckless car driving while he was with him in Pedrena. When I was with him in the Canary Islands in 1995, I recall he didn't once get the vehicle out of second gear. It's not only on the golf course, or in his buggy at Valderrama in 1997, that his driving could be, shall we say, idiosyncratic.

Even in what might be termed the parts of the golf course where he was in his element, trouble, his mental resources drained away. 'The first time I went in the trees,' he said, 'I saw only the green and how I could put the ball on it. Now I see the branches and the roots and the trunk. Experience can be a marvellous asset but it can also be bad.'

Generally, Seve could still play when he was within, say, 150 yards of the green. 'Seve plays shots I don't even see in my dreams,' said Ben Crenshaw, twice a Masters champion. Lee Westwood said: 'He pulled off shots others wouldn't even have thought about, and that was part of the thrill.' The problem was, Seve had usually been in trouble by the time he got 150 yards away. His skills at bunker play, pitching, chipping and putting have long been lauded. The rest was lamented.

As sadly became more evident in recent years, Seve was not shy in talking himself up, no doubt at least in part because everyone else treated his golf like a disease. Comparing himself to Phil Mickelson, he said: 'My short game is one of the best ever. Great technique and great imagination. I have many more shots around the green than he does and I'm a much better putter.' So that's one of the world's best put firmly in his place.

In his pomp, Seve's waywardness – which wasn't always apparent though the tendency was invariably present – was compensated for by his length, hence his strategy for conquering Royal Lytham when he won his first Open in 1979. In those days – this with wooden-headed drivers, remember – he could smash the ball 300 yards through the air. As his length diminished, that was no longer a viable way to go about beating the course. As he was constantly reminding himself of his own fallibility with the longer clubs, it was no wonder his performances with them became less proficient. Of course, it should be acknowledged that you don't win what Seve did if you've never been able to hit a driver or a long iron.

In February 1985, I was with him at La Manga where he was working on his swing with Manuel's assistance. 'I would say, right now, just about everything is wrong,' he said. 'I'm playing like a 4- or 5-handicapper.' Remember, this was within seven months of him having won the Open; less than two months before he would run Bernhard Langer so close in the Masters.

Manuel said: 'Seve has not felt right in himself since the 1980 Masters. His swing may look good but it does not feel right to him.' Seve agreed. 'Yes, that's so. The 1980 Masters was the best golf I've ever played from tee to green. My tempo has been wrong for some time.' As far as the technical aspect of the game goes, that Masters – or at least the first 63 holes of it – would remain the apogee of Seve's career, despite all the other victories that would follow.

In itself, this is no quirk. Jack Nicklaus recalled Gene Littler, a fine player and the US Open champion in 1961, once saying to him: 'It's a long time since I've played real good golf. It must be at least five or six years.' Nicklaus himself, this after he had won three Masters, two US Opens, an Open and a USPGA, wrote: 'I wonder if I have ever hit the ball as squarely or sustained my shotmaking at as high a level as I reached at 20 [as an amateur].'

Seve's first win over Colin Montgomerie at the Seve Trophy in 2000 emphatically made the point that when he was free of the fear of marking a card, when the odd triple-bogey or two wouldn't mean an irretrievably lost cause, he could still play. In the event, when he beat Monty in their singles match, he shot 67 round the Old Course at Sunningdale, missing just three fairways. It was written up, incorrectly, in more than one paper that he had won even though he had played wildly. In Seve's case, his reputation for that went ahead of him more assuredly than one of his better drives.

Of course, the fact that throughout his career he was having to play from the rough meant fans could relate to him more readily than other players because he was in trouble as often as they would be, albeit they couldn't get out of it like he could. Spectators would prefer to see someone play the front nine in a level-par score comprised of two birdies, an eagle and four dropped shots than with nine straight pars.

It was, I think, in part the British adoration for the manner in which Seve set about the golf course that meant when Nick Faldo won his first major championship, the 1987 Open at Muirfield, with a final round of 18 consecutive pars (which only did the trick when Paul Azinger completed his round with two consecutive bogeys), this admirable achievement of consistency and resilience under the severest sporting pressure was slightly derided in some quarters as almost unworthy because it had manifestly not been dramatic. Faldo admitted how he'd think his game was gone forever if he hit it in the places Seve did. For Seve, there was no situation he could get into that he wasn't capable of getting out of.

In his book *On Golf*, the author Timothy O'Grady wrote of a visit to Oak Hill. The club president couldn't wait to show him something. 'He took me to a spot in the trees of the nearly 600-yard long 13th,' wrote O'Grady, 'to describe a shot struck by Severiano Ballesteros during [the 1989] US Open. He was about 40 yards into these woods on the left, with a 10-yard corridor leading out between the trees to the fairway. This corridor was at an angle of around 135 degrees to the direction of the hole. Nearly anyone else would have simply punched the ball back out to the fairway, but Ballesteros took out a 3-wood, hit it low off the dirt and the leaves through the gap, and when the ball got out into the open it rose high into the air and took the 135 degrees left turn to finish around 260 yards up the hole in the centre of the fairway. It was the most astonishing thing, said the president, that he'd ever seen on a golf course.'

At the 1994 Masters, the first of the two Olazábal would win, Seve opened with a 70 to Chema's 74. He was playing with Raymond Floyd, who got to see at first-hand the sort of shot no one else could ever play, even in their dreams. On the 4th, a long par-three, Seve's tee shot left him with a frightening pitch over a bunker to a green that sloped away from him. The ball flew gently through the air and, in a phrase used fondly by the late Dave Marr, sat down by the pin like a butterfly with sore feet. 'The most fabulous par I've ever seen,' said Floyd. 'His short game is fantastic. There isn't anyone in the world even close to him.'

The Zimbabwean tour professional, Tony Johnstone, told Lauren St John how he once saw Seve hitting shots after stamping some golf balls into the ground. 'It's against the bounds of science, but he was hitting shots with a ball that was entirely, 100 per cent, underground. He was hitting these shots and getting them to come out high and soft and land and then run three or four feet. I mean, it can't be done. *It can't be done.* But he was doing it. I could stand there for 50 years and I couldn't ever make that happen.'

Geoff Ogilvy, the 2006 US Open champion, said: 'Seve was all emotion and art. I played with him once. He was past his peak but was so much fun to watch. He still hit a couple of shots where you just went, "Oh, come on, you can't do that!"'

Recalling the man's genius to the American golf writer Jaime Diaz, Rodger Davis mentioned a shot Seve had played in a tournament at Wentworth. 'He'd pushed his drive into these thick pine trees with branches that hung within four feet of the ground. Seve got on his knees and from 185 yards he flew a 4-iron to within 20 feet of the pin. Most pro's wouldn't have been able to carry such a shot 20 yards. Magnificent.'

'Peter Alliss used to say I hit miracle shots,' said Seve. 'I never thought that. Miracles don't happen very often; I was hitting those shots all the time.'

Tiger Woods told *Golf Digest* of his preparation for his first Masters as a pro, that 1997 extravaganza. He played nine holes with Seve on the Monday before. 'Of course I picked his brain. He was incredible. He told me the shots you need to play, the clubs you need to play with. I played with him and Ollie [José María Olazábal].' Then he used that 'G' word again. 'It was awesome to hear genius at work, because I had no clue.'

Such talent. Such genius. If only he'd listened to the right man. Or to anyone – just so long as it was only the one. 'All these teachers,

I appreciate their help very much because they have tried to help me,' said Seve in 1998, 'but some of them frighten me when I see them out there. In fact, they hurt me more than helped me.'

José Maria Olazábal spoke for most tour players and golf teachers when he said: 'I've said it to Seve quite a few times, he needs to go with a coach, just one guy, whoever he decides, and stick with him for five or six months and see if he improves in that time. Having said that, it's hard for him to go and work with somebody because he has done it himself, his own way, for all his career.'

Indeed. Butch Harmon, David Leadbetter, Robert Baker, Mac O'Grady, John Jacobs, Simon Holmes, Stuart Smith, Peter Kostis, Bob Torrance, Mitchell Spearman, Jim McLean, Dennis Sheehy – that's not an inclusive list of instructors who have worked with Seve and it doesn't count his brothers. Come to think of it, I might have given him a tip myself at some point while lurking around on a magazine instruction shoot.

One such, in Miami in 1988, was especially amusing. I was there but, as usual, mostly to help the photographer – Steve Szurlej of *Golf Digest* – lug his stuff around, leaving the writing to someone who could play golf properly, in this instance John Huggan. It was agreed Seve would meet us at 3.30 p.m. We had lunch while we waited. He then showed up at 3 – as you probably realise, late is more frequent than early in such situations. That didn't stop Huggan blurting out 'You're early!' in an accusatory way. I ushered Seve out of the door before he might decide to pull out entirely.

Echoing Olazábal, Butch Harmon, Tiger Woods' long-time coach, said a few years ago: 'The big thing is that he never stuck with one person. He went to everybody and tried too many quick fixes. A swing change takes time but Seve always wanted it right now. He has spent the last several years looking for quick fixes. I have great respect for Seve; I think he's a great champion. If I could get him to step back, take five or six months off and put his faith in one person, be it me or someone else, he could win tournaments again. The guy's short game is still phenomenal. As we're talking, he's one of the best putters on the European Tour. His creativity is unmatched by anybody other than maybe Tiger Woods. His desire to compete and to win is still there.' That reflects it all: Seve's talent and temperament, his impatience and impetuosity.

If Butch Harmon isn't rated the world's top golf teacher, David Leadbetter is. He already had a high reputation in the mid-1980s. When he then helped turn Nick Faldo from one of the best players in Europe into the best player in the world by undertaking an extensive, two-year modification of Faldo's swing, his position as one of the world's best golf teachers was secure.

'Seve has always had to guard against going left,' said Leadbetter in 1990. 'Even when he won the Open at Lytham in 1979, you could see the way he was fighting to hold the club on line. When he won the Open there in 1988, he hadn't been playing well for some time, but once he won that he was off and winning again. With him, it may just come down to confidence. Seve still has a young man's swing and it's hard for his body to cope with the power it generates. He has a perfect grip, a perfect set-up and wonderful rhythm, but he does tend to hit the ball while off-balance, leading to a 'reverse-C' position in his follow-through.'

Leadbetter worked with Seve in Japan in 1991. He came second in one tournament, won another, and then went back to Europe and won the PGA Championship. He finished the year atop the Order of Merit. They then took a further step together.

'Just before the Masters in 1992,' Leadbetter told me in 2005, 'Seve came to Lake Nona [then Leadbetter's Orlando base] and he was looking good. We were working on both shortening his swing but putting greater width into it. We worked on improving his posture, too, not only to improve his swing but also because I was aware of his back problems and felt this would help to ameliorate those in the long term. He went off to New Orleans and had a good tournament there, tied 12th. At Augusta, Billy [Foster, his caddie] was talking early on during the week that Seve could win. The next day, I went on to the range. Billy was there.

That's when it started to go wrong. 'Billy came up to me and said "Fuck,"' recalled Leadbetter. '"What's wrong?" I asked. He pointed to where Seve was – working with Manuel. He was hitting it sideways. He somehow made the cut but he shot 81 on Sunday. I've never worked with him after that and, though I'm not saying how much difference I could have made, he's hardly had a good week since.

'Seve avoided me all that week. About three weeks later, he saw me in Japan again and said that while what I had told him was not wrong, he hadn't followed it through because he felt it was not natural for him – whatever that means – and it was too complicated for him to think about what I'd told him. I think the truth is that Seve is reluctant to credit any teacher with helping him because that would be to admit it had not come from within. I don't think you could say it was obvious his long game would go so badly wrong but you did always know that he was a "feel" player as opposed to a "technical" player, and that he perhaps didn't really have an understanding of the technical concepts of the swing.'

It is hard to see this as anything other than an example of one of his brothers being piqued and Seve – and I realise this sounds incredible given the strength of his character in so many respects – not having the resolution or gumption to do what was best for himself. Perhaps, and again the idea sounds crazy, it was that he would prefer to show solidarity with his family than side with a comparative stranger, even when not in his self-interest.

In July the next year, the Leadbetter experiment having been consigned to the dustbin, Seve's flavour of the month was Simon Holmes, a former protégé of Leadbetter's. I was in the clubhouse at Pedrena (no sign of José Maria Zamora) and I asked Manuel if he was going to the USPGA Championship with Seve in August. 'No,' he said shortly, 'but maybe Seve's friend Simon will be going.' It wasn't intended as a compliment.

I really like Manuel but, like I say, I don't think his influence has been altogether positive when it's come to Seve's swing. This day, he wasn't even very positive about Seve. He believed he was listening to advice from too many quarters and wasn't selective enough about whom. He said: 'I love Seve – he's my brother. But he's lost his charisma. He now believes everything he wants is right.'

Seve was at the beginning of the stage in his career when he had to work hard to keep fighting for pars, which he found so demoralising when for 15 years and more he had been in the mental position of thinking 'birdie' rather than 'bogey'.

Playing golf well to tour professional standard is extremely difficult. Doing it badly is twice as hard. By the mid-1990s, Seve was exhausted at the end of every round. The game had become an ordeal. After his extraordinary Ryder Cup performance in 1995, Seve implemented a strategy he had decided on before going to Oak Hill. On 28 September, four days after he had succumbed to Lehman, he announced he was taking a five-month break from competitive golf.

> I have been a professional for more than 20 years. Everyone knows how much I love the game, and my passion for competition, and I know this mid-career break will be good for my golf . . . I wouldn't want anyone to think this decision has anything to do with an early retirement. It is quite the opposite and I wish to stress this now. The rest will enable me to take enough fresh air and resume my career in the best possible frame of mind.
>
> I have set targets throughout my career. I have fulfilled many of my ambitions. The game of golf has been very good to me. Now my intention is to play until I am 54. Why 54? I think for me this will be a good stage to stop playing, more than 35 years after becoming a professional.

He quit four years short of that.

When Seve did come back in 1996, as we have seen, he didn't set the golf world on fire, even if he was perhaps tempted to torch the flow of articles dissecting how awful his swing was. Maybe it was the company he was keeping. In July 1997, Sergio Gomez, Olazábal's manager, mentioned that Seve was spending a lot of time with José Rivero, who was talking of giving up the game. 'Seve is like a cancer patient,' said Gomez. 'He should not spend all his time with people who have the same illness.'

At the end of that month, Seve played in a pre-Ryder Cup, made-for-TV exhibition against his soon-to-be opposing captain, Tom Kite, at Pedrena. His drive at the first was such a violent hook that it finished in the trees on the far side of the 18th fairway. He shot in the 80s. Kite later said: 'I've never seen a good player drive it the way he did.' No one knew which coach Seve was working with at this point but there was one popular theory going round – that Seve was working with Dennis Sheehy under the mistaken impression that he was Denis Pugh, Colin Montgomerie's teacher.

At the Open two years later, I met Baldomero regarding the proposed autobiography. He said it was likely Seve would only play five or six more tournaments in 1999 so that he could work on his game, ready for 2000. He talked about coaches who had worked with Seve; how he thought they had gradually removed the instinct to simply hit the ball that had made him great to begin with. Baldomero felt Robert Baker was the best – 'He keeps things simple' – and Mac O'Grady the worst – 'Seve was trying to think of a million things. It was impossible.' What was funny about this was that Seve was about to quit working with Baker to go back to O'Grady. Seve hadn't yet told Baker, even though Baker knew, so Seve was taken aback to see Baker and O'Grady having dinner with a couple of mutual acquaintances one evening. 'This is a very strange table,' Seve had said, as sheepishly as he's capable of.

For all his failures as a player over the past decade, when Seve played, people still went to watch him. Granted, given that he went from October 2003 to October 2005 without playing a tournament, this was not easy to do, but the fans were always there for him.

This was not mere car-crash stuff, to see if he could run up double figures somewhere. He consistently drew the biggest galleries for so long because the spectators were hoping he could provide something that no one else in the field could. 'They come to see a shot of genius,' he said. 'They know that I can still produce something special.' When that happened, it was of no relevance that he was eight over par rather than eight under.

In 2000, he told John Huggan for *Golf Digest*: 'What I can tell you is that when I was in my best time, I had so much confidence. I knew I was the best. Whenever I finished second or third, I knew it was a bad result, because I knew I was better than the others. I could always see more shots than anyone else. Some people don't have that. Some people have that. I don't know if genius is the right word, but that is how I am.'

However, there was this, too: 'It is hard to know you don't have the game to win, and that making the cut is the best you can hope for. When you do that, you never get the chance to compete. And you never have rhythm. Then you lose confidence. You are what you believe you are.'

The following year, Ian Woosnam told the *Daily Mail*: 'I don't know how he can keep going. If I played like that, I'd have to go away and sort it out, and if I couldn't sort it out, I'd pack up.'

But Seve was in denial. In March 2002, he had told the *Sunday Telegraph*: 'I think I can win the Masters. You may sound surprised [I should imagine the sound was the paper's golf correspondent, Mark Reason, falling off his chair] but I am very confident this year. I have a very good feeling in myself. I am capable of winning.' The basis of this absurd boast was that he'd been shooting 66s in practice at Pedrena, whereas a year before it had been 76s. Even though Seve obviously knew the difference between practice and reality, he had expected to play well. His subsequently dreadful golf in Qatar and Madeira, followed by 75–81 at Augusta, left him distraught.

He was also awful at the Seve Trophy and the Spanish Open, after which he withdrew from the Benson & Hedges International and the Volvo PGA Championship in England. He could hardly comprehend it. Then, in June, came the Irish Open where Seve was disqualified for signing for that incorrect score – for a 10 at the 18th when he'd actually taken 12. Apparently, he had lost count of how many balls he'd hit into the water. While his owning up was honourable and proper, there were those who wondered if he'd committed the infraction on purpose because he couldn't face the thought of more torture on the morrow.

His record in Europe for 2002 showed he had played nine

tournaments (none in the UK), missing six cuts, being disqualified in Ireland, withdrawing in Switzerland and making one cut. For 2003, his last season of 'proper' competition, his record included another no-show at the Open, a warning for slow play in Madeira, a worst-ever 85 at Augusta, disqualified amid the 'Mafia' row in Italy and another withdrawal in Switzerland. From seven starts, he made only one cut, a tie for 67th in Madeira, which – as we have seen – wasn't an unmitigated blessing in itself.

How did it ever get to this? For the answer to that, or at least part of it, one has to go back to the beginning, to the back injury he suffered aged 14 and the consequent stress put on his back by incessant practice. As long ago as 1977, when he was 20, Seve visited a Madrid specialist who suggested he sleep with a board under a hard mattress. That was easy enough to do. He also advised that Seve take six months off from golf, but there was no way that was going to happen.

In 1978, Seve told *Golf World*: 'I can only practise for about an hour a day. I'd like to practise more but cannot for fear of aggravating the back trouble. It's worrying enough for me to have seen several specialists but I think it is OK if I do not overdo the practice. That could be dangerous because aggravating the trouble could force me off the circuit. I can live with the problem.'

At the 1980 Masters, he had dinner on the Saturday night with some friends, business associates and journalists. One of the latter was Myra Gelband of *Sports Illustrated*. He told her: 'If I talk about my back, then I will think about the pain. Then I will feel it, so I don't talk about it. Only I will know.' He once said to me: 'It's like if you think about something nice, you start smiling. If you think of something bad, you start crying.' In his rented house that week at Augusta, he had brought with him from home a trapeze-like contraption – the 'Gravity Gym' – from which he would hang in order to help get his back in working order.

Essentially, everything he did, or could do short of abstaining from golf for a significant period, was a palliative. Over time it has caught up with him, as time tends to do. He went with his family for eight weeks of treatment in Arizona in late 1993, shortly after his dispiriting performance against Jim Gallagher in the Ryder Cup singles. He attributed much of his poor play at the 1995 Ryder Cup to his back problems. As far as Seve was concerned, the tournament victories he enjoyed in 1994 and 1995, at the end of the winning phase of his career, were achieved despite the pain, glorious flourishes that retaliated against the evisceration of his talents by the passing of the years and the pain in his body.

After he withdrew during the 1996 Players Championship, he had an operation on his back. His playing partner on the day in question, Robert Gamez, was asked if he had noticed when Seve suffered his injury. He said he hadn't seen it. 'The way he was hitting it, I didn't want to watch.'

By March 1997, Seve was at a well-known clinic near Munich, to see the controversial Dr Hans-Wilhelm Müller-Wohlfahrt, the specialist who had corrected the faulty diagnosis originally given to José Maria Olazábal and then treated him to such effect through 1996 that Olazábal, who a year before had feared his career was over – indeed that he might be a permanent cripple – had just resumed competitive golf. I say controversial because the doctor's use of such things as sheep's amniotic fluids and calves' blood had aroused widespread intrigue, but that such eminent athletes as Linford Christie, Boris Becker and the Bayern Munich football team were among his patients (as Michael Owen, Paula Radcliffe and the German World Cup football team would later be), not forgetting what he had done for Olazábal, was vivid testimony to his expertise.

Among the sceptics of this plan was Olazábal. Before Seve went, his friend told him: 'Seve, this man is not the doctor for you.'

'Why not?' asked Seve. 'You don't know what's wrong with my back.'

'No, Seve, but I know you.'

Seve stayed in Munich for two weeks but left because he wasn't feeling any improvement. In this respect, he surely got it wrong; Chema had got it right. Müller-Wohlfahrt's treatment of Olazábal proved that he knew what he was doing. One couldn't help but feel that Seve was looking for a quick fix for what had been a very long-term injury, a mindset beyond optimism or logic. It's the same problem that has dogged his attempted swing cures: his own incurable impatience. Robert Baker once recommended that he see another specialist in this field, another man with a fine reputation, in his case based on alternative, holistic medicine. That didn't work either. 'With those guys,' said Seve, 'you have to believe, and I did not believe.' The end result, as Baker said in describing Seve's problems from a technical perspective, is that 'he can't swing properly because his back's a mess'.

As he has got older, of course, his back has not got better. Many people reading this will have found themselves starting to suffer back pains once they reach their 40s. It's commonplace. The abandonment of good posture in the mists of their youth and, later, all those years of sitting badly at desks and in cars, together with lack of proper exercise, have contributed to the condition. Backs do not tend to get better, they get worse. And if you've had a bad one since your early teens, and you play professional golf for a living, the chances are that yours might be one of the worst of the lot.

Despite the discomfort, often acute, Seve tried to fight on through, sometimes to his own detriment. At the 2003 European Masters, he shot an opening 74 and then spent 3½ hours on the practice range. As a result, he so damaged his back that he had to withdraw from the tournament for the second year running.

In early 2004, Seve resolved to prepare properly for Augusta. 'For the last few years, I have gone into the Masters with almost no competitive play,' he declared. 'That is not good and neither is the fact that I have not been flexible enough to play my best.' Accordingly, his latest assault on his back problems was Pilates. 'It is boring, boring, boring,' he said. 'Lying still doing breathing exercises for 1½ hours a day is not easy. But I believe it is making a difference.'

The second step was to write to several American tour sponsors for invitations. His reward was an encouraging response and a desperate denouement. During the pro-am for the first of these tournaments, the Ford Championship at the Doral Country Club in

Miami, he had to withdraw after nine holes, so painful was his back. He couldn't swing the club. Two weeks later, he didn't help himself by practising further at Bay Hill, where he filled his time later in the week by doing some guest commentary for USA Television. Now he wouldn't play the Masters at all. As we know, he didn't play any tournament for a further 18 months.

By the end of that May, Seve was sounding uncompromisingly bleak. He told Derek Lawrenson of the *Daily Mail*: 'I have to face up to the fact that I may never play again in competition. My back is riddled with arthritis and I have no feeling in the middle of my neck. I have hardly any mobility. There is no cartilage left between my vertebrae and every time I practise, they rub together. When that happens, it goes way beyond discomfort. I know pain, but no one could play golf with this amount of pain.' He also admitted: 'I wouldn't say I am destroyed mentally but I am very low.'

Later in the month, Olazábal told the media in Britain: 'I feel sad for Seve. I feel sad for me. I feel sad for the game. No one has made a bigger contribution to [the European Tour]. He was the one who broke down all the barriers, all the walls. He made the rest of the players of his time believe they could win anywhere. I don't think anyone comes close to him in this part of the world.'

At the end of June, I rang Seve to see if things really were so bleak. In fact, although the press had been full of how he had withdrawn from the Open in light of his back problems, he told me he would be at Troon, albeit not to play in the championship. He had a Callaway commitment on the Friday and Saturday beforehand and on the day prior to our conversation, on some business with a group that had been arranged ages before, he had played golf at St Andrews. He said his back hurt a lot but it was not as bad as had been painted by the *Daily Mail* article. 'I know you writers,' he said. 'The first rule of journalism is to make sure you have a strong story.' He even said his back was improving and that he played maybe three times a week, but to be ready to play in a tournament was a completely different matter from just playing golf. 'I am putting a lot of pressure on myself,' he said. 'I cannot just turn up at the Open and play. When I am ready, I will play in some smaller tournaments.'

At the end of October, he was at the Madrid Open – not playing, but talking a good game about how much he might play in 2005. He was brandishing a copy of the proposed third edition of *Seve Ballesteros* magazine, which included several photos of him working out in the gym. He boasted to journalists that he could lift a mountain bike above his head. Earlier in the year, it was as much as he could do to lift his arms that high without the bike. 'This year is closed,' he said, 'but it is my intention to do next year what I wanted to do this year – that is, to play several tournaments before the Masters, some in America if I can get the invitations, and come back and play in Europe.' As we know, he didn't play any tournament for a further 12 months.

In the interim, there were countless more pills and exercises – swimming, gym time and bike riding – and assorted herbal remedies and alternative medicines. He can never feel comfortable but he feels better if he is standing up and walking around rather than standing still or sitting down. Playing golf caused him as much pain as it did because of the incessant stop-go: hit your ball, walk to it, wait, assess the shot, hit, walk some more, bend down on the green to mark your ball, wait, putt, bend down again to get it out of the hole (eventually), walk a bit more and then bend down again to insert your peg on the next tee. His back has been the cross he has had to bear. Because it's twisted, maybe that's why he's bitter.

In late 2004, Nick Faldo said to me, with reference to Seve's back having been in a mess in the 1980s: 'Poor bugger. And now he's sad. What I'm sad about is that he's sad. When he talks, he talks down about himself. That is sad, because he was frigging awesome. He was one of the world's greatest sportsmen. It's sad to see the way he is right now.'

That he was able to play the Madrid Open in October 2005 demonstrated that at least there had been some improvement. Precisely how he had effected this was a subject on which he was typically enigmatic at the time – 'If I told you that, we wouldn't have much to talk about over the coming months' – but whatever it was had evidently worked to some degree.

In late January 2006, Seve's office announced that his intention to start the new season at the Dubai Desert Classic had been changed. 'Seve wants to practise some more and the other thing is his back,' read the statement. 'He's been doing exercises, but he has some pain. He wants to be at the Masters in April and is hoping to play before then.' He neither played before the Masters or in it, although he did to no great effect manage the French Open and the Open, and the Masters one year later.

As much as his back has hampered his game forever, there is no escaping the technical flaws that have beset Seve's swing. I also asked Faldo if he – who probably knows as much about the technique of swinging a golf club as any player – could ever have foreseen that Seve's game could have unravelled as it has. 'Oh yeah,' he replied. 'Technically he was a feel player with astonishing touch and creative ability. Tell Seve to hit it down the fairway, he can't do it. Tell him there's a tree in front of him and he'd find a way to get it out and around. He has great visualisation skills – to be in the bushes and to be able to conjure up a shot.

'I know it sounds daft, but pro's probably try to hit the ball too straight. When I had problems with my swing, it was like "Go and hit a big hook; 'course you can hit a big hook. Go and hit a big fade; 'course you can – till the cows come home." Then I'd think "So go out and play that way." So I'd go out on to the course and aim at a right-hand bunker and hit a big hook. Obviously you have to do all the adjustments to make it happen, but when we start nitpicking about hitting it five feet right of the pin with a tiny little draw and then you tweak it a little bit, suddenly it's 20 feet left, or it doesn't happen at all. I think this is what may have happened to Seve. He was never technical, then he tries to get technical, and he got bogged down with it all. He went round asking everyone for advice and they gave it to him, and 99 times out of 100 he wouldn't take it because he didn't like it. I think he got lost in all of that.

'I remember at the 1995 Open at St Andrews, I was walking

across the practice ground back to the hotel [and came across Seve]. I remember saying something like: "I'd love to have just a few minutes with you." I had been working on something, I think along those lines – nothing technical, give me a draw, give me a fade – and how to do that. But he didn't seem to want to know.'

Greg Norman disagreed, at least to some degree. 'From a technical aspect, I couldn't see this happening to Seve. I thought Seve had a pretty good swing. But Seve's approach to golf is very much aggressive, swashbuckling. He did a lot of improvisation as he went round. Now is that changing your swing on every shot? In fact, I've seen him do that, where he has made a different swing on each shot. I can't say whether what he did then has technically affected the way he is now. I can't say that.'

He added: 'I can say this. Seve was one of the unique talents that I've ever played golf with. Every time I played golf with him, it intensified me more because of his intensity. He was different to play golf with, not like some guys – whether you beat them or not is no big deal. You wanted to play well against Seve, and you wanted to beat him because he just wanted to beat you so badly every time.' Few would argue with that. Certainly not Curtis Strange.

In 2005, Vijay Singh told *Golf World* (US): 'The thing is to never let yourself slip more than one or two steps. You slip more than two steps, then it takes four steps to get back to the top because everyone else is climbing. That's what happened to Seve, who was like God on the golf course when I was playing the European Tour. He was probably the best player of the whole lot the last 25 years. But he let himself fall too far behind, and then it was just too much work to catch up and the load got too heavy and he kept slipping back down.'

Norman also made another point about Seve, a more glorious memory. He told *Golf Digest*: 'I used to be in awe of Seve Ballesteros and the way he'd deliberately hook or slice the ball 60 yards. He was the best shotmaker I ever saw. We'll never see the likes of him again, because the equipment won't allow it. It's very hard to make the modern ball curve. You've heard this before, usually from a 70-year-old guy who you think is just pining for the good old days. But I'm telling you, equipment has made the game less spectacular to watch.'

That was a perennial complaint of Seve's, and not only after he was brought low by the ruination of his own game. The fact that players hit it so far these days means they can carry a plethora of wedges. Seve had to acquire the skill to play a less-than-full shot if he was playing anything under 100 yards, either going down on the shaft with his grip, opening the clubface wider, taking a shorter backswing, hitting the ball softer or whatever. Today, players have wedges for which a 60-yard carry is a full shot. 'The 60-degree wedge requires no feel and no imagination,' says Seve. 'The lob-wedge has changed golf. Other players could not do what I could with an ordinary wedge.' Him using one of those clubs would be like Michelangelo grabbing a roller to paint the Sistine Chapel.

Nick Price recently told *Golf Digest*: 'Seve was probably the best I ever saw with a 56-degree wedge. He was a wizard. When the more-lofted wedges came along, he lost a lot of his advantage.'

In his autobiography, *My Story*, Jack Nicklaus wrote: 'The more forgiving the tools, the tougher it becomes for the best to rise above the rest. Much as Seve Ballesteros, for example, stood out from the crowd . . . [his] talent and dedication would have separated him even more had all the players still competed with the equipment of my early professional years.'

In January 2006, Tiger Woods was saying to *Golf Digest*: 'You look on Tour and you ask, "Who's a true shotmaker? Who actually manoeuvres the ball or does something different with it?" And there really aren't that many, if any, out here anymore.' You couldn't have a more emphatic example of this than the fact that Phil Mickelson won the 2006 Masters carrying two drivers in his bag – one to fade the ball, the other to draw it. Woods also said: 'I'd eliminate the 60-degree wedge and set a 56-degree limit. For one, it would bring more feel back into the game. Because now guys lay up to exact yardages and hit nothing but full shots. Nobody hits half-shots anymore . . . It's all about keeping the skill factor. At the moment, equipment has brought everyone closer together. It's harder to separate from the field, without a doubt.'

'I see good swings and good players,' said Seve in 2005, 'but nothing that really keeps me watching television for a long time. There is nothing special. With metal woods, it's very hard to shape shots. Balls are now designed to fly straight and always on the same trajectory. When I play, it seems like they are turning to the right but they don't. It is like they have radar and they come back to the fairway. [His ultimate dream, you'd have thought.] Everybody has been equalised by the new clubs, the long putter, more loft on wedges. Something has to be done with the rules.'

Today, golf is a power game. It's like Indiana Jones in *Raiders of the Lost Ark* when Indy, suddenly bored with all that brandishing by the bad guy with the scimitar, takes out his gun and shoots him dead. There's no skill required like that of the evil swordsman in modern golf. By way of illustration, both the 1999 and 2005 US Opens were played at Pinehurst. In 1999, John Daly was the longest driver with an average belt of 286.3 yards. In 2005, no less than 64 players who made the cut were longer than that. Tiger Woods was King Kong with 325.9; 18 others were more than 300 yards. Furthermore, computer technology means that not only is equipment superior to what it used to be, the players can now maximise all the benefits.

Seve's raging against new technology is slightly compromised by the fact that since 2001 he has had a club contract with Callaway, one of the world's leading manufacturers of golf equipment, which markets a comprehensive range of clubs but largely the sort that make the ball easier to hit for you and me rather than developed for superior ball-strikers. But then why wouldn't he? Callaway is not only a very reputable and successful company, Seve was a professional golfer.

Seve Ballesteros, Professional Golfer. That is how he became known to the world and it is how he defined himself. 'We all live and die,' he told the *Sunday Times* in May 2003. 'Everything has a beginning and an end, and it's the same in golf. I continue to compete because it's my profession.'

The American writer, Red Smith, famously paid tribute to Fred Corcoran, one of the earliest golf promoters, with the words: 'Dying is no big deal. The least of us will manage that. Living is the trick.' On a less terminal scale, those were the sentiments echoed by Seve in 1998 when he said: 'The easiest thing in the world to do when things are going badly is to quit – anyone can do that. The most difficult thing to do is to keep trying.'

For the sake of preserving their own memories of him at his peak, and for what they perceived as being for his own good, some fans as well as critics for years urged Seve to quit playing tournament golf. They felt it was not his outbursts against the authority of the European Tour that harmed his dignity so much as the fact that he carried on playing when sometimes it seemed to be all he could do to hit the ball forwards. Well, now they have got their way.

'No one told me when to start playing golf,' he said more than once. 'No one can tell me when to finish.' But now he's decided that for himself.

In the previously mentioned 2002 BBC interview with him, in reply to Rob Bonnet's repeated questions about what he seemed to think should surely be Seve's impending retirement, Seve's scattergun answers went: 'Golf is my life. It has been my life. I like the competition. Retire! Never. The white flag up? Never. That is the last thing; the easiest way. Never. Never. Arnold Palmer is nearly 75 or something like that and he still plays golf. Never. Retire. Never. When I die. Retire. Never. It never rains forever. It has to stop. I can never be as good as I was, but I can produce now and then a good week.'

He added, which sounds poignant now: 'What happened in the past is done. People will always remember me for that. What happens now, what's the difference? I still produce better shots than anyone else there once in a while. I still believe I can win. I am convinced. I know I am very far away at the moment but it possible to change things. I'm 100 per cent convinced.'

But not any longer. If fooling himself was what he was doing, then that's over with, too. Even casual golf at Pedrena is apparently out-of-bounds. A friend asked him if he still played golf for fun. 'No', he answered. 'It's not fun anymore.'

When Bobby Jones, the greatest amateur golfer in history, died in 1971, after spending the last 20-plus years of his life in a wheelchair due to his suffering from the hideous spinal-wasting disease syringomyelia, Herb Wind's tribute read: 'As a young man, he was able to stand up to just about the best that life can offer, which is not easy, and later he stood up with equal grace to just about the worst.'

Seve's fate is not as grim as that but, like Hamlet, he has been well and truly pelted by the slings and arrows of outrageous fortune. To have been great at golf and then to be so comparatively bad must hurt profoundly, but – as it goes – better to have loved and lost than never to have loved at all. While I have never been in the equivalent position to where Seve was at what he did best, and cannot say for sure what he honestly thinks about his circumstances now, at least he did know the glory days. The perspective is different, but they are our memories as well as his.

12. THE BUSINESS END

If being Seve's caddie was regarded as the toughest job in golf, being his manager is no easy task either. As the following indicates, while he hasn't got through them like he did caddies, or even like Elizabeth Taylor has husbands, the relationship between master and manager was frequently fraught.

It was at Turnberry in September 1975 that Seve was introduced to his first manager, Ed Barner, the preliminaries effected by Roberto de Vicenzo. A month later, Seve signed with Barner's company, Uni-Managers International (UMI). Over time, it was a move he came to regret.

Barner was a member of the Mormon Church (not the reason for Seve's regrets), as were Billy Casper and Johnny Miller, two of the best golfers in the world and both on Barner's books. However, Seve was not the only non-Mormon he looked after. Barner also had Lou Graham and Jerry Pate, respectively the then reigning and the next-to-be US Open champions. Given that Johnny and Seve would be the two main contenders at the following year's Open at Birkdale, things were about to look even better for UMI.

Just about the first business suggestion Barner had was guaranteed to raise Seve's hackles. Barner thought Severiano Ballesteros was too long a name. How about Seve Sota, his mother's family name? That went down like a four-putt green. Eventually, Seve Ballesteros was settled on. Incidentally, Barner had done the opposite with Miller – when he'd finished runner-up at the 1971 Masters, he was known as John. Barner thought that sounded cold and anonymous.

A plethora of deals were lined up, often confusingly. Seve had three different club contracts at one point – Slazenger in Europe, Mizuno in Japan and Sounder in America. The result was that he had many more company days to satisfy for his differing clubs, balls and clothing contracts. At one point, he was wearing Slazenger clothing in the UK, Lacoste in continental Europe, Izod in America and Munsingwear in South Africa. Later, that all became Hugo Boss, with waterproofs by Sunderland. At various points during his career, there have been endorsement deals with American Express, Rolex, Range Rover and Sanyo, and associations with the La Manga Club in Spain and the Doral Country Club in Miami. All considered, he must have had as hard a time keeping track of that lot as one of his wilder tee shots.

Seve also formed his own company, Spangolf Enterprises, for which UMI was the exclusive management representative. Seve's original UMI deal, which ran from 1975–80, had called for UMI to keep 25 per cent of the profits from the contracts it arranged. This was renegotiated down to 20 per cent when it came up for renewal in 1981. Basically, neither side was happy. Barner wanted more for his company; Seve felt likewise for himself. The essence was that they didn't really understand each other's point of view and eventually matters got to the stage where they probably didn't bother trying.

Being disenchanted with having his business in Spain managed from California, in 1981 Seve set up another company called Fairway. (I know, but at least it meant he could find one.) Barner was kept out of this company and it operated out of the Madrid offices of Jorge Ceballos, an old friend of Seve's, originally from Pedrena, who had been the executive director of the Spanish PGA and was now a senior executive with Iberia Airlines. 'We didn't exactly know what a golf manager was like, but we learn that very soon,' Ceballos told me in 1985. 'I think that in the beginning, his relationship with UMI helped Seve to be launched into the world of golf, and into the world of contracts and endorsements, but maybe he could have been in better hands. The American way of doing business is really very brutal sometimes.'

The shareholding in Fairway was set up with 85 per cent held by Seve and five per cent by each of his brothers. When Seve's second contract with UMI was up, in 1983, he wanted Fairway to run all his business affairs. However, the relationship between the two principals, Ballesteros and Barner, had been poisoned by the almost perpetual state of acrimony between them. Resolving their separation staggered on until December 1986, at which point peace, if not harmony, broke out – at least it did for a little over 18 months.

Seve was happier with Ceballos in charge, although Ceballos didn't always notice it. He told *Sports Illustrated* in 1985: 'You meet someone like Seve who has everything – family, health, wealth, fame, the best golf swing – and you think he must be thanking God all the time. But he is not a happy person. I look at him and I think, "What is this damn life doing to him?" He is a perfectionist and perfection is very hard to achieve.'

In February that year, over a typically late dinner in Madrid (the restaurant didn't open until 10.30 p.m.), Ceballos talked of the intense demands on Seve's time. 'Social functions really make Seve very tired and really affect his concentration. We have requested sponsors many times not to oblige him to attend dinners and such things, so they can get the best out of Seve. The less bother he gets, the happier he is and the more likely he is to go back again. Seve's soul is on the golf course, not in a cocktail party.'

The next instalment in Seve's empire was Amen Corner, founded in 1986. This mushroomed out of a joint venture between Fairway and the promotions company of an Irish businessman, Roddy Carr, who would later become another of Seve's managers. The company takes its name from the famous trio of holes on the back nine at Augusta National, the 11th–13th, so named by Herb Wind, who took a line from a jazz song called 'Shoutin' in that Amen Corner' in an essay he wrote for *Sports Illustrated*. The name stuck and has since become part of Masters lore. Given that a catalogue of

Seve's heartaches at Augusta makes for a longer list than his happy memories, it may seem slightly perverse that he should name his company after the course (although to call it 'The 15th' would have made even less sense) but it does show the depth of affection he has for the place.

Amen Corner was the vehicle used first to promote the Spanish Open and later other tournaments in Spain – often in association with Turespana, the Spanish State Tourist Board – and Portugal. As you would expect, Amen Corner also promotes the Seve Trophy. The hope of starting a Senior Ryder Cup probably still remains out there somewhere.

By 1986, Seve's new manager was Joe Collet, Ceballos being preoccupied with his other business interests. Collet had previously been with UMI. A while into Seve's contract there, Barner had put Collet in charge of Seve's affairs. Collet could speak Spanish, which was obviously preferable for Seve when it came to discussing the nitty-gritty of business and the legal niceties of contracts. Collet had left UMI in 1983 and when he became Seve's full-time manager, Seve insisted that he move to Spain. Collet and his family went to live in a nearby village called Somo, from where he commuted to the Fairway offices in Santander by ferry across the bay.

Collet set about expanding Seve's portfolio. He arranged for Seve to design golf courses, to create his own line of clothing and to market fashion accessories such as attaché cases, sunglasses, cuff links, belts and fragrances. In line with this upmarket branding, Seve became a resident of Monaco. The taxes were lower, the weather was warmer (which was good for his back), there were better airport connections and he felt unmolested. Other than in Pedrena, where he was left to his own devices because everyone knew him, Monaco was ideal for someone who didn't want to be disturbed, in this instance because he was relatively anonymous. In Monaco, nearly everyone is a celebrity of some sort. 'In Monte Carlo, I can do what I want without anybody talking to me,' Seve said – which would pretty much be the case on the London Underground, albeit without the tax, climate and airport advantages. Eventually, though, he got tired of what was in some respects a fiction. He did an interview with *Hola* in Spain in which he talked up the pluses of living in Monaco, but really he yearned for the familiarity and simplicity of Pedrena, to where he formally returned.

There were setbacks: quitting the PGA Tour in 1985 cost Seve a Nike contract worth $500,000. There were hassles: Collet was compelled to write to Ken Schofield and John Lindsey, respectively the heads of the European Tour and the British PGA, in June 1990, complaining about Glenmuir using images of Seve as a Ryder Cup player in magazine advertisements for their clothing. Seve was contracted elsewhere and Collet suggested that if this didn't stop, 'wouldn't it follow that each of the players could refuse to wear the "team" clothing on the grounds that it infringed on contractual commitments elsewhere'? And there was still Ed Barner.

After winning the 1988 Open, Seve invited a few journalists round to his rented house for drinks that evening. He told them he had had to pay off Barner to get out of his old contract – that is, to resolve a clause in it which stated that UMI would continue to receive financial benefit from the contracts it had negotiated for Seve so long as the agreements with those companies stayed in place. This hadn't been a huge amount of money, given the sort of sums Seve's bank manager was used to handling, but Seve had forgotten that his settlement with Barner included a confidentiality clause that meant he wasn't even supposed to disclose its existence. Barner sued him and Seve had to pay some more, around $1 million, to be rid of UMI.

Joe Collet was getting restless, too. What he saw as Seve's ultra-cautious business strategy meant his personal financial expectations had not been realised, and increasingly Seve's brothers were being brought more into the decision-making process. 'I was already burdened with so much administrative responsibility that it was becoming increasingly difficult to generate new business,' he said. 'Too much time was spent trying to convince the board to adopt my business plans, leaving insufficient time to go after the next deal.'

By 1995, Joe had had enough. On 8 May, Seve issued the following statement:

After a working relationship of 8½ years, Joe Collet and I have reached an agreement to cancel his services as my manager. Joe would like to return to the USA after travelling to Austria where he will work for some time in his own personal business.

For Joe, as well as myself, working together for so many years has been a great experience and with positive results. Joe has always been a great professional, very efficient, honest and above all a good friend.

From 1 July onwards, my new manager will be Roddy Carr. As everyone knows, Roddy is presently vice-president of my company, Amen Corner S.A., and my decision to sign up with him was based mainly on all the good work he has done.

That month coincided with Seve's last tournament victory. As we have seen, in a few months time he would announce his temporary retirement from competitive golf, after the Ryder Cup match at Oak Hill.

Collet, meanwhile, was off to Austria, to work on a project he'd been nurturing for years: the creation of a World Tour. Seve had long been aware of this concept. In early autumn 1994, with his playing fortunes enjoying what would prove to be an abbreviated renaissance, he encouraged Collet to go ahead and set up his version of a World Tour, an attempt to break the commercial stranglehold of the existing tours by giving the participating players equity in a new entity, the International Golf Tour (IGT). Collet also established a players' union, the IPGA. He was confident he would get it off the ground with a softly, harder approach – being conciliatory towards the tours while forcefully persuasive to the players, whom he managed to convince were selling themselves short with the sort of money they were presently making, partly because the way the tours operated meant the players' freedom to maximise their earnings was restricted. That one played well with the troops.

One of the players whom Collet was sure was totally onside for this was Greg Norman. Indeed, Greg liked the idea so much that he made it his own. Towards the end of November 1994, he announced a provisional schedule for 1995 of eight tournaments on his 'World Golf Tour', with purses of $3 million each – trust me, that was big bucks in those days – and, perhaps more importantly, a deal with Rupert Murdoch's Fox Sports for it to televise the tournaments.

Collet was in Japan with Seve at the time and was initially devastated – years of work broken into pieces. Within 48 hours, he had perked up. Norman's idea was not going to fly. Norman thought he had secured the support of José Maria Olazábal (the Masters champion), Ernie Els (US Open champion) and Nick Price (Open and USPGA champion) while they had all been playing in the Grand Slam of Golf event in Hawaii a fortnight before. Greg had been there to make up the numbers, Price having won two of the year's majors, but their commitment, and that of a couple of top Americans he had approached, hadn't been as substantial as he had anticipated. And no other player liked the way Greg had made the numbers add up. As Nick Faldo said: 'It would have been like playing Greg's own tour.' A manager of one of the leading players of the time, among the top 10 of the 40 players Norman was looking for to compete in his events, told me: 'Greg screwed it up. It was not his idea, it was Joe Collet's, and Greg got greedy. If he had given the other big guys [i.e. Seve, Faldo, Price, Langer] a share of the business, it would have worked. No question.'

In February 1995, Seve told me: 'Greg rang me in Japan about the World Golf Tour and was very nice. When I told him that he might know that Joe Collet had been working on a plan for years, Greg said "Yes, I know, and you can be part of our organisation". I think what happened was that Joe told Frank Williams [Norman's manager] about his idea and when he mentioned it to Greg, he decided to announce it without having sorted out anything or talked to anyone. I talked to Nick Price about it in Manila and he said Greg had not explained anything to him.'

Although hampered by the baggage brought about by Norman's premature declaration, Collet was nevertheless undeterred. A bit of time for these wounds to heal, he believed, and his plan could still be accomplished. He moved to Vienna, got on board two young Austrian colleagues and businessmen, Karl Ableidinger and Matthias Nemes, and together they worked the world, trying to convert the non-believers.

In April 1997, meanwhile, Norman played in the Spanish Open, promoted by Amen Corner, on the understanding that Seve would play Greg's tournament in Australia later in the year. Seve didn't keep his side of the bargain, insisting there never had been any such deal. Who knows, but that may have been a Seve pay-back of some sort for Norman's World Golf Tour.

Seve himself remained supportive of Collet, although it was rapidly becoming apparent that the demise of Seve's playing prowess looked permanent. Also, he was himself intrigued that one of the American lawyers Collet had got involved in the project had once served a writ on him on the first tee of the US Open over some business dispute he had with Seve. Not the ideal way for him to begin a major championship. 'I don't know why Joe now works with this guy,' he told friends.

In early 1998, the IPGA took out advertisements in golf magazines in Britain, the United States and the Far East, outlining the goals of the IPGA and carrying an endorsement from Olazábal: 'Something new has to be done in professional golf and this is a very good first step.'

Ultimately, it didn't get a great deal further than that. An IPGA press conference was scheduled during the 1998 Open but was then cancelled. Funds Collet thought would come through did not. Without the money, he couldn't maintain player interest, and in any case the PGA Tour, European Tour and other tours around the world had by now approved the creation of the World Golf Championship events, which were allegedly going to deal with some of the international issues Norman and Collet had been campaigning about. The fact that latterly they have all been held in America rather shatters that notion. 'I don't think this is how all the members of the federation of tours envisaged the WGC events,' said George O'Grady, head of the European Tour.

Joe Collet's idea was perhaps ahead of its time or – given Greg Norman's intervention – some way behind it. But it was out of time.

While all this excitement had been going on, back at the hacienda there had been Seve's business interests to look after. Roddy Carr took on that job in the summer of 1995. Two years later, he explained how it had, or rather hadn't, been working: 'The relationship is not as close as people might expect. I've spent virtually no time with him. I got on with my job and he played tournaments. I never really had day-to-day contact with him. If I needed anything, we met four times a year for board meetings and the odd dinner, but not much more.'

Shortly after leading Europe to victory in the 1997 Ryder Cup at Valderrama, Seve put his faith entirely in the hands of his family. Big brother Baldomero would take over the handling of his business affairs. Despite decades of effort, the International Management Group wouldn't be getting that job.

Through all Seve's changes of managers, the one constant throughout his career has been his stubborn refusal to join IMG on a longstanding basis. IMG did represent Seve in the United States and Canada in 1984, after the severing of the UMI arrangement, but they never got their hooks into him in the way they wanted. Ceballos said simply at the time: 'We have a good relationship with IMG. [They are] very efficient – but very expensive.'

IMG is the most powerful and most influential sports management company in golf. It was founded by Mark McCormack, a Cleveland lawyer, after he started doing some work for Arnold Palmer. This initially consisted of looking over existing contracts and a few other bits and pieces. From small acorns . . .

Gary Player then asked if McCormack would do the same for him. Palmer didn't object so the South African became client No. 2. In November 1961, just after the hottest amateur golfer in the world turned professional, Jack Nicklaus became the third man. Some 25–30 years before people would talk of Europe's Famous 5, this was the original Big 3. The next year Palmer won the Masters and the Open, Nicklaus the US Open and Player the USPGA Championship.

From then until 1976, only in 1969 did none of them manage to win at least one major championship a year. McCormack's business had got off to a strong start and it just got stronger . . . and stronger . . . and stronger.

Fast-forward some 30–40 years, IMG clients were competing against one another for the same, say, course design project. Norman, notably, left when he realised IMG was using him as bait to get lesser clients into tournaments. As he saw it, his celebrity was being used to attract rivals to compete against him.

IMG seemed ideal for Seve; at least they thought so. Seve was wary. He felt that if he wasn't totally in control of his business affairs, he would not be able to choose what he did, which he was not prepared to do. Whatever they claimed to the contrary, a common perception of IMG was that they forced clients into situations that were not always in their best long-term interests but were good news for IMG's short-term revenues. The epitome of this was Bill Rogers, who won the Open at Sandwich in 1981 and then, in the opinion of many, spent the remainder of what was left of his prime years chasing the dollar around the globe. IMG always vehemently denied this, but there was no escaping that it was a widely held view. There was some logic to Seve's scepticism as well – how could you spend your life saying 'No' to IMG? They would then cease to want to be your manager anyway.

Ceballos told me: 'I remember Mark McCormack telling me once that his biggest rivals were people like me, who were close to the athlete – like John McEnroe being looked after by his father. I know far better than Mark and his men what Seve needs to do – his frame of mind, his peace of mind. Athletes are not machines. Sometimes it doesn't pay to travel 30,000 miles to get a $100,000 cheque because you might lose half a million by destroying the possibility of winning a major championship, which is what counts in the end. I think it is better to play 20 tournaments and win 10 rather than play 30 and win two.'

But his anti-corporate set-up with Ceballos in the early mid-1980s didn't mean that Seve's head could not be turned by money. In late April 1985, he was sufficiently seduced by the riches on offer at a skins game in Australia – £450,000 in prize-money, then a huge figure, with a minimum guarantee included – to skip the Madrid Open and fly halfway around the world to play in it. The week after, he pitched up at the Italian Open in Milan and finished tied fifth, including a 64. He could be lured by money but he seldom let down a European promoter.

IMG had paid Seve a lot of money by way of appearance fees but not got anything back from managing him. In the 1970s, IMG had gone to enormous lengths to try to lure Seve from UMI, with appearance-fee guarantees of around $50,000 for him to play 11 tournaments in Europe – a massive figure at that time. Such offers were conditional on Seve not playing certain tournaments that IMG did not promote. Having considered the idea, Seve and Barner said no.

Seve claimed that in 1981, the year he won the World Matchplay Championship – an event founded by McCormack – for the first of five times, and also the year of his near-banishment from the European Tour, IMG did not want to invite him until Ceballos talked them into it. But then his IMG relationship has always been complicated. They hated having to give him money; he loved it. He hated their power base in golf; they loved that.

In 1994, for example, IMG wanted Seve to play in the Trophée Lancôme, a tournament that McCormack had invented and IMG consequently promoted. But there was a problem. Although Seve had played the Lancôme many times, as has frequently been mentioned in these pages, IMG were not prepared to pay him an appearance fee on this occasion. Given all that Seve had contributed to the European Tour, even latterly – in 1994, he had already won a tournament in May, his last two finishes had been eighth and second, and he was about to win in Germany the next week, so it wasn't as if he was washed up as a player at that stage – this attitude was not so much a principled stand by IMG as a distinct snub. Other players were being paid. Seve refused to play. The chief recipient of the sponsor's largesse was Greg Norman. When he withdrew with an illness, there was cash in the kitty for Seve. He played, shot four rounds in the 60s and finished third.

However, the comparison with Norman is instructive in another regard. In his halcyon days, Seve could and should have done more to establish himself as a great brand in golf. Greg Norman has done it wonderfully, and while Seve never devoted as much of his time to the United States, the single biggest market in the world, as Norman has, his unwillingness to make the effort to exploit his name commercially – as Joe Collet repeatedly urged him to do – has cost him in terms of money and opportunities.

At *Golf International* in 2000, we asked McCormack if there was something he hadn't done that he wished he had. He said: 'I'd like to have signed Seve Ballesteros, for sure, at the beginning of his career. As wonderful as he is, as charismatic, as talented, the package of Seve Ballesteros would have been a better one with us managing him than it's been with others. So I'm sad about that. I suppose I can't think of too much else that really jumps out.' IMG had done a marvellous job of marketing Arnold Palmer for over 40 years and was handling Tiger Woods. McCormack considered Seve to be in that sort of league.

In January 2003, McCormack suffered a cardiac arrest while undergoing a minor operation in New York. He never came out of the coma and died in May, shortly after Seve had described the European Tour as being 'nearly like a Mafia' because of what he perceived as its incestuous relationship with IMG. In September 2004, IMG was bought by Forstmann Little & Co for $750 million. (Ted Forstmann was perhaps the only person to emerge with his integrity intact from the famous book, *Barbarians at the Gate*, about corporate greed in America in the 1980s.)

Earlier in 2004, I spoke to Norman about this subject. Norman is often acknowledged to be the best businessman/golfer ever – McCormack made all Arnie's deals and Tiger was a dream waiting to become reality, but Greg left IMG and capitalised on his own potential to the maximum. I asked him whether he thought Seve's name alone was a good brand and, if so, was he surprised Seve hadn't done as much as he might have done to establish his name in that manner

'I don't know,' he said. 'All I can tell you is that when I first made the decision to go alone, you have to bite the bullet. You're bringing people in on a salary. When you are with a management company, you pay them a fee to meet the overheads. When you decide to bring everything in-house, you have the overheads of salaries, insurance, etc. So you have to stay the course. Sometimes you sit back and ask yourself if you have made the right decision. You see the overhead expenses mounting into seven figures. So I can understand why people don't want to do it.'

Given Greg's track record in business, who am I to argue? However, his answer doesn't actually address the issue, since Seve's management is already in-house. Many people look at this situation and reach the obvious assumption: that Seve is a meal ticket for his brothers and extended family. Baldomero has been his long-time manager. Baldomero's son, Ivan, has recently been appointed managing director of Fairway. It's a tough call: is Baldomero in thrall to Seve because of his past brilliance and how he has come to represent the family name, or is Seve intimidated by his elder brother? The truth is probably six of one and half-a-dozen of the other. Vicente, meanwhile, runs the Seve Ballesteros Natural Golf School at the San Roque resort in the south of Spain.

Seve's brothers are golf professionals like him, but never nearly as good. They have not trained to be businessmen. Certainly, he can be sure they won't rip him off whereas he might fear – if still upset by the Barner imbroglio – that an outsider might, but the end result is that he can lose out due to their lack of expertise and, no doubt, because they won't be as firm with him as might sometimes be necessary. They will also be less expensive than an external replacement for Joe Collet or Roddy Carr.

Given what Seve brought to the game – his number of victories, his flair, his (potentially) vibrant personality and his classically Latin good looks – it seems something of a disgrace that he didn't make the top-50 in the *Golf Digest* annual ranking of the game's top earners, published in February 2006. (He's even further off the pace now he's stopped playing.) Tiger Woods was top, with over $86 million of income in 2005. Not only Norman, even Arnold Palmer broke the $20-million mark. José Maria Olazábal was 30th with nearly $5 million. If the research was correct, Seve couldn't muster $3.3 million in off-course earnings. It may have been far less. (Obviously, there were no on-course earnings, although Nick Faldo topped $3.5 million on pretty much the same basis.)

Among his businesses outside Amen Corner is Trajectory, the course-design operation. Seve first got into course architecture by working alongside Dave Thomas, a Welshman who co-designed The Belfry with Peter Alliss, at the Westerwood Golf & Country Club in Scotland. The company has designed over 30 courses world-wide, about two-thirds of them in Spain, with another dozen or so under construction, including the reconstruction of the course at Bridgedown, in Barnet, just north of London, rechristened The Shire London since it reopened in 2007.

In 1990, I flew with Seve from Paris to Marseille – helicopter and then Lear Jet, the only way to do it. He was going for a site visit to what remains the only course he has built in France, Pont Royal in Provence. I have been back since, now there's a proper course there, and think he did a good job. *The Peugeot Golf Guide* gives it 16 out of 20, so I'm not alone. Having said that, it gives the same mark to Novo Sancti Petri, of non-Ryder Cup notoriety, although I haven't seen that. Opinions about the quality of a golf course will inevitably be subjective, beauty being in the eye of the beholder, but I think it would be fair to say that Seve's work has come in for more criticism than praise. His remodelling of the 17th hole at Valderrama is one example, his restructuring of the greens at Crans-sur-Sierre, venue of the European Masters, another. Sam Torrance said of that tournament it was 'for years – before I think the course was ruined – home to one of the most enjoyable events on the schedule'. On the other hand, his Porto Santo on Madeira looks truly spectacular.

He has another entity, Heather & Company, which organises the Seve Trophy, and he has a company called Motivational

Training, which aims to, for example, improve people's business techniques.

At present, he is not doing commentary work for the BBC. He had reportedly been on £15,000 per tournament. In the April 2006 issue of *Golf International*, the former BBC golf anchor, Steve Rider, told Richard Simmons: 'It's a difficult thing to become integrated into the BBC commentary team – and I don't mean in terms of personality, because everyone loves having Seve on the team. But he's a bit like he is on the golf course. There's a certain impetuosity and impatience. You always knew he was going to be there, but he wasn't the most patient man in the commentary box, which led to a few problems. But I expect the BBC will figure out a way to use him. At least I hope they do. He has the passion for the game that comes across in the way he speaks and airs his views.'

Latterly, Seve has done such things as autographing a 3,000-copy limited edition book entitled *Golf, a tribute (Europe)*. This coffee-table tome, so large (60cm × 70cm) that it comes with its own coffee table, retails for £3,000 a copy.

How much is Seve worth? Expert estimates put it at somewhere close to but below £50 million – not bad for a farmer's son from rural Spain. But it could surely have been very much more. Seve has charisma and he is a proven leader. He might have become the most pre-eminent non-American former sportsman in the world (a long title, I know), with the prospect of a non-playing career associated with multinational businesses or even politics. He didn't. He hasn't. Where does he go from here?

EPILOGUE

In an interview in *The Guardian* last autumn, Seve spoke to Donald McRae about a forlorn night he spent in his hotel room in Alabama in May 2007, considering that final step of retirement. 'I felt very alone, and I could hear voices in my head – 'Seve, what the hell are you doing here?' I'd heard these questions a long time . . . but inside I was not accepting it. I changed that night.' The opposite of a 'Eureka' moment, if you like.

When Seve concluded his retirement statement at the Open last summer, mindful of the fact that he was addressing a room full of journalists, he joked: 'If you have any questions, the bar is open.' In fact, he raised it for European golf.

Nick Faldo has said: '[Seve] was the king. The rest of us might have helped to further the cause [of European golf], but we sat at the round table, while he sat on the throne.' He added: 'Seve should have packed it in long ago.' Harsh, but fair.

In an interview on Sky over Christmas, Faldo reminisced about how he and Seve used to be like boxers in the ring. Recently, Seve had asked him if they could now be friends – 'whatever that means,' smiled Faldo, a little like Prince Charles infamously saying 'whatever love is' in those far-off days before he'd married Diana, let alone divorced her. Faldo had replied that of course they could. For him, past conflicts are water under the bridge. His career beyond this year's Ryder Cup captaincy – primarily in golf course design and television work – is settled. Seve may have his own design business but organising the Seve Trophy isn't a full-time job and motivational talks aren't his forte. He has talked about the 2010 Ryder Cup captaincy: 'If the players want me,' he said, 'I would be happy to do it again' – a reprise of what he had said ten years previously (see page 142). But I don't see that one happening.

Peter Jacobsen, an American tour pro who was on the wrong end of the Ballesteros/Gilford victory in the 1995 Ryder Cup, once said: 'I thought Seve would become one of the ambassadors in the world of golf.' The chief executive of the European Tour, George O'Grady, hopes for that. 'It is the fervent wish of everyone at the Tour that an ambassadorial role could be found for Seve, to reflect the charismatic contribution he has made to European golf and the inspiration he has been.' Seve knows this. To borrow from McEnroe again, the ball is in his court. 'We have had our contretemps with him,' O'Grady told me, 'but given what he's done for the Tour, we obviously overlook that.'

Among other things, though, there may be the fact that Seve is too proud and stubborn to push at this open door. It's a shame that sometimes in the past he could not bite his tongue, even if/when he was in the right, and now he may lack the necessary humility to seek a total reconciliation.

Faldo has also said, in an echo of what Mark McCormack had in mind: '[Seve] as a brand name is fantastic and I don't think he has ever really capitalised on that.' That's surely true, too. Like Pele and Madonna, he only needs one name. It's a great name – perhaps somewhat tarnished, but maybe not beyond restoration. One long-time friend of his told me: 'It's not too late to reinvent himself if he wants to, away from the golf course, but he'd have to reorganise his business affairs first, and that will only happen if he falls in love again and that woman tells him what to do.'

Whatever he does, if Seve could learn to free himself from his demons, mental and physical, that he has sometimes encouraged to thrive in his live, he might be able to attain new and different goals, helping to banish the sadder memories and leaving us – and, more importantly, him – with the happier ones. Like all his fans, I hope so.

APPENDIX

Seve's record in the four major championships

Masters Tournament

1977: 74-75-70-72 291	33=
1978: 74-71-68-74 287	18=
1979: 72-68-73-74 287	12=
1980: 66-69-68-72 275	1
1981: 78-76	Missed cut
1982: 73-73-68-71 285	3=
1983: 68-70-73-69 280	1
1984: 73-74	Missed cut
1985: 72-71-71-70 284	2=
1986: 71-68-72-70 281	4
1987: 73-71-70-71 285	2=
1988: 73-72-70-73 288	11=
1989: 71-72-73-69 285	5
1990: 74-73-68-71 286	7=
1991: 75-70-69-70 284	22=
1992: 75-68-70-81 294	59=
1993: 74-70-71-71 286	11=
1994: 70-76-75-71 292	18=
1995: 75-68-78-75 296	45=
1996: 73-73-77-76 299	43

1997: 81-74	Missed cut
1998: 78-79	Missed cut
1999: 78-78	Missed cut
2000: 81-81	Missed cut
2001: 76-76	Missed cut
2002: 75-81	Missed cut
2003: 77-85	Missed cut
2004-6: Did not play	
2007: 86-80	Missed cut
2008: Did not play	

US Open Championship

1978: 75-69-71-77 292	16=
1979: 79-81	Missed cut
1980: 75-Disqualified	
1981: 73-69-72-75 289	41=
1982: 81-79	Missed cut
1983: 69-74-69-74 286	4=
1984: 69-73-74-75 291	30=
1985: 71-70-69-71 281	5=
1986: 75-73-68-73 289	24=
1987: 68-75-68-71 282	3
1988: 69-74-72-73 288	32=
1989: 75-70-76-69 290	43=
1990: 73-69-71-76 289	33=
1991: 72-77	Missed cut
1992: 71-76-69-79 295	23=
1993: 76-72	Missed cut
1994: 72-72-70-73 287	18=
1995: 74-73	Missed cut
1996-08: Did not play	

Open Championship

| 1975: 79-80 | Missed cut |
| 1976: 69-69-73-74 285 | 2= |

1977: 69-71-73-74 287	15=
1978: 69-70-76-73 288	17=
1979: 73-65-75-70 283	1
1980: 72-68-72-74 286	19=
1981: 75-72-74-72 293	39=
1982: 71-75-73-71 290	13=
1983: 71-71-69-68 279	6=
1984: 69-68-70-69 276	1
1985: 75-74-70-73 292	39=
1986: 76-75-73-64 288	6=
1987: 73-70-77-75 295	50=
1988: 67-71-70-65 273	1
1989: 72-73-76-78 299	77=
1990: 71-74	Missed cut
1991: 66-73-69-71 279	9=
1992: 70-75	Missed cut
1993: 68-73-69-71 281	27=
1994: 70-70-71-69 280	38=
1995: 75-69-76-71 291	40=
1996: 74-78	Missed cut
1997: 77-71	Missed cut
1998: 73-75	Missed cut
1999: 80-86	Missed cut
2000: 78-69	Missed cut
2001: 78-71	Missed cut
2002-5: Did not play	
2006: 74-77	Missed cut
2007: Did not play	

USPGA Championship

1981: 71-73-72-70 286	33=
1982: 71-68-69-73 281	13
1983: 71-76-72-67 286	27
1984: 70-69-70-70 279	5
1985: 73-72-68-76 289	32=

1986: 74-76   Missed cut
1987: 72-70-72-78 292   10=
1988: 71-75   Missed cut
1989: 72-70-66-74 282   12=
1990: 77-83   Missed cut
1991: 71-72-71-73 287   23=
1992-3: Did not play
1994: 78-76   Missed cut
1995: 76-75   Missed cut
1996-07: Did not play

The Ryder Cup Matches: Seve's personal record

1979

Fourballs: lost 2&1 to Lanny Wadkins & Larry Nelson; lost 5&4 to Wadkins & Nelson
Foursomes: won 3&2 against Fuzzy Zoeller & Hubert Green; lost 3&2 to Wadkins & Nelson
(all with Antonio Garrido)
Singles: lost 3&2 to Nelson
CUMULATIVE RECORD: 1-4-0

1981

Did not play

1983

Foursomes: lost 2&1 to Tom Kite & Calvin Peete; won 2&1 against Tom Watson & Bob Gilder
Fourballs: won 1 up against Raymond Floyd & Curtis Strange; halved with Gil Morgan & Jay Haas
(all with Paul Way)
Singles: halved with Fuzzy Zoeller
CUMULATIVE RECORD: 3-5-2

1985

Foursomes: won 2&1 against Curtis Strange & Mark O'Meara; won 5&4 against Craig Stadler & Hal Sutton
Fourballs: won 2&1 against Andy North & Peter Jacobsen; lost 3&2 to O'Meara & Lanny Wadkins
(all with Manuel Pinero)
Singles: halved with Tom Kite
CUMULATIVE RECORD: 6-6-3

1987

Foursomes: won 1 up against Larry Nelson & Payne Stewart; won 1 up against Ben Crenshaw & Stewart
Fourballs: won 2&1 against Curtis Strange & Tom Kite; lost 2&1 to Hal Sutton & Larry Mize
(all with José Maria Olazábal)
Singles: won 2&1 against Strange
CUMULATIVE RECORD: 10-7-3

1989

Foursomes: halved with Tom Watson & Chip Beck; won 1 up against Tom Kite & Curtis Strange
Fourballs: won 6&5 against Tom Watson & Mark O'Meara; won 4&2 against Mark Calcavecchia & Ken Green
(all with José Maria Olazábal)
Singles: lost 1 down to Paul Azinger
CUMULATIVE RECORD: 13-8-4

1991

Foursomes: won 2&1 against Paul Azinger & Chip Beck; won 3&2 against Fred Couples & Raymond Floyd
Fourballs: won 2&1 against Azinger & Beck; halved with Couples & Payne Stewart
(all with José Maria Olazábal)
Singles: won 3&2 against Wayne Levi
CUMULATIVE RECORD: 17-8-5

1993
Foursomes: lost 2&1 to Tom Kite & Davis Love; won 2&1 against Kite & Love
Fourballs: won 4&3 against Kite & Love
(all with José Maria Olazábal)
Singles: lost 3&2 to Jim Gallagher
CUMULATIVE RECORD: 19-10-5

1995
Fourballs: won 4&3 against Brad Faxon & Peter Jacobsen; lost 3&2 to Jay Haas & Phil Mickelson
(both with David Gilford)
Singles: lost 4&3 to Tom Lehman
CUMULATIVE RECORD: 20-12-5

1997
Winning captain: Europe 14½, USA 13½

European Tour victories

1976: Dutch Open, Trophée Lancôme [No.1 on Order of Merit]
1977: French Open, Uniroyal International, Swiss Open [No.1 on Order of Merit]
1978: Martini International, German Open, Scandinavian Enterprise Open, Swiss Open [No.1 on Order of Merit]
1979: English Golf Classic, [Open Championship]
1980: Madrid Open, Martini International, Dutch Open
1981: Scandinavian Enterprise Open, Spanish Open, World Matchplay Championship
1982: Madrid Open, French Open, World Matchplay Championship
1983: PGA Championship, Irish Open, Trophée Lancôme
1984: [Open Championship], World Matchplay Championship

1985: Irish Open, French Open, Sanyo Open, Spanish Open, World Matchplay Championship
1986: British Masters, Irish Open, Monte Carlo Open, French Open, Dutch Open, Trophée Lancôme (tied - playoff with Bernhard Langer prevented from conclusion by darkness) [No.1 on Order of Merit]
1987: Suze Open
1988: Open de Baleares, [Open Championship], Scandinavian Enterprise Open, German Open, Trophée Lancôme [No.1 on Order of Merit]
1989: Madrid Open, Epson Grand Prix, European Masters-Swiss Open
1990: Open de Baleares
1991: PGA Championship, British Masters, World Matchplay Championship [No.1 on Order of Merit]
1992: Dubai Desert Classic, Open de Baleares
1994: Benson & Hedges International, German Masters
1995: Tournoi Perrier de Paris (with José Maria Olazábal), Spanish Open
2000: Seve Trophy: playing captain of winning Continental team

Other international victories

1976: Donald Swaelens Memorial (Belgium), World Cup of Golf for Spain (with Manuel Pinero)
1977: Braun International (Germany), Japan Open, Dunlop Phoenix (Japan), Otago Charity Classic (New Zealand), World Cup of Golf for Spain (with Antonio Garrido)
1978: Kenya Open, Greater Greensboro Open (USA), Japan Open
1980: [Masters Tournament]
1981: Australian PGA Championship, Dunlop Phoenix (Japan)
1982: San Remo Masters (Italy)
1983: [Masters Tournament], Westchester Classic (USA), Sun City Million Dollar Challenge (South Africa)

1984: Sun City Million Dollar Challenge (South Africa)
1985: USF&G Classic (USA)
1988: Westchester Classic (USA), Taiheiyo Masters (Japan)
1991: Chunichi Crowns (Japan)
1992: Copa Quinto Lentenario per Equipos (Argentina)

Spanish domestic victories

1974: Under-25 Championship, Open de Vizcaya
1975: Under-25 Championship
1976: Catalunia Professionals' Championship, Tenerife
        Professionals' Championship
1978: Under-25 Championship
1979: El Prat Open
1985: Spanish Professionals' Championship
1987: Larios PGA Championship, Spanish Professionals'
        Championship
1988: Larios PGA Championship

Other top-10 finishes on the European Tour

Second
1976 [Open Championship]
1977 Trophée Lancôme
1978 French Open
        Irish Open
1979 Scandinavian Enterprise Open
1980 Spanish Open
        Bob Hope British Classic
1981 European Open
1982 Trophée Lancôme
1983 Italian Open
        German Open

European Open
1984 European Open
Trophée Lancôme
1986 Suze Open
Madrid Open
1987 Spanish Open
PGA Championship
1988 PGA Championship
European Masters-Swiss Open
Volvo Masters
1991 Spanish Open
Scandinavian Masters
European Masters-Swiss Open
1993 European Masters-Swiss Open
1994 BMW International Open
Masters
1994 Volvo Masters
1995 Open De Canaria

Third
1976 Scandinavian Enterprise Open
Swiss Open
German Open
1977 Spanish Open
Scandinavian Enterprise Open
1978 Madrid Open
1979 French Open
1980 Scandinavian Enterprise Open
1981 French Open
Tournament Players Championship
1982 Scandinavian Enterprise Open
1983 Madrid Open
1984 Irish Open
1985 British Masters
1986 Spanish Open

1987 Madrid Open
    Grand Prix of Europe Matchplay Championship
    German Masters
1988 Monte Carlo Open
1990 Dubai Desert Classic
1991 English Open
    European Open
1992 Belgian Open
1993 Dubai Desert Classic
1994 Trophée Lancôme
1996 Oki Pro-Am

Fourth
1978 Benson & Hedges International
1980 Irish Open
1982 Car Care Plan International
1983 French Open
    European Masters-Swiss Open
1984 Spanish Open
1985 PGA Championship
1986 Italian Open
    European Open
    Sanyo Open
1987 Monte Carlo Open
1988 Madrid Open
1989 PGA Championship
1990 English Open
1991 Volvo Masters
1993 Alfred Dunhill Open
1996 European Masters-Swiss Open

Fifth
1974 Italian Open
1976 Portuguese Open
1976 Irish Open

1977 Italian Open
1978 Spanish Open
1979 Italian Open
1985 Italian Open
1990 Italian Open

Sixth
1975 Portuguese Open
     Spanish Open
1976 Spanish Open
1977 Irish Open
1979 European Open
1983 [Open Championship]
1985 Trophée Lancôme
     Portuguese Open
1986 [Open Championship]
1987 Scottish Open
1988 German Masters
1990 Spanish Open
1994 PGA Championship

Seventh
1979 Martini International
1980 Tournament Players Championship
1983 Spanish Open
1984 Madrid Open
1985 European Open
1989 Italian Open
1990 Monte Carlo Open
     Trophée Lancôme
     Grand Prix of Europe

Eighth
1975 Madrid Open
     Swiss Open

1976 French Open
    Benson & Hedges International
1977 Benson & Hedges International
1980 German Open
1991 Scottish Open
1994 Spanish Open
    European Open

Ninth
1979 Madrid Open
1982 Bob Hope British Classic
1987 Dutch Open
1989 Spanish Open
1991 [Open Championship]

Tenth
1979 PGA Championship
1986 German Open
1991 Monte Carlo Open
1994 Chemapol Trophy Czech Open
1998 Dubai Desert Classic

INDEX